Practical Marketing

Practical Marketing

An Asian Perspective

Wee Chow Hou

Addison Wesley Publishing Company

Singapore • Tokyo • Seoul • Taipei • Reading, Massachusetts
Menlo Park, California • New York • Don Mills, Ontario
Wokingham, England • Amsterdam • Bonn • Sydney • Madrid
San Juan • Milan • Paris

© 1997   Addison-Wesley Publishers Ltd
© 1997   Addison-Wesley Publishing Company

All rights reserved. No part of this publication may be reproduced, stored in a retrieval system, or transmitted in any form or by any means, electronic, mechanical, photocopying, recording or otherwise, without prior written permission of the publisher.

Many of the designations used by manufacturers and sellers to distinguish their products are claimed as trademarks. Where those designations appear in this book, and Addison-Wesley was aware of a trademark claim, the designations have been printed in initial caps or all caps.

Cover designed and illustrated by Michael Chan Chian Fu, Singapore
Text designed by Lesley Stewart
Typeset by Times Publishing Graphics
Printed in Singapore

First printed in 1996.

Library of Congress Cataloging in Publication Data

Wee, Chow Hou.
    Practical marketing: an Asian perspective / Wee Chow Hou.
        p. cm.
    Includes bibliographical references and index.
    ISBN 0-201-62857-0
    1. Marketing.   2. Marketing—Asia.   I. Title.
    HF5415.W363   1997
    658.8'0095--dc20   96-25487
                                                                CIP

Preface

There is no shortage of good marketing texts in the market. You can find them in practically any bookstore in Singapore and other Asian cities. However, many of these texts are very academic and lengthy in nature, making reading for the practitioners and students tedious and difficult.

On the other hand, there are also many so-called practitioner's marketing books. These books, while readable, lack depth and are often narrow in perspective. At the same time, there are very few books that adopt an Asian perspective. This perspective is important in view of the growing importance of Asia. Over the past ten years, many Asian economies ranging from the four newly industrialized economies of Taiwan, Hong Kong, Singapore and South Korea, to the semi-developing economies of Malaysia, Indonesia, and Thailand, have all experienced tremendous economic growth that is unparalleled in any part of the world. With the opening of China and other centrally planned economies like Vietnam, Myanmar, Laos, and Cambodia, Asia is definitely on the path of an astronomical economic growth. It is more than timely that a book with an Asian perspective be written.

Since 1979, I have been very active in conducting executive training and in-house programmes to over 100 large organizations in the Asia-Pacific region and the rest of the world. The types of courses that I conduct focus largely on marketing and strategic planning. Since 1990, and with the increased opening of China, I have also began to conduct similar training in Mandarin. With my strong academic training from North America, and my understanding of the Chinese culture as well as of the region, I have accumulated a lot of practical knowledge about marketing and doing business in the region. This book contains much of my training materials as well as knowledge and expertise gained from years of conducting executive programmes. It is written primarily for the manager who may not have any marketing knowledge or experience. For the marketeer, I believe there are many concepts and thought-provoking reminders that he or she will find useful for streamlining the decision-making process. Certainly students of marketeers will find much to think about in this book.

About the Author

Dr. Wee Chow Hou is Professor of Business Policy, Dean of the Faculty of Business Administration and Director of the Graduate School of Business at the National University of Singapore. He was a former Merit, Colombo Plan and Commonwealth scholar, the winner of the Academy of Marketing Science (USA) 1984 Ph.D. Student Paper Award as well as of the 1985 Doctoral Thesis Award.

He has over 200 publications in various international, regional and local journals and proceedings, and is the senior author of *Sun Tzu: War and Management* a best seller that has been translated into Korean, Indonesian, and Chinese. Dr. Wee is currently on the editorial boards of *Advances in International Marketing* (USA), the *Asia Pacific Journal of Management* (Singapore) and the *Journal of Strategic Marketing* (UK). He is also Associate Editor of *The International Executive* (USA), and a Consulting Editor on the Asia-Pacific Series of Addison-Wesley Publishing Co. Inc. (USA).

Dr. Wee has consulted to and conducted executive training for more than one hundred major organization in sixteen regions and countries including Fortune 500 companies, and many of the large corporations in the Asian-Pacific Region.

He also sits on the boards of several national level committees, organizations and companies.

Contents

Contents

Contents

1
New Directions in the Asian Marketing Environment

1.1 Introduction

One of the most noticeable economic developments in the world in the 1980s has to be the fast economic growth rates recorded by many countries of Asia. More significantly, these high growth rates are expected to be sustained for the rest of the century, so much so that the Asian region is now receiving increasing world attention. With the opening of China, the gradual embracement of a market-oriented economy by countries like Vietnam, Myanmar, Cambodia and Laos, and with the awakening of India, Asia is likely to emerge as a strong economic region. In fact, the emerging view is that the total income of countries in the Asian region may even overtake that of the Organization of Economic Cooperation and Development (OECD) countries within the next thirty years. For sure, China is now the third largest economy after the United States and Japan. According to one estimate, China will have about one hundred and fifty million people (located mainly in the new economic zones and coastal cities) with a per capita income that will approximate US$4,000 by the year 2000. And by the year 2010, the total Gross National Product (GNP) of China may even rival that of the United States!

The importance of Asia to the world has even prompted *Fortune International* in its November issue of 1993 to carry on its cover page the title, "The Battle for Asia: Japan and the West Square Off in the World's fastest growing market." Obviously, American, European and Japanese companies have begun to court the Asian consumers with great zeal. Even Australia, despite its traditional ties with the western world, has begun to align itself more with Asia, and has been very aggressive in promoting Australian products and services to the region, including massive export of tertiary education.

1

1.2 High Economic Growth Rates

The Asian region is fast becoming an economic force to be reckoned with. It is led by Japan and its key players are the four Newly Industrialized Economies (NIEs) which comprise Taiwan, South Korea, Hong Kong and Singapore. The new players are the semi-NIEs: Malaysia, Philippines, Indonesia and Thailand. Its increased economic presence is further augmented by another group of fast growing Less Developed Economies (LDEs). The LDEs, led by China, have begun to gradually open up to the western world for foreign investments and technology.

These NIEs, semi-NIEs and LDEs have recorded healthy growth rates over the last few years. More significantly, the economic growth rates of these countries are unlikely to slow down in the foreseeable future. Table 1.1 shows a compilation of estimated growth rates for 1994 and 1995, and the forecasted growth rates of 1996 of the Asian economies vis-a-vis other developed economies. It can be seen that with the exception of the Philippines, all the Asian economies recorded very high growth rates for 1994 and 1995. In general, most of them are expected to grow between 5 to 10% for the rest of this decade.

In contrast, several of the western developed economies like the United States, Canada, Britain, Australia, and Germany experienced lower growth rates in 1994 and 1995. Many of these economies are expected to grow at no more than 4% annually in the near future. Interestingly, Japan, the only Asian economy among the developed nations, while encountering some economic slowdown, is expected to recover before the turn of the century.

With high economic growth rates, these economies represent a vast potential market for world investors. In fact, the economic significance of the Asian region to the western world had been very well articulated by Singapore's former Prime Minister, Lee Kuan Yew, in a speech[1] at a banquet hosted by the Lord Mayor of London in May 1990.

Despite the 1990/91 Gulf crisis and the concessions that were given to the East European countries by the European Community (EC) as a result of the collapse of the Berlin Wall in December 1989, the Asian region is likely to remain a significant market in the world. This

---

1. The text of this speech was reported in *The Straits Times* on 26 May 1990.

2

TABLE 1.1 Estimated and forecasted economic growth rates of selected Asian economies vis-a-vis other developed economies

	Estimated % 1994	Estimated % 1995	Forecasted % 1996	Per capita GNP for 1995 (US$)
NIEs				
Taiwan	6.5	6.8	6.2	11,240
Hong Kong	5.5	5.4	5.3	21,560
South Korea	8.4	7.4	7.0	8,700
Singapore	9.5	8.9	7.5	22,500
Semi-NIEs				
Thailand	8.3	8.2	8.3	2,320
Philippines	2.0	4.3	4.5	990
Malaysia	8.7	8.9	9.0	3,560
Indonesia	6.5	6.8	6.7	790
LDEs				
China	11.6	10.3	10.2	460
India	4.5	4.9	5.3	360
Myanmar	4.0	6.3	6.5	620
Vietnam	7.9	8.4	8.5	280
Laos	7.2	7.5	8.0	290
Pakistan	4.9	4.8	5.0	460
Sri Lanka	4.9	5.6	6.0	560
Developed Economies				
Japan	1.2	2.3	3.5	38,750
Australia	2.0	3.6	3.5	17,800
New Zealand	4.8	5.0	5.1	15,010
United States	3.8	3.0	2.0	25,950
Canada	4.0	4.1	3.8	21,000
Britain	3.4	3.3	3.1	18,500
Germany	2.9	2.8	2.5	25,100
France	2.3	3.0	3.1	24,200
Switzerland	2.2	2.4	2.0	40,300

Sources: 1. Asian Finance, various issues
2. IMF publications
3. Key Indicators of Developing Asian & Pacific Countries

is because the region as a whole has become much more dynamic, and the respective governments of the countries in Asia, are committed to economic development. For example, the Malaysian and Indonesian governments are now working closely with the Singapore government to develop the Singapore-Johore-Riau triangle, which is also known as the South Triangle. At the same time, Malaysia and

Indonesia are also exploring with Thailand, the feasibility of developing a North Triangle. It is envisaged that with the current development of the South Triangle and the likely development of the North Triangle, there will be economic spillover effects to other parts of Malaysia, Indonesia and Thailand.

Besides these developments in Malaysia, Indonesia, Thailand and Singapore, other Asian countries are also jumping on the bandwagon of economic modernization. China has begun to make attempts to repair the damages the June 4, 1989 Tiananmen incident. It is now focussing more attention on attracting foreign investments and on revitalizing its industries. Its efforts are beginning to pay off. Within a short time of less than five years (up to early 1994), it has become the largest benefactor of foreign investments. It even made a concerted, though unsuccessful, attempt to bid for the 2000 Olympics as a sign to the outside world of its committment to further open up its economy. Another significant step was its move to unify its yuan with its foreign exchange certificates (FEC). This move effectively abolishes the state controlled exchange rate for its currency that had existed for over forty years under the socialist central planning system. The Chinese yuan is now floated in the currency market and its value determined by market forces.

The conversion of the dual exchange rate system to a single currency one is only part of the overall efforts to push China towards a market-style economy. Many other measures such as new tax laws and the overhaul of the Chinese banking system are also taking place concurrently. All these are intended to enable China to become a strong economic power in the 21st century.

Besides China, previously war-torn and poverty-stricken nations like Vietnam, Myanmar, Laos and Cambodia are also beginning to realize the folly of their closed-door policies, and are beginning to open up their borders for foreign investments and economic development. They have put aside their political ideologies in favour of economic reforms and the development of a market economy. Vietnam, in particular, has been very aggressive in pushing for economic reforms. Like China, Vietnam has discovered that it can no longer isolate itself from the rest of the world. Thus, it has gradually adopted a more market-oriented policy, and is fast attracting foreign investments from companies in the region as well as from the rest of the world. Interestingly, despite the bad experiences of the Vietnam War, many American companies have shown strong interest in doing business in Vietnam. In fact, companies like IBM, Motorola, DHL, Pepsi, and Coca-Cola have already set up offices in Vietnam, They are waiting for the lifting of the trade sanctions against Vietnam. Thus, when President Clinton announced the lifting of trade embargo against Vietnam on 4 February 1994, these companies became among the first American companies to reap the rewards of their wait. They wasted no time in making their moves. For example, the cola war between Pepsi and Coke began almost on the same day that the trade embargo was lifted! Indeed, with American trade and economic involvement in Vietnam, the rate of growth of that country is likely to accelerate further.

1.3 Varying Stages of Economic Development

What is significant about the Asian region is that its members are clustered into distinct stages of economic development. For example, Japan is clearly in its own class with a 1995 per capita income of US$38,750 (see Table 1.1) which places it among the most developed and richest economies of the world. It is followed by the four NIEs with per capita incomes ranging from US$8,700 (South Korea) to US$22,500 (Singapore). The four NIEs are followed by the four semi-NIEs of Thailand, Philippines, Malaysia and Indonesia. At the bottom of the pack are seven other Asian LDEs.

In aggregate, the various countries in the Asian region form a four-step economic ladder, with each group complementing the other. Owing to the different stages of economic development, the countries within the region are able to service each other in terms of trade, investment, labour supply, and even the transfer of technology. Moreover, as many of them are enjoying high economic growth rates, they are able to fuel the growth of each other, adding more dynamism to the region. The result is greater economic synergy. For example, Japan is probably the most active in investing in the four NIEs, semi-NIEs and the LDEs.

What is more significant is that the four NIEs are now actively investing in the semi-NIEs and the LDEs. In turn, semi-NIEs like Malaysia and Indonesia have begun to invest in the LDEs like China. Even China has begun to invest in the more developed economies of Asia. For example, one of the leading Chinese investment companies, China's International Trade and Investment Corporation (CITIC) is a major shareholder in Hong Kong-based companies such as Cathay Pacific Airways, Dragon Airlines, and BC Development.

Besides CITIC, many other Chinese companies are now actively investing in other Asian economies such as Hong Kong, Taiwan, Thailand and Vietnam.

Besides investments, the more developed economies of Asia are now able to supply industrial goods, machinery and equipment to their poorer neighbours. In return, as the semi-NIEs and LDEs are very rich in natural resources and primary produce, they are able to provide the necessary raw materials and supplies. In addition, they are also able to export their excess labourers to ease the labour-shortages in Japan and the four NIEs. For example, the Philippines has become a major exporter of foreign workers. In fact, remittances from its domestic maids working abroad have become its main source of foreign exchange earnings. Similarly, a high percentage of construction workers in Malaysia, Singapore, Taiwan and Hongkong now comes from Thailand and Indonesia.

1.4 Increasing Income and High Savings

With sound economic development over the past several years (for some Asia-Pacific countries, their track records stretch over twenty years), and with sustainable growth rates in the future, the Asian countries are likely to witness continuing increase in their incomes. In fact, per capita incomes in Japan, the four NIEs, and the semi-NIEs have been rising rapidly over the last two decades. In particular, as of end 1995 (see Table 1.1), the per capita incomes of the four NIEs are fast catching up with some of the European countries like Britain. In the case of Hong Kong and Singapore, they have even overtaken Australia, Britain, Canada and New Zealand in per capita GNP, largely as a result of the depreciating currencies of the latter countries over the past few years.

Besides increasing incomes, many of the Asian economies are characterized by high savings and low inflation rates. As can be seen in Table 1.2, the savings rates in these economies range from 27% (as in the case of Taiwan) to 48% (as in the case of Singapore). Even China showed a savings rate of 36% for 1995. These rates are far above those recorded by the developed economies. Their high saving rates together with their export-driven strategies have enabled these economies to build up substantial foreign exchange reserves. With the exception of South Korea, the other three Asian NIEs are net creditors, and have no foreign debts. The large reserves of these Asian economies ensure that they have a buffer against any rainy day,

TABLE 1.2 Selected economic indicators as of 1995

	Reserves (excl. gold) in US$bil.	Foreign Debt US$bil.	Savings % of GDP	Inflation Rate ('95)
NIEs				
Taiwan	100.3	0.0	27	3.3
Hong Kong	49.3	0.0	30	8.5
South Korea	27.3	54.0	35	4.2
Singapore	56.5	0.0	48	1.7
Semi-LDEs				
Thailand	30.3	62.1	37	5.4
Philippines	6.7	37.3	15	6.8
Malaysia	25.4	23.3	34	3.9
Indonesia	13.0	90.0	37	10.5
LDEs				
China	62.7	100.0	36	15.0
India	23.5	85.2	24	8.5
Myanmar	0.6	5.3	12	26.7
Vietnam	0.6	24.7	8	19.8
Laos	0.1	1.1	4	6.8
Pakistan	2.6	26.1	14	12.1
Sri Lanka	2.5	6.4	16	8.5
Developed Economies				
Japan	155.4	0.0	34	0.6
Australia	12.4	121.8	19	4.5
New Zealand	4.1	35.2	19	4.6
United States	75.7	555.7	15	3.2
Canada	14.3	236.0	19	2.9
Britain	40.7	0.0	15	3.5
Germany	82.1	0.0	28	2.4
France	26.6	0.0	21	1.6
Switzerland	31.5	0.0	29	2.1

Source: Asiaweek, 1995 & 1996, various issues

as well as the potential to develop even further. Their healthy economic conditions contrast sharply with those of some of the developed economies like Australia, Canada and the United States which are now saddled with huge foreign debts (see Table 1.2).

What is significant about these Asian countries is the way they utilize their savings. Unlike the western world, which in the past, used their large reserves to build up substantial social and health care programmes that have boomeranged somewhat disastrously, these

Asian countries have cleverly channelled their savings to the development of infrastructures and productive facilities (like schools) that would, in the future, yield high social returns. In addition, they have also invested in other countries, either to protect their existing market share, or to secure promising future markets. Theirs is a long term goal: to ensure their competitiveness in the long run, and thus the protection and increase of their reserves in the long run.

These countries have deliberately avoided excessive spending on health and social welfare programmes. Instead, countries like Singapore has even gone a step further. Not only has it asked the employee to share part of the health bill, it has also embarked on a campaign in promoting a healthy lifestyle that includes the banning of smoking and the discouragement of excessive drinking. With the increasing success of Singapore in enforcing such "desirable" social policies, it would not be surprising to find other Asian economies following suit in due course.

Barring any major political mishaps, the current high savings rates of many Asian countries are likely to continue. As the economies of Vietnam and the other Asian LDEs like India begin to open up and develop further, it is likely that their savings rates will increase correspondingly. And as their exports pick up volume, they are likely to increase their foreign exchange reserves as well. This is because their cultures favour a thrifty and prudent lifestyle, and their governments have not been known to be very generous with social welfare schemes. Together with the existing high savings of Asian economies, they are likely to form a strong economic force to be reckoned with.

1.5 Education and Learning

Asian countries have also begun to invest substantially in education and training. In the past, owing to various economic and political problems in many of these countries (like those in the semi-NIE and LDE groups), education and training received scant attention. However, to support faster economic development and to increase competitiveness, education and training have become necessary in these countries. At the same time, with rising incomes, education and training have become more accessible and affordable.

There are several points about education and training that deserve mention. First, basic education is now provided to the masses in many of the Asian economies. As a result, the literacy rate among Asian countries has been raised significantly over the last 10 years. Second, there has been increasing focus on technical education and training as keys to a more productive workforce. Third, Asian countries are less inhibited (by culture or religion) in pursuing languages that have high utility and commercial value. For example, as a result of the opening of China, many Chinese have begun to learn the English language with great enthusiasm as it is the language of communication with the western world. At the same time, many of its Asian neighbours have begun to learn Chinese (the official language of China) so as to do business and gain political access to China. Fourth, the link between education and economic rewards has been firmly established through elaborate salary structures. It is thus no surprise that commercial and private tuition is a thriving business in Japan and the four Asian NIEs. These reasons, and the reverence for scholarships in most Asian cultures, have made the pursuit for education a relentless one.

It is important to highlight that the positive learning attitude is not owing to the individual or his Asian culture. Political leaders in many Asian countries do not hesitate to borrow good ideas and policies from their neighbours. A good example is that of China and Vietnam. They have begun to actively adopt the Singapore model for their economic development by adopting many of the policies practised by Singapore such as in the areas of infrastructure development, public housing, air and sea port development, and even the compulsory savings scheme concept. In the case of Malaysia, it has now allowed the teaching of technical subjects in the universities to be in English (as opposed to Bahasa Malaysia in the past) as an attempt to ensure that Malaysian workers do not lose out as a result of language constraint. In addition, Malaysia is known to pattern many of its industrial and economic policies after those of Singapore. For example, their Employee Provident Fund (EPF) scheme resembles that of Singapore's Central Provident Fund (CPF), and their Human Resource Development Fund (HRDF) has similar features to that of Singapore's Skill Development Fund (SDF). Thus, political ideologies and cultural inhibitions are gradually giving way to economic pragmatism and market realities. The ability to shed such inhibitions will ensure that these countries will continue to develop at an even faster pace.

This positive attitude with regard to learning also extends to other areas. While some countries tend to be very defensive about foreign technology and ideas, it is not the case with many Asian countries. On the contrary, they have been very liberal in the importation of foreign technology and ideas. For example, they encourage foreign investment as a major means to generating employment, minimizing the use of local capital, and to gaining access to international markets and technology; they allow the employment of expatriates so as to fill in gaps in the skills of the locals as well as to provide the motivation for the locals to upgrade; and they are even prepared to change local laws and regulations (for example, in adopting laws on protecting copyrights and patents) in order to attract more multinational corporations (MNCs) to invest. Some countries like Singapore and Malaysia even encourage MNCs to set up overseas research and development offices and operation headquarters. The result is that many Asian countries are able to leap-frog forward very quickly as the learning process is shortened considerably.

1.6 Implications

The macro changes experienced by countries in the Asian region hold tremendous implications for the marketeer. This is because there are now morenew opportunities available to the shrewd marketeer who is able to capitalize on these developments. The rest of the book will be devoted to highlighting many salient issues that are relevant to the marketeer operating in the new Asian context. At this point, I will only highlight some major implications for consideration.

1.6.1 The Marketing Function Has Arrived

Prior to the increasing affluence of the Asian region, a firm may be primarily concerned with producing a fairly good quality product and then distributing and selling it through the most efficient channel. To some extent, this approach is still applicable to some Asian countries like India, Vietnam and Sri Lanka. However, the production-oriented approach is reactive in nature and tends to focus primarily on the product. It is suitable when the expectations of the consumers are low. Moreover, as compared to the consumer who tends to be very dynamic, the product tends to be relatively static. As such, when a firm focuses mainly on the product and production, it is less likely to make major changes over time. Take the example of white bread. As a product, it has hardly undergone any significant changes over the years. Yet, as a result of changing consumer demands, it is now a highly differentiated product. Thus, brands like Gardenia and Sunshine are not only able to capture substantial market shares in the white bread industry, but are able to price their bread at a premium. In essence, as the Asian consumers become more sophisticated and demanding, a more proactive stance is needed — that of a marketing approach.

To begin with, the marketeer must now pay close attention to consumer analysis, and make attempts to monitor the consumer's changing tastes and preferences. For example, as consumers become more complex and sophisticated, there is a need to be concerned with market segmentation and targetting. Similarly, as various marketeers begin to bring in a greater quantity and variety of products and brands to satisfy the consumers in this region, there is a need for product differentiation. Not only does a firm need to create actual differences along various product attributes vis-a-vis its competitors, it also has to develop perceived differences as well — many of these may be intangible cues like brand names and images. Positioning through detailed market and consumer analysis and product differentiation is fast becoming an important dimension of the marketeer's task.

The marketeer must also constantly review his product, pricing, promotion, and placement (distribution), strategies — commonly known as the 4Ps of marketing — to find how he can create or develop competitive advantages as a result of changes at the macro level. For example, improved education will have an impact on the decision-making processes of the people. With better education, the Asian consumer is now in a better position to decide on product choices and quality, and is more capable of forming his own opinion and judgement. On the other hand, as he is now richer and more educated, there are also more ways for the marketeer to reach out to him. Radios and other forms of audio broadcasts were used extensively in the past. Today, the more expensive audio-visual means like televisions and cinemas are used very effectively. Of late, cable television provides another new avenue for the marketeer to reach out to the three billion viewers in Asia. These can be complemented by printed media like newspapers and magazines that are targetted at specific audiences.

In the area of distribution, new avenues must be explored beyond the traditional channels which may be losing their effectiveness in reaching out to the Asian consumers. In Singapore and many major Asian cities, the corner grocery stores are gradually being replaced by modern supermarkets (like NTUC Fairprice), chain stores (like

Econ Minimart and 7-Eleven) and mini-supermarkets operated by gasoline chains like Shell, Esso, and Caltex. Indeed, the shift away from traditional channels of distribution can be seen by the mushrooming of many modern shopping centres, supermarkets, departmental stores, and specialty stores in cities like Bangkok, Jakarta, Kuala Lumpur, Taipei, Seoul, Beijing, Shanghai, Manila, and so on. With greater affluence, the Asia-Pacific consumers are demanding a more conducive shopping environment. It is perhaps in response to, as well as in capitalizing on these new challenges that Takashimaya — one of the largest retail giants in Japan — decided to set up a mammoth department store in Singapore in 1993.

Packaging of products is another area that needs improvement. Here, the Japanese companies have clearly excelled. The amount of details that Japanese manufacturers put into packaging, say, a box of candies, is indeed remarkable. Similarly, one is easily impressed by the thoroughness and overall appeal of gift wrapping of Japanese retailers. By paying attention to packaging, Japanese marketeers are able to create a very expensive and high quality image for their products. This "created value" inevitably enables Japanese marketeers to place higher price tags on their products. The Japanese are not alone in exploiting the power of packaging. Of late, companies in this region are beginning to pay attention to this area, even for products like compact discs and books. Consumers are now willing to pay a premium for better packaged products.

1.6.2 Managing Change

In a fast growing market like Asia, there is a need for managers to learn how to cope with and manage change. This is particularly relevant to subsidiaries and agents of large MNCs which have their headquarters in the United States and Europe. As mentioned earlier, in contrast to Asia, these countries are barely growing. It would thus be unwise to manage their businesses in the dynamic region of Asia from a distant headquarter where its market is hardly changing, or worse, even shrinking. This is because the skills and resources required to manage in a fast-changing market environment are very different from those required in one where there is minimal growth. In addition, being absent from the region, it would be difficult to capitalize on the opportunities that may arise. This is because in a high-growth economy, not only are there plentiful opportunities, but they also come and go at a fast pace. Thus, unless one is close to the area of action, one is likely to miss the boat.

A good example of a missed opportunity for the western companies can be cited from the airline industry. While many American and European airlines did not see the need for expansion owing to their ailing and stagnant economies back home, many Asian economies have set up new airlines to capitalize on the air travel in Asia. Over the last few years, many new airlines have emerged in Asia, such as Eva Air (of Taiwan), All Nippon Airways Airlines (of Japan), Dragon Air (of Hong Kong), SilkAir (of Singapore), and Sempati Air (of Indonesia). More significantly, there have been at least six new airlines that have emerged since China opened up to the outside world, and new economies like Vietnam, Cambodia and Burma are re-establishing their airlines to gain more international exposure.

Fortunately, there are enlightened American companies like Motorola, Coca-Cola, McDonald's, and Allied Signals which have begun to restructure themselves to take advantage of the market opportunities offered by Asia. Motorola has even established regional research and development, and copyright headquarters in the region. By decentralizing and providing more automony to overseas headquarters, companies like Motorola would be able to respond to the changing needs of the Asian market quickly and effectively. In this way, it will be able to introduce and adapt new products and services to the region faster. Motorola, for instance, has been able to benefit substantially from the sale of pagers and cellular phones to the region largely because it is well organized in accessing the Asian market.

Without doubt, in a fast growing region, the response to the changing business environment has to be swift and decisive. As such, many decisions must be made close to the market place. In addition, there is a need to monitor the new needs and wants of the consumer. The adoption process for new products and services in a fast growing region may be shortened considerably so that the marketeer can seize the opportunities that emerge. After all, the consumption gap is narrowing very quickly between countries in the Asian region and the developed countries. Thus, what were luxuries that appeared to be beyond the means of the Asian consumer may now become affordable. In essence, the marketeer must keep a very close watch of the market, and proximity to it would be a definite advantage. In addition, he must not be bound by past events and experiences. Instead,

13

he must be proactive and innovative in his approach to the Asian market. Those who choose to wait and operate from a distance will only live to regret doing so.

1.6.3 Exploiting the Regional Market

In the past, companies in Asia used to target their products for the European and American markets. In fact, many of them had to rely on these markets for the survival of their businesses. Some of them even exported a hundred percent of their output, while others became suppliers of parts and components. This orientation towards the European and American markets will have to change because the European and American markets are now growing at a very slow rate. In some industries, they are even stagnating or, worse still, declining. Furthermore, as a result of the success of the export-oriented policies of the Asian NIEs and LDEs in the past, many American and European manufacturers are today lobbying heavily for greater protection of their local industries. As such, it would be increasingly difficult to penetrate these markets. In sum, it is no longer viable for Asian companies to rely on these traditional markets.

On the other hand, as discussed earlier, the Asian market is now growing by leaps and bounds. Companies of Asian origin must now re-orientate their businesses to capitalize on this vast potential. Unfortunately, this is where many Asian companies, because of their past reliance on the businesses of the western MNCs, are weak at. In the area of brand development, for instance, Asian companies are lagging way behind their counterparts in Japan and the West. This is because many of them chose to become licensees of established western and Japanese brands. In the past, such a strategy made good business sense as it would allow these Asian manufacturers to have access to the western and Japanese markets easily. However, as the Asian market develops, there is a need to have good brands for the marketing of products and services. Owing to the lack of Asian brands, it is no surprise that many Asian consumers turn to Japanese and western brands. This is particularly true of consumer products.

This is where Asian companies must make attempts to improve themselves, especially in focussing their business and marketing attention on Asia. A paradigm shift is urgently required if they want to do well in the future. In particular, they must now pay increasing attention to the marketing function and invest in brand development. Fortunately, the Asian market is very large and still growing, so that there is still time for the more enterprising Asian companies to develop a strong presence in the region.

1.7 Conclusion

Perhaps the advent of the marketing era in Asia can be best illustrated by the experiences of the western fast food industry. In a region where culture and traditional values are high in a country's priority, and where strong attempts have been made to resist western culture and influences, the tremendous successes of the western fast food chains demonstrate conclusively that the power of marketing transcends various cultures and value system.

When the western fast food chains first entered the Asia-Pacific market, many skeptics argued that Asians would never develop a taste for hamburgers or pizzas, and that their presence would only be a passing fad. Their arguments were not unfounded. The prices of these western fast food were by no means low. In fact, they were and are much higher than local fast food. The same cup of coffee in a local restaurant would cost more in a western one. One can even go further to challenge the nutritional value of hamburgers, hot dogs, fries, and pizzas. How can any Asian, who has grown up on rice and noodles, ever fall for such "junk" food? Any logical person would think not.

However, history has an interesting way of unfolding itself. Today, western fast food outlets like those of McDonald's, Burger King, Kentucky Fried Chicken, and Pizza Hut — amongst others — are familiar sights in any major city such as Singapore and in Hong Kong, Malaysia, Philippines, and even Japan and China — all rather different societies in terms of dietary habits. Yet, in all these countries, these western fast food outlets have not only done well, but in some cases, they have even out-done the local fast food operators as well. How did they succeed? The answer is definitely not in the food, but in the way they approach the market.

Among other reasons, the strong marketing orientation of these western fast food chains must be singled out as one of the key factors for success. All these chains study their markets carefully before establishing their footholds. True, they have encountered hiccups in some instances, but they never fail to focus on the Asian consumer whose income is rising, and lifestyle changing. They rely heavily on marketing research data to monitor their performances, and never

15

hesitate to adopt innovative and creative ways to reach out to the consumers. This is shown by the incredible number of sales gimmicks that they come up with constantly to attract and entice customers. Immense efforts are also invested to build and extend consumer loyalty. For instance, McDonald's cleverly "buys" the loyalty of its young consumers — the kids — by "selling" them small souvenirs, toys and other products that carry the McDonald's logo! It focuses heavily on influencing the mindsets and winning the hearts of the kids who in turn, can "persuade" their parents to lunch or dine at McDonald's.

What is interesting about the McDonald's experience is the way it involves the consumers in the purchasing process. The extent of its success can be clearly seen when one considers the fact that it is able to make the customer queue up patiently for his or her food, make payment before consumption without questioning the prices, help the restaurant to upkeep its cleanliness by clearing empty trays and cups, and so on, and at the end of it all, to comment that the service is fantastic despite having paid a high price for a lot of self-service!

The western fast food chains also constantly try to come up with new products and exciting promotional campaigns that are normally very well-timed in terms of launching (for example, just before the school holidays for children). In addition, they choose the locations of their restaurants very carefully — often conveniently located in high volume traffic areas. Finally, they also pay close attention to in-store service and comfort for the consumers. In essence, by adopting a total marketing approach, they have been able to levy a price premium for their products, including the soft drinks and beverages!

The success of the western fast food chains clearly demonstrates that the era of marketing has arrived in the Asian region. The western fast food chains have altered the attitude toward the consumption of beef, hotdogs, cheese, bacons and French Fries; they have shown that with effective marketing, even the traditional strong-holds of the various local food industries in the Asian region can be challenged. This being true in the case of the food industry, is likely to be true of other industries as well.

2

Understanding the Changing Asian Consumer

2.1 Introduction

Without doubt, the focus of any marketing effort in a market economy has to be the consumer. He is the one who will determine the success or failure of any product or service. Hence, there is a need to understand his attitude and behaviour. Such an understanding would be much easier to gain if the consumer's taste does not change drastically. Unfortunately, this is not the case. This is especially so in the case of the Asian consumer. As a result of increasing economic growth experienced by many of the Asian countries, there has been drastic transformation in the consumption pattern of their consumers. One only has to travel to the major cities of these countries to experience the rate at which these consumers are changing.

For instance, who would have expected that as a result of the opening up of China, many of its consumers in the coastal and major cities have become so fashion- and brand-conscious within a very short period of time? Barely ten years ago, designer brands were unknown to the Chinese. Today, the major streets of Beijing, Shanghai, Shenzhen and Hangzhou are lined with upmarket boutiques and fashion stores. western fast food restaurants too, are now a common sight in these cities. In the area of jewelry consumption, the Chinese are no longer contented with gold, but are now going for platinum.

In the same way, the growth of the telecommunication industry in Asia where pagers and cellular handphones are concerned, has been nothing short of spectacular over the last ten years. On a per capita basis, economies like Hong Kong and Singapore now rank highest among the world in terms of ownership for pagers and handphones! The phenomenal growth in the telecommunications industry in Asia has even prompted companies like Motorola and Northern Telecom to establish regional headquarters in Singapore and elsewhere in the region.

What has happened to the new Asian consumers? This chapter will explore some of the fundamental shifts in taste of the fast changing Asian consumers. The need to do so is very obvious — there are about three billion of them in a region that is now widely recognized as the fastest growing in the world.

2.2 Increasing Western Influence

With their emphasis on economic development, particularly with importation of foreign capital, technology and personnel from the developed countries (largely the western world) it is inevitable that the people in the Asian region comes under western influence. This influence is further augmented by the various mass media like television programmes, cinema shows, magazines, and newspapers. Cable News Networks (CNN), for example, is telecasted even in countries like China, Indonesia and Thailand. In fact, recognizing the potential of Asia, satellite broadcasters and cable systems operators such as Rupert Murdoch's News Corporation, and Home Box Office (HBO) International are setting up operations all over Asia to capture this vast market of three billion potential viewers — a market size that is likely to prove more important than that of the United States and Europe combined in the next ten to fifteen years.

The advent of these western mass media, especially that of satellite broadcasting and cable television, provides a new and powerful way to reach the minds of consumers in Asia. They not only influence the attitude and behaviour of the Asian consumers, but have the capacity to alter and change their outlook and lifestyle as well. Today, many television programmes and movies shown in this part of the world are imported from western countries. The audiences are thus constantly being bombarded with western culture, values and lifestyles and generally, a materialistic outlook.

In the past, when incomes were low, the western lifestyle as portrayed on television and magazines were regarded as fantasies. However, with increasing affluence, these fantasies are fast becoming realities; consumers are acquiring more and more of the western lifestyles, tastes, and behaviour. A good example is the yuppies. In many ways, their life-styles and value systems are mirror those of their counterparts in the West. They prefer buying western branded products, model their homes along European or American designs, patronize western theatres and fine arts, consume French wines, and so on. In fact, the Asian yuppies even surpass their western counterparts in several ways — they employ domestic maids, are keen owners of pets with pedigrees, and are ardent purchasers of exclusive golf and social club memberships.

The power of the western media in influencing the Asian consumers has now become a concern among Asian political leaders. In some countries like Malaysia, Indonesia, Thailand and Singapore, attempts by the government are made to reduce the influence of the western media by regulating the number of broadcasting hours, increasing local contents in media and resorting to censorship. However, until such time that the Asian countries are able to develop their media industry to a level of sophistication comparable to that of the West, they will have to bear and withstand the onslaught of western influence for some years to come.

2.3 Emergence of Consumer Credit

Another noticeable development in Asia in the recent years is the emergence of consumer credit. This is brought about to a large extent by the increase in incomes over the years and an optimistic expectation of the economic future of the region. Assimilation of western values and the influence of the marketeer in promoting credit are also responsible for this change. For instance, banks and related financial institutions and even companies often advertise a wide array of credit facilities that are available to consumers. Some financial institutions like Citibank even grant unsecured personal loans within twenty-four hours to an application by phone!

Fifteen years ago, consumer credit was rather alien to even the city dwellers of the NIEs and semi-LDEs. Thrift is definitely a virtue in the past when borrowing was considered demeaning and a social taboo. Today, the same city dwellers in the NIEs and LDEs would be considered by their peers as old-fashioned and out of touch with the times if they do not have a bank overdraft. The phenomenon of living on credit is especially prevalent among yuppies who pride themselves on the number and the variety of colours of credit cards that they possess, as well as the kinds of credit lines they enjoy from the banks (from personal loans to share financing). Apparently, for them, leveraging is now the way to live.

The rise in consumer credit in Asia can be seen the mushrooming of credit cards. In recent years, the growth of credit cards in the region has far exceeded that of the world, both in terms of the number of cards and the volume of sale cards. In view of the strong economic performance of the region, it is likely that the growth trend of credit cards is likely to continue in the future. The trend, especially that of easy access to credit, has caused some governments in Asia to tighten up credit and extol the virtue and importance of thrift and of thrift.

With more money and credit, the new Asian consumer is in a position to demand more from the marketplace, both in terms of quantity and quality of products and services offered. Marketeers, have not failed to take advantage of this changing trend. For example, banks are now more willing to grant more and larger consumer loans and overdraft facilities for purchases of properties, cars, and even shares. The repayment period has also been extended. For example, while car loans in Singapore rarely exceeded five years in the past, they have now been extended to eight to ten years. In addition, some banks are even willing to finance the cost of the Certificate of Entitlement (COE) for the purchase of a car (as of December 1993, the cost of a certificate averaged about US$35,000). Similarly, mortgage payments on housing loans have been extended to thirty years in some Asian countries. In the case of Japan, the mortgage payment can even be stretched to two generations! Further more, owing to the business optimism in some of these Asian economies, banks are even prepared to take mortgages and extend loans on a "balloon" scheme basis — that is, the repayment amount increases over the period of the loan.

Banks are not the only ones cashing in on the live-on-credit mentality of the Asian consumers. Consumer onsumer credit is also given through the various hire-purchase arrangements and instalment plans for the purchases of various consumer durables such as television, hi-fi systems, furniture, pianos, computers, and so on. Even services relating to hospitalization, honeymoon, and vacation packages can now be purchased through instalment plans.

2.4 From Needs to Wants

With increased income and education, the Asian consumers, especially those from Japan, the four NIEs and the city dwellers of the semi-NIEs and LDEs, have moved beyond a "needs-driven" to that of a "wants-driven" society. In other words, he is no longer contented with satisfying his basic needs. This drive by "wants" takes various forms. For example, what used to be considered as a luxury item is now deemed essential. The motorcar fits this description. If any, the growth of cars has been stunning, doubling in population within a period of ten years in many instances. Japan's car population went up from thirty-one million in 1980 to fifty-one million in 1990. In Bangkok, cars increased from 450,000 in 1977 to 900,000 in 1987, and then to two million in 1990. In Taipei, the car population has reached an unmanageable number of 1.9 million in 1990, with 463,200 registrations in 1989 alone. The same story is repeated in other Asian cities like Beijing, Shanghai, and Kuala Lumpur. Such high growth rates are not surpassed anywhere else in the world. In fact, the tremendous growth in car populations has reached a proportion that the governments in these countries have now to resolve the massive traffic congestion problems that have built up in cities like Jakarta, Bangkok, Kuala Lumpur, Beijing, and others.

Despite the congestion problems, the demand for cars has not declined in many Asian countries. On the contrary, many American, Japanese and European car manufacturers are entering into alliances with local partners to set up factories in countries like China, India, Malaysia, Taiwan and Indonesia. In the case of Malaysia, it has succeeded in securing a good market share for its first national car, the Proton Saga, has since launched Proton Wira, and has several other automobile plants in the pipeline. Clearly, the car is fast within the reach of the average household in Asia.

Besides cars, the "down-grading" of luxuries to necessities extend to products like television, hi-fi systems, refrigerators, air-conditioners, ovens, washing machines, and many other consumer durables. Many of these items used to be considered as "treasures" by the Chinese in the early 1980s when China had just opened up its economy. Today, the Chinese consumers in all the major cities would deem the same items as necessities! What is more startling is that in some societies like Hong Kong, Taiwan and Singapore, the consumer is after his second television set, second car, second telephone number, second maid, and so on.

Owning a vacation home like a condominium unit or house in another country has now become a reality among the richer Asian consumers in Hong Kong, Taiwan, Malaysia, Indonesia, South Korea, Japan, and Singapore. Besides developers within the region, Australian, British, and even American real estate operators have begun to actively market their properties in these countries. Many of these properties come complete with resort facilities and management contracts. The largest group of investors of private properties in Australia are now Asians. Interestingly, in order to attract the Asian buyers, the Australian developers and real estate agents even employ geomancy experts to assist them in their marketing efforts!

2.5 Aesthetic but Conspicuous Consumption

The drive from needs to wants is also supported by another interesting trend. The new Asian consumer is beginning to shift from a **functional** orientation to a more **aesthetic** orientation in his consumption behaviour. In the past, the average consumer probably operated on a "big, more, and cheap" mentality, and was very concerned about the functional aspect of the product. But today, he is more concerned with aspects like brand name, style, colour, design, packaging, and other add-on features — the aesthetics. In other words, consumers today are willing to pay more for what they perceive as "personal value" or reflective of their personalities — both may have little to do with the functional aspects of the product or service. This, to a large extent, accounts for the emergence of the high fashion industries like designer clothings, costume jewelry, branded watches, and interior decorations for homes. Many of the international designer houses have come in droves to the region in recent years.

The move from a "quantity" to a "quality" approach provides new challenges to the marketeer. This is because there are many intangibles within branded products and services that make rational evaluations almost impossible. For example, how does one place a value on brands like Pierre Cardin, Bally, Dunhill, Chanel, Goldlion, Valentino, Christian Dior, and so on? While it is true that such brands deserve premiums owing to their better quality, it is debatable how much that premium should be. This is where the marketeer can gain if he can build up a strong image for a brand. Thus, there is now more scope for creative advertising and promotion, greater possibilities for product differentiation (even if it is only by brands) and distribution (like having boutiques and specialty stores), and greater leverage for pricing (that is, pricing is not restricted to the basis of functional attributes of the product itself).

The pursuit for the aesthetics and gracious living has also created changes to the demand for new products. For example, over the past few years, the demand for wine consumption went up considerably in many Asian markets. This is because the Asian yuppies perceive wine consumption as modern, refine and stylish than the consumption of liquor which is considered as conventional, hard, and strong. In the same way, light beer has successfully made its market presence felt owing to the emergence of light drinkers (including women).

A somewhat parallel development to the aesthetic orientation and the pursuit of gracious living is the trend toward conspicuous consumption. Many Asians, because of their sudden accumulation of wealth, have yet to fully understand and appreciate what gracious living entails. To them, it means a higher standard in material life. Thus, they buy paintings, patronize the theatres, collect antiques, subscribe to exclusive clubs, employ foreign maids, engage tutors of all sorts for their children, keep pets with pedigrees, purchase expensive imported and branded products, consume exotic coffee and wines, and so on. As ways to reflect such a lifestyle. For example, Mercedes cars, Rolex watches, and Mont Blanc pens, Bally shoes, Dunhill ties, and Motorola cellular phones have successfully taken advantage of their high images and egoistic appeals to generate fairly substantial premiums over their competitors. Some brands like Mercedes and Rolex have even become symbols of **societal arrival**.

The ostentatious and egoistic consumption behaviour of the Asian consumer has also spawned the development of many leisure industries like golf, tennis and social clubs. Membership to these clubs are priced excessively high when compared to those in the western world. Whereas golf is a sport for the average consumer in the West, in Asia it has been elevated to a pursuit for the rich and famous to engage in for networking and socializing. Such memberships are thus marketed as symbols of success and initiation into the societal order. For example, a membership at the Singapore Island Country Club costs about US$150,000 as of early 1994!

As an attempt to meet the insatiable demand for such egoistic affiliations, more and more golf courses have been built in this part of the world, even including China. Of late, there has also been a new trend emerging — the demand for marina membership as a result of the increasing ownership of leisure boats and yachts. In fact, the richer Asian consumer today pride themselves with claims to spending weekends and holidays at sea fishing and socializing on their own boats.

2.6 Increased Demand for Discretionary Products and Services

The aesthetic orientation has also led to the emergence of many new service industries: those relating to music, theatres and the fine arts. Fifteen to twenty years ago, few consumers in this part of the world would dream of taking a vacation. Today, annual vacation (at times more than once a year) has become a social norm, especially among consumers in the more developed economies within the region. More significantly, the nature of the vacation has also changed. It is no longer mere sightseeing. Instead, the new Asian consumer has begun to opt for more varied vacation packages that include activities like cultural shows, free time for self exploration and relaxation, camping, mountain climbing, bungee jumping, scuba-diving, fishing, golfing, factory visits, amongst others. He is also more willing to venture to farther and more exotic sites, even unexplored ones. The result is that more and more resort areas have sprouted within this region over the past few years to cater to the new Asian holiday maker.

The changing preferences in vacationing of Asian consumers have led Club Mediterranee, the French leisure group, to step up its investments in the region. As of 1995, Club Med operates resorts in Thailand, Malaysia, Japan, and Indonesia. In the near future, it plans to develop new resort villages in Vietnam, China, Singapore, Okinawa (Japan), Korea and Taiwan. In order to cater to the special needs of the Asian tourists, Club Med is said to be modifying its vacation packages so that they would avoid the Club's reputation for "sun, sea and sex" (which generally do not appeal to many Asian vacationers). For example, instead of providing a week-long stay at one resort, it intends to shorten a stay to only a few days, and to include sightseeing and other activities. In addition, recognizing the penchant of Asians for food, it has also included Asian menus. To overcome the language barrier, it has begun to train its guides to ensure that different Asian vacationers in the group can feel comfortable in the various organized activities. Given the passion of many Asians for golf and gambling, it would not be surprising if Club Med include such activities in their new resort villages.

Besides the demand for vacationing and travel, the richer and better educated urban consumers in Asia have also developed tastes for the fine arts, concerts and theatres. These industries never flourished in the past. For example, ten years ago, it would have been unthinkable to stage multi-million dollar concerts for western artistes like Michael Jackson, Diana Ross, Pavorotti, and Placedo Domingo. Today, despite their high fees, these artistes are able to perform before packed audiences. More significantly, even home-grown Asian artistes are beginning to be appreciated. In the past, many Asian artistes had to migrate to Europe or America to make a living. Today, they can command hefty performance fees and enjoy comfortable lifestyles.

Besides concert performers and singers, artists like painters, calligraphers, sculptors, musicians, composers, symphony conductors, choreographers and even deejays are beginning to win greater respect in their communities. Their works are also of increasing market values. For example, well-known Chinese painter, Wu Guan Zhong, an artist of international stature whose his paintings are exhibited around the world and are priced in the six-figure range. Wu is not the only artist who is enjoying high premiums for his works. There is now a thriving market for Asian (in particular, Chinese) paintings, calligraphies and antiques as there are now more and more serious collectors. This has prompted world renowned art auction houses like Sotheby to set up offices in Hong Kong and Singapore.

The appreciation for the fine arts has given rise to many related industries like music and dance studios, musical equipment and supply shops, exhibition halls, as well as classes for the teaching of painting and calligraphy. Today, writers (including those from Asia) of fiction and other related subjects have found increasing appreciative readership. The consumers are reading more (as a result of widespread and higher education) for relaxation and leisure.

In the future, it is likely that a greater number and variety of hobbies will emerge as a result of the overall pursuit for a more cultural and balanced lifestyle. Thus coins, stamps the collection of and other related artefacts will probably find increasing followers in Asia. Similarly, landscaping and the growing of rare plants and flowers will probably become activities pursued by the rich. As it is, the pursuit for exotic hobbies has taken various forms which are very interesting. For example, a single pot of "Damo" orchid plant was auctioned off in Hong Kong in 1993 for more than US$550,000! It is not uncommon for orchid plants to sell for tens of thousand dollars in Hong Kong, Taiwan, Japan, and even China. Similarly, rare fishes like the Japanese Koi (*nishiki* carp that can live up to one hundred years or more), the Discus and the Arawana are bought for thousands of dollars each! In 1993, a Singaporean family bought a "lionhead" dog for more than US$65,000! Strange as they may be to many westerners, all these are nonetheless examples – not isolated ones either – of the purchasing power of the new Asian consumers.

2.7 Premium on Time and Health

Like his western counterpart, the Asian consumer is also beginning to feel the pressure of not having sufficient time. There are several causes for this. To begin with, more and more women have entered the labour force. While this has created more double income families (and hence, greater spending power), it has also reduced the time available for household chores. There has also been a conspicuous decline in the size of the family as a result of successful family planning, thus making eating at home less practical. All these have resulted in the trend of families to eat out very frequently, with some even opting for home catering and home delivery of food.

The squeeze on time has resulted in a demand for products and services that offer convenience and time-saving features. Such products include vacuum cleaners, washing machines, dish washers, and microwave ovens. The preference for products that have automatic or remote control features is one of the most interesting manifestation of pursuit for convenience. Today, many household durables like television, laser disc players, hi-fi systems, amongst others come complete with remote control facilities. Even the household gate can be activated by remote control!

The pursuit of a more gracious lifestyle has also placed a premium on time. This is because any time saved on doing household chores and other "non-productive" work can be diverted to the pursuit of hobbies and leisure activities like sports and games. This is probably one of the reasons for the tremendous demand for domestic help and maids among many urban and more affluent Asian consumers. In fact, on a per capita basis, economies like Hong Kong and Singapore are probably ranked among the highest employers of foreign domestic maids. Besides domestic maids, other products and services that can enable the consumers to save time have become increasingly popular: automatic telling machines (ATMs), for basic banking functions, electronic payments (no queueing needed) through banks (GIRO services), electronic booking of seats for theatres and cinema shows, telephone enquiry services, and so on, are fast spreading in many Asian cities.

Recently, another time-saving product that has had a warm reception from many affluent Asian consumers is home entertainment systems. Together with easy purchase and rental of laser discs and videos, movies can now be watched in the comfort of the home. This has helped the Asian consumer to save time on having to travel to watch a movie. It is likely that home entertainment systems will become increasingly popular among the urban dwellers of Asia. This is because in many Asian cities like Bangkok, Jakarta, Taipei, Hong Kong, Kuala Lumpur and even Beijing, traffic jams and conjestions have become serious problems to the extent that social outings — like going to the cinema — can become very time-consuming, frustrating and stressful. Marketeers of home entertainment systems should capitalize on the situation to promote their products, working towards a wider acceptance of them.

Advanced technology also offers tremendous opportunities for the shrewd marketeer to introduce new products and services to the fast learning Asian consumers who place an increasing premium on time. For example, electronic shopping through teleview in countries like Singapore is now a reality. It would not be long before such technology will be made available to other large Asian cities. In fact, large retailers should use technology to provide better services to consumers. For example, they could provide free delivery of goods through tele-shopping or electronic shopping. In doing so, they not only provide convenience to the shoppers, but also help them to save time, to levy of course, the marketeer then for such services provided. As it is, fast food operators like Pizza Hut levy a charge for home delivery service, and taxi operators levy a surcharge when their services are booked in advance through telephone booking.

In the area of health, many skeptics, a few years ago, thought that self-dispensing drug and health food stores never find enough customers. However, judging by the speed in which such stores have been springing up in countries like Singapore, Hong Kong, and even cities in Thailand, Indonesia, and Malaysia, the pharmaceutical business is going to be a fast growing industry. Even China is no exception. Recognizing the vast potential that China offers, Janssen Pharmaceutical set up a joint venture company in Xian in the 1980s.

Today, it is still facing challenges to cope with the demand of the domestic market alone.

Similarly, few would dream that bottled mineral water will ever have a market when in most Asian cities, it is possible to drink water directly from the taps. Yet, the sales of bottled mineral water in the last few years have silenced the harshest critics. Complementing the growth of self-dispensing drugs and mineral water is a whole range of health food businesses like salad bars, yogurt, low calories restaurants, and so on. Like their North American and European counterparts, the Asian consumers are becoming more health conscious. They have also begun to take on a proactive orientation and pre-emptive stand where health is concerned. Health clubs, aerobics lessons and various exercise classes are now very common in many Asian cities.

One of the interesting trends that have emerged in recent years as a result of the premium placed on health is the growth of the insurance industry. In particular, life and accident insurance policies which were shunned by Asian consumers in the past, have now become widely accepted. Of late, as a result of increasing health care costs and longer life expectancy, policies that cover critical illness (commonly known as crisis cover) and hospitalization have become popular among the more affluent Asian consumers. Over time, it is likely that such health-related type of insurance will spread to the rest of the population.

2.8 Future Oriented

The Asian consumers are becoming more future-oriented. Owing to better education, Asian consumers are no longer myopic in their goals. In other words, they are more capable of making independent decisions, and are less hampered by events of the past or superstitions. Such an outlook has been affected to some extent by advances in technology. Today's consumers are better informed of what is going on in the world at large. Higher incomes and more education have heightened awareness of events and happenings around them. Thus, like their western counterparts, they have become more conscious of their environment. Inevitably, the conduct of business will be affected by such consciousness of the environment. For example, the cigarette industry is facing increasing difficulty in trying to survive in countries like Singapore where the government, with the support of the people, are pursuing anti-smoking campaigns with great fervour. Besides Singapore, many other countries in the region have also ban cigarette advertising and sponsorship. Other businesses that are causing pollution should take heed of what is happening to the cigarette industry — their turns may be next. On the other hand, **recycling** business (of bottles and other non-polluting containers) may make a comeback in the not too distant future.

The future-oriented outlook of the consumers has also sparked off other forms of business opportunities. The consumer is more willing to borrow and live on credit. This is because he is more confident of his future, and is prepared to leverage. In addition, his optimism also prompts him to be more adventurous in some of his purchase decisions in terms of stretching his financial means. This is most evident in the area of housing. Many consumers today are prepared to take larger mortgages that stretch over longer periods. Some of them have even ventured into investing in assets that have long term appreciation value like antiques, coins, stamps, and paintings.

To some extent, the Asian consumer's future-oriented outlook should not come as too much as a surprise to anyone who understands the Asian culture. By tradition, many Asians have always taken a very long term view of life when compared to their western counterparts. This is evidenced by the practice of "investing" heavily in their children in the area of education as well as allowing the children to stay with them (rent free) for as long as they remain single. In fact, even after their child's marriage, Asian parents do not object if their son or daughter and his or her spouse choose to live with them. Here lies some possibilities for the enterprising marketeers to capitalize on such Asian practices. One area is that of marketing of properties. For example, property developers could build and design homes that cater to extended families, and yet provide privacy for the immediate family unit. This can be done by creating a "home within a home" concept. Houses could be designed with separate entrances and facilities for each home, yet built within the same compound.

It is interesting to note that the more affluent Asian parents have also begun to buy properties for their children as a hedge against future inflation of housing. This is particularly true in the urban cities of Asia where property prices have been skyrocketing in the 1980s. Ironically, in doing so, they have helped to maintain or even drive up existing property prices. Indeed, the concern for the future of their children is not confined to buying properties alone. Many Asian

parents have begun to purchase education insurance policies as a
hedge against future increases in the costs of education and to ensure that their children will not miss out on having a tertiary education owing to the lack of funds. Such a mentality of the Asian consumer
can definitely be exploited for the marketing of new products and
services. The range of possibilities is limited only by the creativity
and innovativeness of the shrewd marketeer.

2.9 Don't Rule Out the Impossible

Without doubt, some of the major factors causing the change among
Asian consumers have got to do with the higher levels of income and
education, greater exposure to the lifestyles of the western world
through the mass media, a more globalized society (brought about by
advances in communication and technology), and the marketing efforts made by firms (such as introducing more and newer products
and services). These factors have, in aggregate, created major shifts
in consumer attitudes and behaviour. What is important for the
marketeer is not to take these things for granted. As a result of the
fast pace of change, it is not wise to rule out what seem impossible.
Perhaps one of the most interesting developments over the last few
years in the Asian region has to be the wide acceptance and popularity of the *karaoke* (which means "empty orchestra" in Japanese).

Most critics have argued, and understandably so, that the *karaoke*
cannot survive in the typically reserved cultures of Asia where most
people are shy and inhibited. Yet, this unusual and comical, bellow-
ing-your-heart-out form of entertaining others (or amusing oneself)
has given a new lease of life to lounges, bars, restaurants, and other
entertainment outfits, and created a new industry for the sale of
karaoke equipment and related items. More significantly, the *karaoke*
craze has spread through countries like Japan (the originator), Hong
Kong, Philippines, Thailand, Singapore, Malaysia, Indonesia, Taiwan,
South Korea, China — the list goes on! In addition, there is now a
wide range of related services which include highly customized set-
tings for mass singing in.

The *karaoke* is not the only example. It was previously assumed
that Chinese consumers would never like cheese. As such, when Pizza
Hut entered the Asian market, there was great skepticism about its
ability to survive in the face of competition from the Asian fast food.
Yet, since coming to Asia, Pizza Hut has been opening up restaurant

after restaurant in countries like Singapore, Hong Kong, Taiwan, and even China. Similarly, Asians were never known to have a taste for western food like salads, yogurt, and spaghetti. However, these foods are now widely accepted. In cities like Hong Kong, Singapore and Taipei, salad bar restaurants are beginning to become viable businesses. Of late, even pubs and taverns that cater to an increasingly Asian clientele have begun to appear in these cities as well.

Within each country in Asia, the changes at the consumer level have also caught many marketeers by surprise. As mentioned at the beginning of this chapter, the Chinese consumers in the major cities of China are today living a lifestyle that rival those of the NIEs. The hostility of the Vietnamese against the Americans was simply overwhelming after the Vietnam war. Any product that was made in America was literally thrown out. Yet, barely thirty years later, the Americans are now planning to invade Vietnam again, this time in the economic sphere and they have met with a warm reception. With the lifting of the trade embargo against Vietnam in February 1994, American companies are planning to invest between US$5 to US$10 billion within the next five years. As it is, many American consumer products like Pepsi-Cola and Coca-Cola have found ready acceptance by the Vietnamese consumers. The big battle for the Vietnamese consumers has really only begun with yet more American companies deciding to throw in their stakes.

The above examples show that what is once thought impossible or unlikely to happen, can and does happen. And when it does happen, those who are more prepared for it stand to gain by capitalizing on the opportunities that emerge, while those who are slow to react or who simply adopt a "follow strategy" tend to benefit less. It is important to point out that in a fast growing market like Asia, the consumers are very dynamic and their tastes and preferences can change very quickly. Thus, while there many opportunities appear, they disappear as quickly as they appear.

While capitalizing on opportunities, the marketeer must also be sensitive to the respective needs of the Asian consumers and their governments. A good example is that of the experience of Rupert Murdoch after he acquired control of Star TV. As a result of his over-enthusiastic remarks on what television can do to change politics in Asia, he was forced to back-paddle when the governments of China and Malaysia took offense to his statements. Recognizing the importance of the Asian consumers, especially those from China and India to his business, Murdoch even hinted in February 1994 that world renowned stations like the British Broadcasting Corporation (BBC) would risk losing a key channel in his network if it did not tone down its biased coverage on the Asian countries. Indeed, the power of the Asian consumers whom many western skeptics would never have expected, is finally a reality.

On the other hand, Japanese consumers are posing different challenges to their marketeers. While the purchasing power of the Japanese consumers has been increasing steadily since World War II as a result of their rising incomes, this increase finally slowed down in the 1990s. As a result of its prolonged economic slowdown since 1991, Japanese consumers are now becoming more price- and value-conscious, forcing marketeers to slash prices and cut frills. In fact, in retail marketing, no-frills shopping is now on the rise. To some extent, the Japanese retail scene is mirroring what happened to the American market in the 1980s. Such new trends are likely to leave a significant impact on how the Japanese consumers will shop in the future, even after they emerge from the slump.

2.10 Conclusion

In summary, the Asian consumers are no longer "pushovers". To a large extent, many countries in the Asia Pacific region are experiencing the arrival of a consumer society whereby they will begin to dictate what they would like to consume. No doubt, marketeers can always bring out more new products and services, but they will have to battle a lot harder for the consumer dollar. This is particularly so with increased competition and greater accessibility of technology — both acting to shorten the life cycles of products and services in the market. The marketeer would have to adopt a more proactive stance and a more professional approach to the marketplace if he hopes to be successful. Besides developing an indepth understanding of his consumers through consumer analysis, he would need to apply marketing tools like market segmentation, product differentiation, and positioning to aid him in developing more effective marketing strategies — topics which I shall cover in the next three articles.

3
Market Segmentation: Knowing the Basics

3.1 Introduction

Given a choice, and with unlimited corporate resources, a company would go after the entire market and become a monopolist. However, with very few exceptions, most companies have to contend with competitors and operate with limited corporate resources. At the same time, the marketplace is generally not made up of a homogeneous set of consumers. The Asian market is a very good example. It is much more diverse and heterogeneous than the American and European markets. There are the four clusters of economies in terms of stages of economic development to begin with— Japan at the top, followed by the four NIEs, the semi-NIEs and the LDEs. Besides countries differing in terms of stage of economic development, people in Asia are also of many different races, cultures, religions, and languages. The Indians are significantly different from the Chinese who are in turn very different from the Malays. In India alone, there are apparently over eight hundred different dialects.

Even among the Chinese, there are substantial differences in the way they think and behave, despite the fact that they may share the same cultural roots. For example, there are distinctive differences in behaviour, ideological thinking and lifestyles among the Taiwanese, Hong Kongers, Singaporean Chinese, Malaysian Chinese, Indonesian Chinese, Thai Chinese, and the Chinese of the People's Republic of China. The Thai and Indonesian Chinese have largely been assimilated into their respective local cultures, and have even adopted local names, customs and religions. Many of them do not even speak the Chinese language.

The Asian region is more complex than any other region in the world. This effectively means that from a marketing angle, there is a need to develop products and services to appeal to the different sets of consumers. This heterogeneity of consumer demand would compel a company to rationalize its corporate resources in order to make the most of the market. The process in which a company tries to adjust its products and services and marketing efforts to meet the different demand situations of the market is called **segmentation**. Specifically, market segmentation is the process in which a company divides a potentially large market into distinctive segments of consumers, and then selecting one or more of these subsets as market target or targets to be reached with a distinctive marketing mix strategy. This is because a company has limited resources and it is not feasible to go after the entire market. Moreover, with a distinctive strategy that is focused on one particular market segment, the effectiveness would be greater than using a general strategy. It is not easy to ascertain how well or successful a market has been segmented. I would like to advocate that a thorough market and consumer analysis be carried out first and that seven basic criteria be met when carrying out a segmentation exercise.

3.2 Market and Consumer Analysis

3.2.1 Macro Level

Prior to performing a segmentation exercise, the marketeer must have a macro view of the market or markets that he plans to serve. This would involve understanding the general trends and patterns of the consumer market. At the same time, he must also know whether the market lends itself to segmentation. For instance, prior to the adoption of market-oriented policies, countries like China and Vietnam were centrally-planned economies. With central planning, there was little scope for segmentation as it was not possible for the marketeer to develop customized strategies to reach the target market audience. Not surprisingly, the concerns were more for production and distribution. Customer orientation and responsiveness to the changing dynamics of the market forces were completely alien to these economies. At the same time, there was little income disparity among the masses and consumption behaviour was centrally determined to a large extent. Of course, with the market mechanism gradually coming into operation, there is now much more scope for the marketeer to segment his market so as to cater to the different needs of his consumers. This is now very evident in China where marketing strategies, especially in the areas of advertising and distribution (such as selling through departmental stores and boutiques), are beginning to be applied effectively.

There are many factors that the marketeer might want to address before deciding on how to segment a market. For example, at the macro level, many markets in Asia are characterized by the following:

- A fast growing market;
- Increasing consumer spending power;
- Movement from needs to wants in terms of consumption behaviour;
- Pent-up demand for consumer durables;
- Powerful influence of advertising and promotion;
- Increasing disparity of income between urban and rural consumers;
- Big underground economy;
- Increasing number of consumers having multiple sources of income;
- Preference for foreign products over domestically produced ones;
- Increasing brand awareness and consciousness;
- Emerging "herd" mentality in consumption behaviour;
- Increasing readiness to try new products or services;
- Increasing trend towards western lifestyle; and
- Emergence of consumer credit and hire purchase.

It is important for the marketeer to note that changes in consumer preferences do occur in aggregate and that there are discernible macro trends to allow him to develop appropriate and effective marketing strategies to exploit these trends. This is really what segmentation is all about — the marketeer must understand what the market is made up of before deciding which particular segment or segments would be best for him to tackle. So, with the fast growing market of China, marketeers are finding it worthwhile to study the market closely in order to better serve the consumers. The responsive and proactive marketeers are not only able to read the trends, but pioneer new marketing products and services as well. Thus special stores and boutiques carrying all kinds of designer brands are now sprouting up in the major cities of China, many of them recording overwhelming sales which come largely from the nouveaux-riches.

Another example to illustrate the need to understand the consumer at the macro level is the case of how the western fast food industry entered the Asian market. One of the early entrants was that of

Kentucky Fried Chicken (KFC). It first entered Hong Kong in the 1970s, but failed because it did not understand the dietary habits of the Hong Kong consumers, especially with regard to the taste of chicken. Hong Kong people generally prefer moist and tender chicken meat while KFC's meat was tough and dry. Furthermore, it entered the market too early. The Hong Kong people then were not ready for western fast food as they were much less affluent then, and the western lifestyle had yet to take root. Kentucky Fried Chicken learnt its lessons from Hong Kong. When it decided to come to Singapore a few years later, it studied the market carefully. This time around, it modified the taste of its product to suit the Asian palate, even including the provision of chilli sauce for the Singaporean market. The result: it is one of the biggest chains in Singapore, and has since extended its success story to include many other Asian cities, including China.

3.2.2 Micro Level

Specifically, there are basically six questions that the marketeer should address. Firstly, **who** are the likely customers or the **target audience** that the marketeer aims to sell his products and services. Before any marketing strategy can be developed, the marketeer must have a clear understanding of the consumers that he is marketing to. It is the beginning of any consumer analysis.

Secondly, **what** do they look for in the product or service? In other words, what product or service features appeal to them? What is important from the marketing perspective is to translate the product or service features into benefits that are relevant and meaningful to the consumers. This is because consumers buy products and services for the benefits that they bring to them. More often than not, such benefits may not be tangible but are social or psychological in nature. For example, consumers may buy expensive and branded products to show that they have "arrived", or to project their personality and lifestyle.

Thirdly, **when** do the consumers normally buy the product? Is there seasonality in the purchasing pattern, and are there preferences with regard to week of month, day of week and time of day that they purchase the product? Is convenience an important factor underlying the purchase of the product, or can the purchase be delayed? Answers to these questions will assist the marketeer in making decisions on advertising and promotion, distribution, and even pricing.

Fourthly, **where** do consumers buy the product? The answer to this question would assist the marketeer to decide on the type of distribution system needed, and the location of the distribution outlets. In fact, as a result of increasing affluence in many Asian economies, the distribution function is facing tremendous challenges in recent years. It is also likely to undergo many changes in the years ahead, and marketeers would be wise to pay close attention to this area.

Fifthly, **why** do consumers buy the product? This involves understanding the motivation behind a purchase. In the past, when the Asian consumers were generally poor, purchases were made largely to satisfy basic needs. However, over the last ten years, many Asian consumers consumption are motivated by wants, not needs. This makes the purchase decision more complex and the marketing job more demanding and challenging.

Finally, **how** do consumers go about buying the product or service? This refers to the process in which decisions are made. For example, is the purchasing decision taken independently or jointly, or is it influenced by friends, peers or family members? Are credit terms necessary for payment? Are purchases done in bulk or singly? These and many other related questions have to be addressed in order to develop a more effective marketing strategy.

The marketing of Gardenia bread in Singapore and Malaysia is a good example of how a company has successfully used consumer analysis to develop an effective marketing strategy. Prior to the appearance of Gardenia bread, the white bread markets of Singapore and Malaysia were dominated by small bakeries that were located in almost every residential area. However, these bakeries did not attempt to give a brand to their bread, and no attempt was made to differentiate one bakery from another through marketing or advertising effort. The bread was sold largely on the basis of price and freshness, and consumers would patronize the bakery that offered them convenience either in terms of opening hours or nearness to their homes or offices. This system of selling the white bread remain unchanged for at least thirty years!

Then came Gardenia. It did a thorough study of the consumer market and discovered that it had changed drastically. Among other findings was that with decreasing family size, increasing affluence and education, consumers wanted a different kind of bread. They wanted the white bread to be nutritious and to remain fresh for a few days (owing to the decreasing family size, and hence decreasing quantity consumed daily). Consumers were now even willing to pay a premium if such qualities could be guaranteed. In essence, the time was ripe for placing a brand on the white bread so that it could be identified by the consumers. Gardenia capitalized on these new needs and developed a marketing strategy that not only captured over 50% of the white bread market in Singapore, but did so with about 40% premium over similar type of white bread that were sold in the neighbourhood bakeries!

A thorough consumer analysis would provide very useful insights to the market segment, as well determine type of marketing strategy to be used. There are many ways in which to segment a market. They include using demographic variables, psychographics and lifestyle approaches, benefits, or even usage pattern. Basically, the marketeer can use one or a combination of several segmentation approaches to decide on the market segment or segments that he wants to address. These approaches are very well covered in many basic marketing textbooks, it is not my intention to rehash them. Instead, I would like to advocate seven basic criteria that should be kept in mind when the marketeer performs a segmentation exercise.

3.3 A Market Segment Must be Identifiable

To begin with, a segment must be **identifiable**, that is, it must be possible to describe it by some characteristics. For example, one can choose to describe a market segment by demographics (such as age, income, sex, occupation, housing type, and so on, psychographics (such as skeptics, pragmatics, idealists, and so on), behaviour or lifestyle (such as the socially active, leaders, followers, relators, spenders, savers, misers, and so on), usage patterns (such as heavy, medium, light and infrequent), and benefits sought (such as convenience, economy, image, etc). Whatever characteristics that are chosen to describe the segment, they must be relevant and useful to the problem at hand.

If a segment cannot be described, it becomes difficult subsequently to design the marketing strategy as the target is undefined. Perhaps, one of the useful ways to help the marketeer to identify the market segment is to conduct a thorough consumer and market analysis as discussed earlier. On this, it is interesting to note that while many American companies have complained about the difficulty of penetrating the Japanese market, few of them are willing to make efforts to understand the Japanese market. As a result, they are unable to correctly identify the needs and wants of the Japanese consumer. A good example is the marketing of American rice to the Japanese consumers in the early 1990s. Despite strong Japanese government support, the Japanese consumers rejected the American rice. The problem was not that American rice was low in quality. Rather, it simply wasn't the kind that Japanese liked. They preferred the short grained, glutinous variety which they use in their diet.

The failure to identify the characteristics of the Japanese segment was a lesson to the American rice exporters. It is important not to project the tastes, preferences, and wants of one market onto another. Given the great diversity of races and cultures within Asia, the marketeer must make an attempt to identify and describe his market segment so as to develop more effective marketing strategies. This is where it is useful to invest in market information gathering and research.

3.4 A Market Segment Must be Measurable

Second, a segment must be **measurable**. In other words, it must be quantifiable. If the segment cannot be measured, then the size of that segment becomes an unknown factor, and this makes it impossible for the marketeer to justify if it is worthwhile to develop a different marketing strategy for that segment. It must be emphasized that quantification also includes the ability to measure the various characteristics that are used to described that segment. For example, if we want to segment a market by usage pattern, then we must be able to measure the various degrees of usage like heavy, medium, light and infrequent. While this may still be manageable, the issue of measurement can become more complicated when psychographic and lifestyle variables are used to describe a market segment. How would one go about measuring what constitutes a skeptic, pragmatist, idealist, and so on? It is a question that only well-trained researchers can answer.

The difficulty in the measurement of psychographic and lifestyle variables has caused many marketeers to favour the use of demographic variables for segmentation. This is because it is always easier to quantify a market segment through demographic variables as the data to these are readily available from many publications. Often, such published data are also authenticated when they are released by official or government agencies.

Currently, in the Asian market, marketeers are likely to favour the use of demographic variables for segmentation purposes for various reasons. First, for many products, especially essential consumer durable, demographic variables like income is still the best way to determine the purchasing power of the consumers. Second, the income disparity between rural and urban areas in Asia is very conspicuous, and they are also reflected in the consumption behaviour of the consumers. Third, Asian marketeers themselves have not reached the level of sophistication to use non-demographic variables for segmentation purposes. For example, psychographic data have to be obtained from primary sources using various research methods. Besides being difficult and costly to collect, they require a well-trained marketeer to interpret and apply the findings as often the conclusiveness and exhaustiveness of the information can be challenged.

However, it is important not to rely too much on demographic variables. This is because the amount of information provided is often sketchy. In an era when the Asian consumers are more affluent and educated, they are likely to become more aesthetically oriented in their consumption behaviour. Thus, it is important to use additional criteria (for example, lifestyle and behavioural variables) for the purpose of market segmentation. This is particularly necessary when there is a need to better understand the activities, interests, and opinions of the consumers.

3.5 A Market Segment Must be Substantial

The third important characteristic of a market segment is that it must be **substantial**. This is because the purpose of segmentation is to design a distinct marketing strategy for that segment. If the size of that segment is not large enough, then the costs of developing a separate strategy to target at it may become rather high, and it would then no longer be efficient to commit corporate resources for such an exercise. For this reason, it is not surprising to find that many marketeers are very excited about the Asian market, especially with the opening of China and the awakening of India. The former has 1.2 billion people, while the latter has eight hundred and fifty million. These two markets alone would push any marketeer who can peddle one-dollar item into the billion dollar annual revenue league if it just succeeds in selling one such item to each consumer of India and China a year! Pepsi-Cola and Coca-Cola definitely believe they can do it, judging by their increasing investments in Asia.

Measuring the size of a segment should not be confined to ascertaining the number of consumers within that segment. More significantly, the consumers must have purchasing power. In other words, it is the volume of sales (in terms of units and dollars) that matter, not the number of consumers! For example, it is well known that many countries in Africa have large populations. However, their low level of incomes and widespread poverty rule them out as markets of any significance. On the other hand, China, which used to be an insignificant market, is now a market that is heavily courted because of its open door policy that has brought much prosperity to the people. The ability of the people to buy low ticket items like soap, detergent, toothpaste, shampoo, beverages, amongst others has even prompted many American companies such as Procter & Gamble, Coca-Cola, and Pepsi-Cola to set up factories in China. In recent years, even manufacturers of big ticket products like cars and discretionary items (products that are not really necessary for day-to-day consumption) like beer have begun to establish themselves in China.

It is important to stress that substantiality is largely a result of economic development. For example, in the 1950s and 1960s, the Southeast Asian market was considered to be a very small market by many American companies. This was because Southeast Asia, despite its large population base, was developing at a very slow pace. As a result, American manufacturers of cars, appliances and other consumer durables simply ignored the market. The Japanese manufacturers, however, saw the vast potential of the region and moved in to build up the market. Today, the Japanese manufacturers are reaping their handsome rewards from this three hundred and sixty million consumer market. It is heartening to note that the Americans have learnt their lesson from their experience in Southeast Asia and are now paying close attention to the Chinese, the Indian, and even the Vietnamese markets. Without doubt, these are new Asian markets of the future, and any shrewd marketeer who wants to establish an international presence cannot afford to ignore them. In due course, each of these markets will lend themselves to even greater segmentation.

3.6 There Must be Similarities Within a Market Segment

The fourth characteristic of a market segment is that consumers within that segment must be **similar**, as judged by the various descriptive measures used to identify them. If there are substantial differences among consumers within that segment, then the marketeer has under-segmented the market. In this case, there is a need to re-examine whether further segmentation is possible without violating the criterion of substantiality mentioned earlier.

Even in international marketing, it is possible to find similarities between consumers from different countries and cultures. In fact, I dare venture to state that from the marketing perspective, there are more similarities in the consumption behaviour among the rich consumers from different countries (and cultures) than between the rich and poor consumers within the same country (and culture). These rich consumers, despite their differences in cultures, like to travel in style (like flying first or business class), buy French wines and perfumes, patronize the fine arts and theatres, purchase branded goods and expensive clothings, belong to exclusive clubs, and carry gold credit cards. Such similarities have allowed many corporations to cluster these multinational customers into one segment, and use standardized marketing strategies to reach them.

Besides the rich and famous, the yuppies are also exhibiting strong similarities in lifestyles and consumption behaviour across different countries and cultures. For example, the Asian yuppies, despite their having acquired wealth rather late when compared to their counterparts have nevertheless quickly acquired similar consumption tastes and preferences to those of their western counterparts. This partly accounts for the mushrooming of condominiums, golf courses and designer brands in the Asian markets.

To be fair, the use of standardized marketing strategies across consumers of different nationalities is not confined to luxury items and services. Coca-Cola (a soft drink), Pampers (a brand baby diapers), and McDonald's (a hamburgers fast food chain) have found that there are global segments for their products. In fact, it is amazing to find that the success formula of McDonald's has been duplicated in almost every city of the world!

On the other hand, one must not assume that just because China, Hong Kong, Taiwan and Singapore are largely made up of Chinese, they can be approached by using the same marketing strategy.

Despite many similarities, there are also many differences among the consumers between these markets as well. Hong Kong consumers, for instance, who are Cantonese (one of the Chinese dialects) tend to be more susceptible to auspicious numbers and vowels (in Cantonese of course) phonetically similar to phrases of good wishes when it comes to the naming and pricing of products. They also tend to be more superstitious. Given a choice, Hong Kong stock brokers would choose to drink 7-Up (which in Cantonese, sounds like "moving upwards") than one of the colas (which sound like "going down") to begin the new year!

Despite the large Chinese populations in all four countries, there are distinctive differences in the food consumption behaviour among them. For example, coffee consumption is more prevalent in Singapore than in the other three markets where consumers prefer Chinese tea. Even then, the types of Chinese tea commonly consumed by the mainland Chinese, the Taiwanese and the Hong Kong people also differ somewhat "Tim Sum", a meal taken through long hours in the morning and especially during week-ends is peculiar to Hong Kong. Smelly beancurd, a hot and sweet type of beancurd drink taken with *you-tiao* (fried dough sticks) are Taiwanese favourites.

3.7 A Segment Must be Different from the Others

Segmentation arises because of the recognition that there is heterogeneity in demand among consumers in the market place. For example, in the vehicle market, distinctive segments are made up of purchasers of sports cars versus those of saloon cars. Similarly, the profiles of buyers for small, medium and large cars differ quite significantly. Even in terms of benefits sought, distinctive segments can be found for those who prefer economy features versus those who opt for prestige and status. For instance, in the two-litre car market, the purchasers of Hyundai Sonata and Mitsubishi Galant are definitely different from those who buy the Mercedes 200E or the BMW 520i.

It is therefore important that besides achieving similarity within a segment, the marketeer must also ensure that there are substantial **differences among segments**. For example, if the consumers of two separate segments have a lot of common characteristics, then the marketeer has probably over-segmented the market. In this instance, it is more appropriate to combine the two segments into one,

43

and use a common marketing mix strategy. At times, however, over-lapping of segments may be inevitable. In this case, the marketeer may want to seriously consider treating the overlapping segment as a separate market, especially when it is substantial enough. Figure 3.1 shows some of these possibilities.

To some extent, establishing differences across segments should not be too difficult an exercise for many products and services in Asia. For example, there is a clear disparity in income between those consumers who reside in the major cities versus those in the rural areas in countries like China, India, Malaysia, Thailand and Indonesia. In the case of China, the income disparity is even seen between those living in the coastal cities and those in the areas that are further inland. Many Chinese consumers in the coastal cities are enjoying a lifestyle close to that of Singaporeans!

Besides incomes disparity, there are also vast differences among Asian consumers in terms of religious, cultural and racial backgrounds. In the case of food marketing, there are strong differences between the market for *halal* (for Muslims) versus non-*halal* food. For this

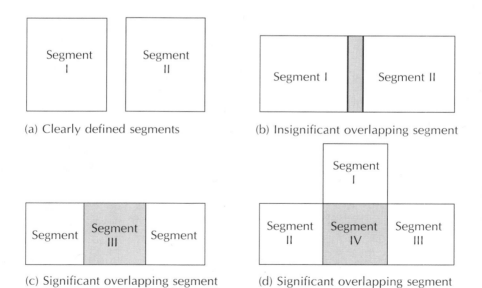

(a) Clearly defined segments

(b) Insignificant overlapping segment

(c) Significant overlapping segment
(The overlapping segment can
form the 3rd segment)

(d) Significant overlapping segment
(The overlapping segment can
form the fourth segment)

Figure 3.1 Defining market segments

reason, Burger King which has pork in its burgers would never be able to market its products to the Islamic populations of Malaysia and Indonesia. Similarly, many western fast food chains that sell beef burgers are not likely to appeal to the large Hindu population of India which regard the cow as sacred. Interestingly, chilli which is a favourite in the dietary habits of the Southeast Asian Chinese, are frowned upon by many Taiwanese, Hong Kongers and mainland Chinese. And the Japanese appear to have unique tastes — judging by their passion for *Sushi* or raw fish.

Allow me to reiterate that Asia is much more heterogeneous than Europe, and clear differences exist among the economies even when measured by levels of affluence. As we saw in the previous chapter, Japan is in a league of its own in Asia, in terms of stage of economic development. It is followed by the four NIEs and the several semi-NIEs and LDEs. Each group of these economies clearly form a segment by themselves, and the marketing strategies needed to reach the consumers in each would differ. Besides economic differences, cultural, social, racial and religious differences also abound. Thus the marketeer should never underestimate the complexity of the Asian market.

3.8 The Market Segment Must be Accessible

The sixth characteristic of a good segmentation exercise is that the segment must be **accessible**. This means it is possible to reach out to that segment by various channels and promotional means. There is no point identifying a substantial segment if there is no way of reaching out to the consumers in that segment. For example, a marketeer may identify a fairly large market of elderly people for his product. However, that segment will remain only a potential market if the marketeer cannot find the appropriate distribution channels and promotional media to reach them. It may be that the elderly consumers may be illiterate or physically handicapped so that they are not able to go shopping. The problem will be aggravated if the price is also beyond the purchasing power of the market of the elderly.

Of course, if the segment is very large, the marketeer might find it worthwhile to invest in finding ways to distribute and or promote the product. However, at times, this is not even possible. For example, prior to the opening of China, many companies already knew that it was an important international market. It was not until a change of political direction took place that this important international segment was accessible to the outside world. The same can be said about Eastern Europe before the collapse of the Berlin Wall.

Accessibility includes taking into account the characteristics and purchasing power of the consumers in a segment. For example, there is a great diversity in incomes among the different markets in Asia. The marketeer must therefore take into account if it is suitable to adopt a uniform pricing policy for his products, or should he adopt a more flexible pricing strategy. McDonald's, for example, does not insist on uniform pricing policy despite having standardized marketing practices for almost all its operations. Thus, while the prices of McDonald's burgers are relatively high when compared to other local competitive products in China, they are nonetheless much lower when compared to prices in Singapore or the United States.

Besides income disparity, the level of literacy can also hinder accessibility to the consumers. Unlike western Europe and North America, the literacy levels among many Asian economies are not only lower, but there is also great disparity among the educated and the illiterate within each economy. Coupled with differences in income, the task of reaching out to the Asian consumers can become a very challenging one for marketeers of some products. Take the case of cigarettes. There is a large population of smokers in many of the developing countries in Asia. However, they are physically spread over large areas country, and many of them do not have high incomes to allow them to even buy cigarettes by the pack or to be able watch a cigarette advertisment on television. Instead, the marketeers of cigarettes have to rely on large bill boards (sited along the streets) and pictorial posters in advertising. In addition, to reach these large pool of scattered smokers, cigarettes have to be sold by the stick through many road-side stalls and small grocery shops that have appeared all over the country.

3.9 A Market Segment Must Not be Too Volatile

Finally, a segment, to the extent possible, should be **durable**. In other words, it should not be too volatile and the composition of that segment should not keep changing. When the composition of the segment is stable, it is easier to **manage** as the marketing mix strategy need not be changed or modified frequently. **Durability** and **manageability** are two possible reasons why biased managers rely more on demographic variables for purpose of segmentation. However, it is important to point out that consumers do not change their lifestyles, interests, opinions and activities overnight. Neither do they change their usage patterns or benefits preferences drastically within a short period of time. Thus, marketeers should still venture beyond demographic variables in analysing their consumers.

Segment stability is something that may not be achievable for the Asian market in the next ten to twenty years. This is largely because with high economic growth rates and increasing affluence, consumer tastes and preferences are likely to change in very quickly. In fact, new segments are emerging every day in Asia. Take the case of the beer market in China. Barely ten years ago, the mainland Chinese were only used to their own local brands such as Tsingtao. In terms of total beer consumption, it ranked seventh in the world. However, in 1993, its beer production reached 12.25 million tonnes, second only to the United States. More significantly, there are now more than thirty large beer producers in China, marketing foreign brands like San Miguel, Becks, Pabst Blue, Budweiser, Carlsberg, Tiger, Kirin, amongst others. The success of these foreign brands indicate that there are new segments of beer drinkers that are emerging in China. In the same way, new market segments are also forming in the beverage industry in China, especially where colas are concerned. This has prompted both Pepsi-Cola and Coca-Cola to plan for ten more factories in China by year 2000.

Marketeers aiming for action in Asia certainly need to constantly monitor their consumers closely. This includes not only monitoring the demographic variables, but focussing on the psychographic factors as well.

3.10 Conclusion

In sum, segmentation is a response to the existence of differences in the market place. It is therefore, a reactive approach rather than a proactive one. In addition, the main focus of segmentation are the **consumers** and the **market**. However, it should not prevent a creative marketeer from exploring niches in the market like discovering the certain latent needs of consumers. For example, one Japanese company successfully marketed a bread-making machine in Japan when it discovered that Japanese consumers love the freshness and fragrance of homemade bread. Similarly, the karaoke was specially designed to satisfy a desire of the Asian consumer to express himself or herself publicly and as a form of an"ice-breaker" in social functions.

Given the increasing affluence of the Asian economies, it would be useful for the marketeer to discover only latent but emerging needs and wants of the consumers. This is where the consumption experiences of the developed economies would provide useful insights on what are likely to come in the developing Asian economies. For example, after studying the lifestyles of major cities in the developed countries, including Singapore, some enterprising Malaysian property developers were able to successfully market up-market condominiums in Kuala Lumpur, Penang, Malacca, and other cities. In doing so, they were able to exploit emerging market opportunities despite the fact that Malaysia has abundant land, and many skeptics doubted the feasibility of condominium living.

In the same way, with the increasing number of yuppies in the major cities of Asia, there will a corresponding increase in the demand for products and services that will serve this new segment. In fact, of late, there are signs of new market segments emerging, namely, "yubbies" (babies of yuppies), "yuppets" (pets of yuppies) and "yupmaids" (domestic help of yuppies) in some of these Asian economies like Hong Kong and Singapore. These new market segments provide ample opportunities for those marketeers who are able to exploit them to their advantage. It would not be long before such new market segments emerge in the other Asian economies.

4

Product Differentiation: Finding Competitive Advantages

4.1 Introduction

While market segmentation focuses on the market and the consumers, product differentiation centres on the analysis of competitors and their products or services. It is a process whereby a company chooses to deliberately create differences between its products from those of the competitors. This need to create differences occurs when there are multiple suppliers of the same product (or service) in the marketplace. In the case of the Asian market, this is very quickly becoming a reality. More and more competitors have moved into the market. Take the case of Singapore. Up to the 1970s, there was only one western fast food chain in Singapore, namely A & W. However, within a decade, all the major western fast food chains have moved in. The result: each of these chains, including the local food operators, began to make efforts to differentiate their product offerings from those of their competitors. Today, all these food operators compete aggressively by employing a wide spectrum of marketing tools and techniques. Interestingly, the experience of the fast food industry in Singapore has been repeated in many economies in Asia, including China.

Apart from the example of fast food industry, there has also been a proliferation of new products and services in many of the economies of Asia. These new competitors include countless number of well established foreign brands and suppliers. Thus, without doubt, the Asian market is getting more and more competitive, and in the process there is a pressing need for a marketeer to differentiate his product or service offerings from those of his competitors.

In creating differences, whether actual or perceived, the company is trying to establish its own presence, and protect it from competition. In economics jargon, it is trying to create its own demand curve

49

so as to exert control over its sales, and reduce price sensitivity. Not surprisingly, therefore, product differentiation is often heavily supported by advertising and promotional campaigns. These are necessary to influence the opinions and attitudes of consumers.

4.2 Actual Differences

Certainly, every company would like to make their products or services different from those of other companies. However, to do so successfully would require a thorough understanding of their competitiors' products or services, including their strengths and weaknesses. More often than not, many companies can analyze their own products or services, but pay little attention to those of their competitors. When they do, they tend to concentrate on the weaknesses of their competitors' products, rather than acknowledge their strengths. The result is that they are unable to truly differentiate their products, and when they do, the differentiation could be very superficial.

4.2.1 The Japanese Experience

Among international competitors, the Japanese manufacturers are perhaps the gurus in detailed product differentiation, especially in terms of studying actual differences between their products and those of the competitors. They are known to strip a competitive product down to its smallest part in order to find ways to make Japanese products different and better. For example, when the Japanese car makers first entered the world market in the 1950s and 1960s, they never competed directly against American and European cars. This was because Japanese cars were of a lower quality. But, the Japanese car makers having noticed that American and European cars were sold without a comprehensive list of options such as air-conditioner, radio or stereo set, radial tyres, sports rims, and so on. The buyer had to pay for every option that he wanted. The Japanese car makers decided to market a car that was equipped with lots of accessories at a relatively cheap price as compared to the American and European models. In their differentiation strategy, the Japanese focused heavily on price and on the fact that their cars were fully equipped. As a result, they succeeded in capturing a sizeable share of the American and European automobile market.

It is important to point out that the differentiation strategy adopted by the Japanese car makers did not remain the same over time. As Japanese cars improved in quality over the years and with increasing cost of production, price was no longer an effective criteria for differentiation. In particular, with the increasing appreciation of the yen, Japanese cars did not remain cheap. Moreover, American and European car makers also began to package their cars with the usual accessories. The Japanese car makers then chose to compete head-on with their American and European competitors. They focused more and more on product attributes, engineering and state-of-the-art technology. A good example is the approach taken in the marketing of Lexus by Toyota Car Company. All its advertising and promotional materials place very heavy emphasis on the state-of-the-art features that have been incorporated into the car. More significantly, to show that such capabilities are different from those offered by the competitors, potential customers are invited to test drive the car.

Interestingly, the earlier price differentiation strategy used by the Japanese automakers in the 1960s and 1970s is now adopted by their South Korean and Malaysian competitors who are producing much cheaper cars. In fact, some European cars like the Alfa Romeo, Seat, Fiat, and Lancia — which have become relatively cheap when compared to the Japanese models – have begun to adopt price differentiation strategies as well. Of course, they do not rely on price as the only basis for differentiation. Many of these car sellers highlight various car features, accessories, performance characteristics, and so on in comparison and as differentiating criteria.

4.2.2 Explore Various Differences

To develop a more effective differentiation strategy, the marketeer must explore beyond the price, and actual content or physical make-up of the product or service. These include other aspects like features, ranges, styling, presentation, packaging, size, colour, method of operation or usage, and so on. Marketeers of cars, for example, go into great lengths to demonstrate product features like four-wheel drive, turbo-charge, fuel injection, anti-brake system, cruise control, air-bags, reinforced car cage, and so on. Hi-fi equipment sellers use sound room and other scientific evidence to prove the quality of their products. Furniture dealers will take pains to illustrate the uniqueness of their designs and the quality of the materials used for the construction in order to convince their customers. Even enclycopaedias, computer software, and many other products are now sold by direct comparison with competitive offers.

What is important to note is that in highlighting the differences, the marketeer must be ble to present them in the form of **benefits** to the consumer. This is because consumers generally do not purchase the product but the benefits that come with it. Hence, sheer differences alone are of no value to the consumer.

It is worthwhile to note that product usage demonstrations through the setting up of promotional sales counters or participation in trade exhibitions can be quite beneficial to new market entrants or competitors. This is because through demonstrations, the sales personnel can effectively bring out the full benefits of the product and its related features. In fact, this is how some of the very expensive foreign brands of cookware like Frissler and AMC, and vacuum cleaners like Miele, Hoover and Electrolux (they were initially relatively unknown although they were already very established in their home markets) managed to penetrate markets like Singapore, Hong Kong and Malaysia successfully. With the increasing number of new products — many of which can be quite complex to the first time buyer — being introduced to the Asian market, methods of marketing involving demonstration of use of the product concerned will become increasingly important in the near future. It is thus of no surprise to note that many major cities in Asia are busy building large exhibition or trade or convention centres. Afterall, they not only provide an effective way of reaching out to the consumers, but allow the marketeers to demonstrate their products to large groups of captive audiences.

Demonstration of benefits are not confined to products. Even for services, their benefits can be demonstrated. For example Singapore Airlines (SIA) is well known in the world for its superb inflight service, and its modern, new and efficient aircrafts. Its inflight service has become almost legendary to the extent that even other airlines talk about it! Such an achievement was made possible through ceaseless training of its airline crew, paying attention to details, conducting research to improve service levels, and constantly obtaining feedback from its customers. All these account for why SIA has consistently been ranked as the top service international airline in the world for many years. To maintain its leadership position, and even to distance itself from its competitors, SIA also invests heavily in advertising and promotion, including taking part in major world events like the Rose Parade in the United States. As a result of its ability to demonstrate its high quality of service and offerings, SIA has been able to enjoy a premium over other airlines in many international routes.

4.3 Perceived Differences

Product differentiation can also be created as a result of differences in consumer perception. It is true that actual differences among products can often be demonstrated, and that consumers should base their purchase decisions solely on the actual value of a product. Unfortunately, despite actual differences and attributes that can be, it is also equally true that many consumers operate more on perception in many of their purchase decisions, especially for services where sampling, trials and testing are usually not possible. For example, perception plays a very important role in one's selection of a holiday package, in consulting a doctor or surgeon, a training course to attend, and so on. Even in the case of products, perception can play an important part in influencing a person's decision-making process. This is particularly so when the product is perceived to project the consumer's image, personality, income and social status. Examples of such products include cosmetics, designer's clothings, watches, pens, amongst others.

4.3.1 Projection of Social Status

Perception may play a bigger role in many Asian societies than in the West. This could be largely attributed to the concept of **face** which is very important to many Asians, especially the Chinese. They are very concerned about how others view them socially. Thus, it becomes important to project a good image of oneself so as to gain "face". This phenomenon is aggravated by the fact that most homes in many Asian societies (China, Taiwan, Hong Kong, Japan, South Korea, Thailand, and Singapore) are relatively small and modest in comparison to those in the West. In addition, except for the very rich, it is also difficult to show off one's wealth by the size of one's home as these tend to be quite similar. It is thus not surprising that many Asians turn to the acquisition and consumption of material goods and services to project their "face" and social status instead. In particular, it is not confined just to the quantity of things (which is objective) that one possesses but the quality of the things (which is subjective) as well. This is where perception becomes important to the marketeer of products.

Let's consider the Rolex watch. It is perceived by many Asian consumers to be a status symbol of the successful. Furthermore, because of its workmanship, it is viewed more as an investment than a time-telling equipment. The result: it commands a premium over other brands of watches. Over the years, Rolex developed its marketing strategy to perpetuate and enhance such perceptions of the product by using celebrities and highly successful people in advertising the product and by sponsoring very high-class events like golf and concerts. These efforts not only help to differentiate the watch, but distance it from its many other competitive brands in the marketplace. Rolex's differentiation strategy has become so successful in Asia that the brand has become legendary.

Interestingly, Omega used to enjoy a status next to that of Rolex in the 1960s and 1970s. It was a watch coveted by many Asian consumers when a Rolex was not within their means. Unfortunately, Omega failed to capitalize on its unique position. Instead of moving in the route of exclusivity, it chose to mass produce its watches, hoping to enjoy the price premiums that it had created. It's strategy boomeranged. Today, Omega is facing tremendous problems of trying to regain its lost brand image in Asia. Indeed, it faces increasing competition from an increasing number of competitive brands that have made their inroads into Asia over the past decade.

Where cars are concerned, a Mercedes Benz is definitely different from other brands of cars like the BMW, Volvo, Audi, Saab, Alpha Romeo, Toyota, and so on in terms of physical characteristics. However, beyond the actual differences, a Mercedes Benz is perceived by many Asian consumers (especially the businessmen) to be a symbol of high social status and quality. To many Asian consumers, the possession of a Mercedes Benz marks one as a member of the social elite and the economically powerful. In contrast, many other brands have been perceived at most to represent various stages leading to success. Such perceived values have allowed the distributors of Mercedes cars to market them very differently from the other brands, including placing a hefty premium on them. In some countries like Singapore and Malaysia, the premium is as much as 10% over competitive brands.

The entrenched status symbol of luxury cars like the Mercedes, BMW and Jaguar cannot be brushed aside easily. Let me illustrate. In an attempt to challenge the luxury car market that has been traditionally occupied by the European car makers like Mercedes Benz, Japanese companies decided to take them head on. Toyota, for example, launched its Lexus model several years ago. While it has achieved considerable success in the United States, the Lexus did not have the "big bang" impact in markets like Singapore, Malaysia, and Hong Kong. This is because in these markets, Japanese cars were never perceived as symbols of social status. If any, they were meant for the ordinary car owner. Thus, despite having state-of-the-art features, and supported by aggressive marketing campaigns, it would take some time before Japanese luxury cars like the Lexus will be admitted into the exclusive club of the rich and famous in Asia.

4.3.2 Perceived Quality and Price

Besides watches and cars, perceptual differences also play a big part in the purchase decisions of many other products where actual differences are difficult to establish or where the consumers tend to be concerned about the image aspects that the products may confer. Examples of such products include cosmetics, fashion wear, designer clothing, jewelry, and other branded big-ticket items. For these products, the perceived value or quality is very much dependent on the buyer's perception.

Interestingly, many consumers tend to associate highly priced products or services with high quality. There is nothing wrong with such a perception, so long as the high price is the result of the high quality. The problem is that most consumers are unable to ascertain the appropriate premiums for the better quality products or services. For example, it is true that most designer brand clothings are of higher quality. However, how much that higher quality is worth is something that many consumers are unable to ascertain. This inability to place an accurate premium on a higher quality product on the part of the consumer has enabled marketeers to have tremendous leverage in pricing. This leverage is even greater when the product contains attributes that are not easily verifiable, as in the case of cosmetics, and other image-related goods.

Not surprisingly, marketeers are willing to invest large sums of money trying to build up the image of their products. In fact, this is the case in China. While many local manufacturers are still reluctant to spend money on advertising and promotion, many overseas companies have exploited the various available media to promote their products. The result is that many Chinese consumers perceive foreign products to be better and are willing to pay higher prices for them. Today, more and more Chinese manufacturers are beginning to realize the need to address the perception aspect. Afterall, in the sphere of marketing, it matters little how good you actually are; what is more important is how good others perceive you to be.

4.3.3 How Perceived Differences Come About

There are many ways in which perceptual differences arise. To begin with, it can be created largely by the efforts of the marketeer through advertising and promotional campaigns. This is a proactive approach. Through consistent advertising and promotions, a marketeer can re-inforce an existing image that the consumers may have of its products or company. Alternatively, he can even alter the image over time. For example, the current strong international image of SIA has been the result of years of building up and reinforcement through its various media campaigns. As a result, SIA has been perceived to be a premier airline offering superior service.

In newly opened economies like Vietnam and China, percieved differences play an important role in the decision-making process of consumers. This is because it is derived largely from advertising and promotional efforts of marketeers and by verbal communication. Thus, it is important for early entrants into these markets to engage in intensive advertising and promotion. In fact, this has been the case of many large overseas brands that manage to enter the Chinese and Vietnamese markets. As a result of their aggressive advertising, many consumers have begun to favour foreign brands over local brands (which are not inclined to invest in advertising) in many product categories, including even beer and soft drinks!

It is important to note that the standing of a company and its products in the perception of its consumers can also be the result of the efforts or non-efforts on the part of its competitors. For example, if the competitors are advertising and promoting their products aggressively, a company can be perceived as a laggard if it chooses to do nothing. Similarly, if a company is always late in coming out with new products or designs or models relative to its competitors, it may also create an unfavourable impression in the eyes of the consumers. Thus, the marketeer should never ignore the actions of his competitors. Afterall, this is the essence of product differentiation. Many Chinese manufacturers are beginning to be awakened by the threats posed by foreign competitors when they witnessed the quick erosion of their market shares, especially over the last five years.

The past experience in his usage of a product can affect a consumer's perception. For example, if the experience has been unfavourable, it would affect future purchases of the product. This can become particularly troublesome if the original product was indeed not quite up to the standard or quality, but the new product is now vastly improved. To the consumer, his original impression of the product's quality will persist. Thus, the marketeer must make marketing efforts to alter such a perception. Otherwise, the damage can be quite serious, especially if the consumer is an opinion leader whose views are expressed verbally!

China again presents a very good example. In the past, many Chinese manufacturers paid little attention to improving the quality and packaging of their products. This was tolerated when there were no foreign products to compare with. However, with the influx of imported goods, the inferior quality of Chinese products show up very glaringly. Despite efforts to improve their quality, such perception persisted even up to the 1990s. For example, Motorola produced some identical products both in China and Singapore. However, the Chinese consumers perceived the quality of the product made in Singapore to be far superior to the very same product made in China.

Prior to China, other Asian economies like Hong Kong and Taiwan also went through similar experiences in the 1970s and 1980s. Products made on their own country were perceived to be inferior to imported goods, and it took them almost twenty years of efforts to change that perception. Of course, it could be that the products were indeed poorer in quality. However, if efforts are not made to correct such perceptions, they linger longer than they should after improvements in the product have already been made.

There are other influences on perceptual differences such as changes in tastes of consumers, the effects of word-of-mouth communication, influence of opinion leaders or agencies, and so on. The marketeer must therefore address all these sources if he wants to influence the views of the consumers toward his product or service. When perceived differences do exist in favour of the marketeer, they should be exploited. When actual differences also exist and can be substantiated, the scope and possibility for successful differentiation are even greater, and the marketing strategy to be devised can be quite distinctive. This is because both the actual and perceived differences would provide useful inputs to the marketeer to design a package of benefits that are unique only to his product or service.

Note that I use the term "benefits" rather than product attributes or characteristics. This is because the consumer is more interested in what benefits the product can offer him. Thus, it is important to market from the perspective of benefits when dealing with consumers.

4.4 Differentiate Beyond Product Attributes

A company should not confine itself to the product or service attributes in pursuing a differentiation strategy. In today's highly competitive environmment, a company should try to find advantages among its other 3Ps of marketing: placement (distribution), pricing and promotion. For example, many brands of cookware like Meyers are distributed through departmental stores. However, some other brands like Frissler and AMC have opted for direct selling as this would allow them to demonstrate the effectiveness of their products better. The result is that they are able to price their products higher than those sold through departmental stores.

Cookware is not the only example. Some brands of vacuum cleaners like Miele are also being sold directly to the consumers as opposed to the conventional distribution channels like departmental stores and supermarkets. Similarly, there are now specialty stores selling products like coffee, drugs, clothings and gifts. Interestingly, exquisite and high-priced pens such as Parker, Waterman, and Mont Blanc are now sold directly as well, especially to corporate clients. In doing so, the marketeers try to make their products more exclusive by targetting at selective customers.

By breaking free from conventional distribution methods, these innovative marketeers have managed to capitalize on new opportunities and gain advantages over their competitors. The setting up of self-dispensing pharmacy stores (as opposed to the traditional prescribed methods) in shopping areas or centres and business districts in many cities of Asia by Guardian Pharmacy is a good example of how it has successfully established itself through differentiation beyond the products alone. In the same way, NTUC Fairprice supermarkets in Singapore have taught the conventional wet markets and the local grocery stores a few important lessons on how to achieve higher profits through greater efficiency and productivity in distribution. In fact, the concept of chain stores has become so successful in some Asian countries that franchising is now very popular.

Another way to create differences is through pricing. Interestingly, this does not mean that one has to differentiate by offering a lower price. Instead, a higher price is not necessarily a handicap. In fact, it can be an important variable for differentiation. Many readers may recall the very effective advertising campaigns that were run on the BMWi model several years ago. The following are some examples of the captions used:

"Rumour has it that the new BMW 735i is expensive.
That's not true. It's very, very expensive."

"This is an advertisement for the wealthy.
(Please ignore it, if you are merely rich)."

While many readers of such advertisements may be turned off by the arrogance and snobbery of the statements, they nevertheless appeal to those who fit such descriptions and who want to be different — the target audience of BMW cars! In fact, other marketeers have cleverly exploited concepts like "the good things in life don't come cheap" and "high price, high quality" in differentiating their products from competitors.

In the service industry, Citibank has also shown that a high price strategy need not be a disadvantage so long as new advantages can be **created** that are of benefit to the consumers. This is demonstrated in its consumer loans in several Asian markets. Citibank charges one of the highest loan rates (that is, high pricing policy). Yet it has managed to secure sizeable market shares in the highly competitive banking industries of Asia against the local banking giants. Instead of focussing on price, Citibank creates advantages in the areas of convenience and speed of service. It allows consumers to phone in for applications for loans and is able to grant loan approval within a few days! Such benefits are of tremendous value for consumers who need loans urgently to capitalize on fast changing opportunities like in the stock and property markets. When a consumer can make more money, paying higher loan interest becomes a non-issue!

Finally, the marketeer must not forget that promotional and advertising means can also be used for differentiation. Instead of using media like television and newspapers, a company could consider opting for more selective modes like direct mailing. At times, direct mailing can also double up as a distribution channel as well. For example, some companies in Asia have used direct mailing successfully in selling products and services like insurance, magazine subscriptions, coins, cassettes, compact discs, costume jewelries, and even cookware.

With today's computer and information technology, there are even greater opportunities for the innovative company to develop new and more ways to differentiate his product or service. For example, he could make use of information technology to market his products or services (such as through Teleview or INTV in the case of Singapore), as well as speeding up the order processing and delivery. In one Asian country, a supplier of liquified petroleum gas (LPG) has successfully worked with Telecoms and other agencies in marketing its cylinder gas by combining various technologies. The process is quite simple but interesting. When a consumer phones in to a retailer to place an order, it is automatically processed by a computer which in turn transmits the order to a fax machine that is mounted in a delivery truck (fully stocked with LPG gas cylinders) on the move. The driver cum delivery man can thus easily deliver the gas without even having to contact the retailer or the consumer! Without doubt, this company has successfully differentiated its total product from those of its competitors by using a comprehensive approach!

4.5 Distinguishing Differentiation from Segmentation

It is important to point out that both product differentiation and market segmentation are marketing tools available to the marketeer to develop his overall positioning of his product or service. Positioning will be discussed in the next article. It is useful to note that a product differentiation strategy can be pursued with or without a market segmentation strategy. For example, it is not easy to segment many commodity-type products. However, this does not stop marketeers from pursuing product differentiation strategies.

Gasoline manufacturers of brands like Esso, Shell, Caltex, BP, and Mobil have never ceased to develop new additives to their products so as to claim better performance for cars. Gardenia tries very hard to differentiate itself from Sunshine in the white bread market. Lux, Imperial Leather, Palmolive, Fa, Camay, and many other brands of soap try to establish their own identities in the minds of consumers. Even soft drinks (like Coke, Pepsi, Sprite, Seven-up, and F&N), beer (like Anchor, Tiger, Heineken, Carlsberg, and Budweiser), stout (like ABC versus Guiness Stout), retail banking services (like those of

Citibank, UOB, POSB, DBS, and OCBC) and detergent (like Fab, Breeze, Dixan, and Persil) have tried to generate various actual and perceived product or service attributes in order to differentiate themselves from their competitors. The objective is to position themselves in the "top of the mind"of the consumer when he wants to purchase such products or services. It is interesting to note that some suppliers of rice and sugar have also begun to place brand names on their products as an attempt toward differentiation.

In contrast to product differentiation, a market segmentation strategy can only be pursued when there are already differences among consumers which in turn create heterogeneity in demand. If demand is homogeneous, there is no need to pursue a segmentation strategy. For example, it is difficult to segment the market for products like rice, sugar, salt, white bread, gasoline, detergent, toilet and tissue papers, and many other commodity-type products. However, while segmentation is not possible, it does not prevent the marketeer from pursuing a differentiation strategy — that is, although the product is targetted at the same market segment, it can still be differentiated from other competitive products. In sum, when a marketeer uses a segmentation strategy, it should be accompanied by a differentiation strategy. On the other hand, a differentiation strategy can be pursued with or without a segmentation strategy.

5

Positioning: Jostling for Competitive Advantages

5.1 Introduction

The word "**positioning**" has been commonly used in marketing. Unfortunately, it is often misunderstood, and narrowly applied. The result is that marketeers are at times confused by what the term means exactly. Perhaps, over-usage of this term in advertising has partly contributed to this confusion. In advertising, the term is often used in association with the positioning of brands in the mindsets of consumers. While this is not incorrect, it does not represent the full picture. Brand positioning is only one aspect of the overall positioning strategy of a firm. Positioning encompasses much more than a brand name.

What is positioning? Simply put, it refers to the **competitive stance** that a company deliberately chooses to adopt relative to its competitors and the market, and is defined within the context of the environment after taking into account the availability of corporate resources. Positioning therefore affects the overall marketing strategy of a company in that the latter is designed on the basis of how the company chooses to position itself, its products and services. For example, a company may choose to build a hotel in response to a boom in tourism and a severe shortage of hotel rooms (an environmental influence). However, it has a choice as to what type of hotel it wants to build — whether to cater to the business or leisure travellers (a basic decision in segmentation). At the same time, it has to also decide on the quality of service (if it is to be a five, four or three-star hotel) it hopes to provide (a differentiation decision). Of course, if the company has abundant resources, it would have more options. Whatever decisions are made, the subsequent marketing strategy of the hotel would have to reflect its competitive position relative to others in terms of how it wants to market the attractiveness of its location to its targetted tourists or visitors, the type of service or product it offers and would like to offer, its pricing policy, the advertising and promotional campaigns to be used, the kinds of public relations and sales promotions to launch, and so on.

Positioning can also be applied at the macro level of competition between countries and the comparative advantages. For example, as a result of the opening up of the less developed economies in Asia like China and Vietnam, the increasing competition posed by semi-developed economies like Malaysia and Thailand, the rising costs of labour and factors of production, the limited domestic market, and the rising value of the Singapore dollar, the government of Singapore has deliberately positioned its industries away from competing directly with those in emerging Asian economies. This is done through abandoning the more labour intensive industries in favour of the mid-level to very advanced technology industries. In addition, Singapore has also begun a systematic effort to encourage its companies to spread their investments over markets in the region. In sum, positioning is a **concerted attempt** to find and establish competitive edge.

A good way to illustrate the process of corporate positioning is shown in Figure 5.1. Note that the purpose of positioning is to provide inputs for the formulation of the marketing strategy. It is important to highlight that positioning is both a **proactive move** (resulting from differentiation through competitive analysis) and a **reactive response** (resulting from segmentation through consumer and market analysis) on the part of the marketeer. In fact, market segmentation and product differentiation as previously discussed are integral components of the **positioning** strategy. As I have dealt with market segmentation and product differentiation, I would like to focus my discussion on the other two issues that relate to positioning — corporate resources and constraints and environmental factors.

5.2 Analysis of Corporate Resources and Constraints

The strategies to be developed by a company would be relatively easy if it has unlimited resources. Unfortunately, almost every company, no matter how richly endowed, is faced with limited resources and constraints. For this reason, it has to decide how to position itself relative to its competitors after taking into account its available

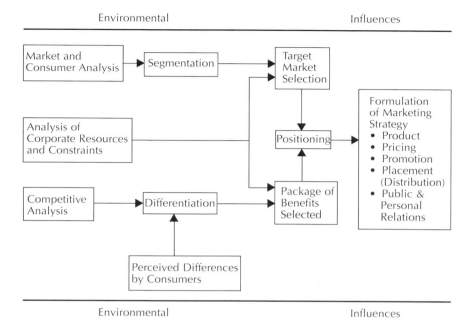

Figure 5.1 Corporate positioning and formulation of the marketing strategy

resources and constraints and the environmental factors. In general, there are nine factors — I call them the 9Ms as they all begin with the letter "M" — that a company has to deal with. These 9Ms are shown in Figure 5.2.

1. Management (Leadership)
2. Manpower (Personnel or Human Resources)
3. Money (Finance)
4. Machinery (Production Systems)
5. Methods (Technology)
6. Materials (Supplies, Inventories and Parts)
7. Muscles (Political Clout)
8. Means (Contacts)
9. Markets (Cusomters)

Figure 5.2 The 9Ms faced by a company

Note that no matter how rich a company may be, it is bound to face constraints in some of the 9Ms. For example, while many economies in Asia are now providing numerous business opportunities, local companies are saddled with problems of finding suitable manpower and management to exploit the markets. In addition, they also face constraints in finance. This is especially true in that many of these companies do not have sufficient number of local partners who can provide adequate financing to match that of foreign investors. Having to pump in the bulk of financing themselves obviously would limit the speed and scope in which these newly opened markets can be exploited.

5.2.1 Need to Prioritize Opportunities

Without doubt, if a company has unlimited resources or faces no constraints, it can choose to enter many markets or market segments, and within each of them, introduce as many products and brands as possible. Unfortunately, no matter how big a company is, it will face limitations in terms of availability of finance, quantity and quality of corporate leadership and workforce, access to supplies, materials and markets, access to distribution and promotion channels, knowledge of technology and production know-how, extent of business networks, ability to penetrate new markets, and so on. For this reason, a company has to prioritize and rationalize the allocation of the resources at its disposal so as to achieve the best results. This is particularly necessary when the opportunities in the market are abundant. In fact, this is the challenge facing many companies operating in Asia today.

The opening up of so many Asian economies within such a short period of time have provided countless business opportunities. The sheer market sizes of economies like China, India, Indonesia and Vietnam are indeed mind boggling and too tempting to any marketeer. However, it is simply not possible for a company to get its finger in every pie. I would even caution that if a company gets over-stretched without recognizing its own limitations, all its fingers might get burnt one day! If anything, this is the time to guard against "corporate greed." This is because while opportunities may be plentiful in these economies, there are no shortage of business minefields as well. In particular, doing business in these economies require muscles (political clout), means (contacts), money (financial investment) and the right market (customers). There are no shortage of business competitors as well.

5.2.2 Avoid Head-on Competition

Owing to the limitations of corporate resources, and to the fact that there are many competitors in the market, there can only be one company occupying the number one position. The rest will have to jostle for a good position in the mindset of consumers. Here it is important to point out that it does not mean by not being the top company, it is not possible to be the most profitable. A good example of a very profitable company which is not the top company is SIA. For the past five years and up to the end 1994, it was still the most profitable airline in the world, although it is out-ranked in terms of size by many other airlines. Among its other factors for success, is SIA's effective positioning strategy that encompasses product differentiation — an inflight service that other airlines talk about, and having the youngest fleet among international airlines — and market segmentation – focussing more on business travellers and long haul flights. In essence, it has a positioning strategy that is very different from most of its competitors.

Similarly, when the Japanese companies first entered the international markets, they did not try to position themselves head-on against the western giants of the respective industries. Instead, Japanese manufacturers carefully studied the market, the consumers and their competitors. They also had a good grasp of their own corporate resource limitations. The result? They chose to enter markets that were ignored or where competition was weak, and they positioned themselves at the lower end of the market through cheaper pricing.

In choosing not to go head-on against the western corporate giants but to focus on areas ignored by the competitors, the Japanese companies were able to gain several advantages. First, as they were building smaller models of the same products as their western counterparts, they were able to use the same technology and learn faster from the West. They needed only to concentrate on improving the design and style, and to make them cheaper (and hopefully, better). Second, as there were hardly any competitors in the small products market, they were able to have all the time on earth to improve themselves without being threatened by their western counterparts. This was possible despite the fact that they could be producing poor quality products then. Third, as there was little competition, they were given, by default, unlimited access to the market or markets available. In particular, as Japanese products were small and cheap, they were able to seek out markets that were not besotted by the larger products of the western manufacturers. In fact, the Japanese companies found customers in many developing economies in Asia and elsewhere. Finally, as a result of the advantages cited above and the unrestricted building up of their market shares in specific product areas, the Japanese companies were able to develop enough expertise and strengths over the years to challenge the market leaders gradually.

History has shown that Japanese manufacturers have chosen the right positioning strategies. In many product categories like cameras, cars, photocopiers, motocycles, hi-fi equipment, refrigerators, and television sets, the Japanese had appropriately positioned themselves away from direct competition against the established leaders. When the western companies concentrated on building big cars, large motorcycles, huge refrigerators, and so on, the Japanese focused on building small models of the same type of products.

To a large extent, Japanese companies still avoid head-on competition against their stronger competitors today. For example, in the aerospace industry, despite having technological capabilities to build aeroplanes, the Japanese have yet to enter the industry in a big way. This non-confrontational approach in competition is also true of Japanese computer, medical equipment, telephone, and other high technology industries.

5.2.3 Positioning Strategies are Not Static

It is important to note that the positioning strategies of Japanese companies did not remain static. They were dynamic changed over time. Over the years, as their corporate resources increased, Japanese companies began to challenge their competitors head-on. In some industries, they have practically dominated these industries. For example, in cameras and home video equipment, the market is literally flooded with Japanese brands. In the case of cars, the Japanese car makers avoided the western manufacturers for many years. They concentrated largely on the lower-end market. However, as Japanese cars gained widespread acceptance, and as their quality improved, they began to position themselves in direct competition against western automakers in the luxury car market. This new positioning strategy started in the mid-1980s. By the 1990s, Japanese luxury cars like the Lexus have begun to penetrate the traditional domain of the western models like Mercedes, BMW, Jaguar and others.

Today, the successful positioning strategies of Japanese companies are carefully studied and copied by other Asian companies in South Korea, Taiwan and even Malaysia. For example, when South Korea decided to enter the automobile market, it went for the smaller and cheaper models. This was because South Korea had the advantages of labour and low production costs, but lacked the technology and expertise to produce the larger and higher quality cars. By focussing on the small car market, South Korean car makers like Hyundai and Daewoo were able to chip away the market shares of Japanese models. In the same way, the Malaysians have begun to enter the lower-end car market with their Proton Saga and Proton Wira. They are now in turn, winning over the market shares of the South Koreans.

In a nutshell, while market and consumer analysis may reveal that there are unfulfilled needs in certain market segments, and competitive analysis may reveal possibilities for product differentiation, a company must take into account its corporate resources. This is because if it has limited resources, it is not possible to sieze all the identified opportunities.

Taking the example of Japanese companies again, it is important to note that while they successfully identified market niches, they did not try to penetrate the market on their own. In fact, in the early years of its foreign market entry strategies, the Japanese companies relied heavily on their western and American partners, including using their channels of distribution and brand names. It was when they had gained sufficient market share and built up sufficient corporate resources that they decided to introduce their own brands and penetrate the markets through developing their own channels.

5.3 Environmental Influences

Positioning strategies cannot be decided without taking into account environmental factors. One good example of how the environment can impact the positioning strategies of companies is the Green Movement and its related agencies in championing the protection of the environment. The impact was so great over the past ten years that many global companies began to position their products and services as environmentally friendly and harmless. British Petroleum (BP) even changed its corporate colour to green while many other companies began to use re-cycled products and sponsored many events to protect the environment. The aim: to position themselves as companies that care for the preservation of nature.

In Asia, the environmental factors are undergoing tremendous changes. Some of the major environmental factors that can impact the positioning strategy of a company include business and economic, political and legal, social and cultural, and technological factors.

5.3.1 Business and Economic Factors

Understanding the impact of business and economic forces on positioning is important for any successful marketing. For example, when the Japanese car manufacturers first penetrated the ASEAN countries in the 1960s, they chose to focus their attention on the lower end of the market by offering cheap and smaller-size models. Of course, they were also constrained by corporate resources as we earlier pointed out. However, it is also correct to point out that they understood that the consumers in Asia at that time could not afford large and expensive cars as their per capita incomes were much lower. Then, the ASEAN drivers in the 1960s were interested in having affordable means of transport, not brands of car that could raise their social status.

However, as the standard of living increased in these countries, the Japanese automakers gradually brought in improved and more expensive models, and positioned their cars at the higher end of the market. What is interesting to note is that in the earlier years, the Japanese used price extensively for positioning their cars against the more expensive European models. As their cars became more expensive, largely because of the appreciation of the yen and higher production costs, the Japanese began to position their cars along new factors like quality of built, engineering innovations and features, higher performance capabilities and so on. It was not that Japanese cars acquired such attributes overnight. In fact, they have constantly been increasing in quality over the years, surpassing the American and European counterparts in many aspects. The point is that they have chosen the right moment — through understanding the environmental forces – to change their positioning strategy. In fact, they began to develop car models that were intended to compete head-on against established brands like Mercedes and BMW as early as the late 1970s. Today, with models like the Lexus, they have begun to claim superiority in car engineering and technology — that is, they are aiming to take over the leadership in the auto industry.

It is also interesting to note that the Japanese car makers are very adaptive in their positioning strategy. When they first marketed their cars to countries like China in the 1980s, they adopted the same positioning strategy that was used in the 1960s in ASEAN markets. Despite having already achieved excellence in quality, the Japanese deliberately priced their automobiles low so as to penetrate the Chinese market. In doing so, they were able to appeal to larger market segments. They reduced the number of the extra features so as to deliver a product that was within the economic means of most Chinese businesses. They understand that positioning strategies must be dynamic and must match the economic and business conditions of existing markets. This is seen by the fact that by the mid-1990s, the Japanese brought in their Lexus to be sold in direct competition against the Mercedes and BMWs in the Chinese market which has now the economic means to purchase luxury cars.

5.3.2 Political and Legal Factors

Political and legal factors can also affect the positioning strategies of companies. At the macro level, it may not be possible for some marketeers to gain access to certain markets if they are not willing to conform to the statutory and legal requirements of the markets concerned. For example, to sell cars to China, they have to be of the left-hand drive models, while many other markets in Asia operate on right-hand drive. Similarly, voltage requirements for electrical appliances vary among Asian markets. This is also true for units of measurement — whether they are in the metric or imperial system.

To be successful, the marketeer must conform to the legal requirements of each market. In other words, he must be flexible especially where manufactured products are concerned. Here, it is important to take note of the contrasting approach taken by the Japanese against that of the American and the European manufacturers. The Japanese manufacturers would go all out not only to meet the legal requirements of the local market, but would even tailor the product features to suit the needs of the intended consumers. This can best be illustrated with the examples of cars and consumer appliances.

The legal requirement for cars to be sold in ASEAN countries like Singapore and Malaysia (two relatively small markets) is that they have to be of the right-hand drive type as these two countries follow the British traffic system of driving on the left-side of the road. To sell their cars in these markets, Japanese car makers not only shifted their car steering wheel from left to right, but they also shifted the ignition hole, wiper and light indicators accordingly so as to suit the driving habits of the driver. Ironically, even great western car manufacturers like the Mercedes, BMW, Saab and Volvo failed to match the "attention to details" of their Japanese competitors. Instead, they only meet the legal requirement of shifting the steering wheel to the right. Many of the other features like signal light indicators, wiper switches, ignition hole, and even park-brakes are located on the wrong side!

For electrical appliances, Japanese manufacturers will ensure that the voltage is compatible with local requirement. In the case of many western manufacturers, they would rather rely on adaptors to do the job. The reason: there is no legal requirement that the standards must be met within the specifications of the product. Thus, these western manufacturers choose the easier way out to solve the problem. The result: they fail to win the patronage and loyalty of many Asian consumers!

5.3.3 Social, Religious, and Cultural Factors

It has been mentioned in the first article that the various economies in Asia is more heterogeneous than those in Europe. This is particularly true where the their social, religious and cultural aspects are concerned. For example, while the East Asian economies of China, Japan, South Korea, Taiwan, Hong Kong, and Singapore have strong Buddhist influences; they are counterbalanced by the Islamic countries of Brunei, Malaysia, Pakistan, and Indonesia; and the Hindu culture of India. Moreover, the often cited Confucian value system that believed to govern Asia, is really only applicable to the some of the East Asian economies.

Recognizing such diversities, the prudent marketeer must learn not to use the same strategy for the different economies. Instead, he must adapt and re-position his strategy accordingly. For example, not only is pork not consumed by Muslims, any food-related items to be marketed to the Islamic economies like Malaysia and Indonesia must be positioned as *halal*. For this reason, western fast food chains like McDonald's and Kentucky Fried Chicken are able to sell their product offerings very successfully to the Muslim consumers in Malaysia and Indonesia. In contrast, owing to having bacon on its menu, Burger King, despite its success in other non-Muslim economies in Asia, has been unable to market its products to the Muslim consumers. Unlike McDonald's which has a global orientation in its strategy (which implies a proactive effort to exploit the world as its market), Burger King seems content to remain as an international company (which implies reacting more to available market opportunities that exist in the world). The result may well be that Burger King may be knocked out of competition in many markets before it can even begin. One wonders whether Burger King has ever thought of positioning its products to Muslim consumers at all.

With regard to western fast food, it is very interesting to note how the various chains like McDonald's, Burger King, and Kentucky Fried Chicken have chosen to position themselves against their Asian counterparts. Unlike in America and Western Europe, various types of cheap and tasty Asian food are easily available. In fact, many streets and roads are often lined with such stalls and food outlets. It would be difficult for western fast food chains to compete head-on against these local operators on the basis of food. There would be no contest. Instead, the western fast food chains have cleverly positioned themselves as a lifestyle phenomenon by offering other benefits like courteous service, air-conditioned comfort, hygienic and efficient food preparation, clean toilets, brightly lit dining areas, modern and attractive ambience, constant but varied promotional offers, and so on. They play down the food aspects (such as taste and nutritional value) of their product offering. By positioning their burgers as a lifestyle offering, these western fast food chains were not only able to capture sizeable market shares by targetting mainly at yuppies with young children, and teenagers, but they were able to do with their burgers higher prices than the local food!

Understanding social trends can often provide ideas not only for the development of new products and services, but also enable the marketeer to develop the appropriate positioning strategy. For example, when the Sony Walkman first entered the market, it was positioned as a personalized entertainment system in that it could follow the owner wherever he went, and yet did not encroach on the privacy of others around him as the music can only by heard by him. In the same way, the karaoke became a big success largely because of correct positioning — by appealing to the latent needs of Asian consumers to seek ice-breaking social activities that can also allow them to showcase their talents.

In the early 1980s, the Swiss Electronic and Watch Company Ltd (SMH) launched the Swatch watch to compete in the highly crowded and competitive lower-end watch market that was dominated largely by Japanese brands. Despite the fact that many Swiss watch makers were squeezed out of the low-price segment by Japanese brands, SMH proved that it could still succeed with a cleverly crafted positioning strategy. The appeal of SMH's Swatch watches come not from its low price and high quality. This is because these two attributes are easily matched by Japanese watches like Seiko, Citizen and Casio. Instead, SMH through its constant innovation and creative designs has positioned itself more as a fashion and collectible item that reflects one's personality, and yet with the potential to appreciate in value over time because of the limited production of each model. By positioning the watch as a personal and lifestyle item that contains the elements of fun and fashion, the Swatch brand not only appeals to a wide spectrum of wearers, but also encourages the buyer to acquire more than one watch. In sum, SMH succeeds with its Swatch watch largely because of its ability to exploit the changing social and cultural trends in the market.

The beer market is another good example. Recently, light beer made a strong entry into many Asian markets by positioning itself to women and the occasional social drinkers. With the governments in many Asian countries coming down rather hard on drunken driving, marketeers of light beer may want to re-think how they can position themselves even better so as to capture a larger market share of the beer market. What is interesting about beer, regardless of whether it is light or heavy, is that it is positioned largely as a product for the white collar and professional workers. In contrast, stout is positioned largely as a product for the blue collar workers with strong "macho" personalities. As a result of such deliberate positioning strategies, the beer drinkers in Asia have become more and more distinguishable from stout drinkers.

5.3.4 Technological Factors

The advances of technology in recent years has been very mind-boggling. In particular, the advances made over the last fifty years (after the Second World War) has probably surpassed the total advances made prior to 1945. One only needs to witness the developments made in computers, biotechnology and robotics to realize the quantum leaps made in technology. The results of such advances have serious implications for the marketeer, especially in the management of his products.

Take the example of the micro-chip. As a result of its invention and possible widespread applications, it has revolutionalized the ways in which companies define their traditional competitors in their lines of businesses. The personal computer is getting smaller and yet operating at greater speed and greater capacity than the way we think. A personal computer is now small enough so that it can easily be classified as a calculator. Yet it offers much more than a calculator (note the wide varieties of organizers that are being marketed). At the same time, the computer is also merging very quickly with the television and the hi-fi system, especially with the advent of the sound blaster. Soon, it will even become a home entertainment product. Indeed, the possibilities are limitless! How then should such a product be positioned? More importantly, traditional producers of calculators, televisions, and hi-fi systems should seriously think of how to re-position themselves in order to take on the new challenges posed by the personal computers.

The technology in the telecommunications industry is equally amazing. No longer is the business confined to conveying oral messages through the telephone line. Today, written messages (through the fax machine) and images are transmitted every second and every minute. Soon, entertainment programmes such as the video-on-demand (VOD) will become a reality. As of early 1995, VOD was already undergoing pilot testing in markets like the United States, Germany, Hong Kong and Singapore. Before VOD comes on stream, cinema operators, video and laser disc rental shops, and even cable TV service providers better start to think seriously about how to reposition themselves or face market obsolescence. Here, it is important to point out that the future of the technology development in the telecommunications industry is likely to be closely integrated with that of the computer industry. The combined effects of these two technologies will create situations that could be very nightmarish for the marketeers of traditional product. Thus, they should start to systematically position themselves away from such future threats.

An interesting lesson may be learned from the watch industry. When new technology such as the first quartz watch invented in the 1960s appeared, many traditional Swiss watch makers ignored the impending threats. In the 1970s, watch manufacturing made quantum leaps when semiconductor technology and quartz crystals were combined, making mass production and economies of scale possible. The result was that the watch became a mass produced item that was priced very cheaply. Many traditional mechanical Swiss watch makers who competed at the lower-price market segment were over-whelmed by their Japanese competitors like Seiko, Citizen and Casio. This was because the Swiss relied heavily on manual but skilled labour to assemble their watches. With much higher labour costs and no economies of scale, they were unable to compete effectively. Some Swiss watch makers tried turning to electronics but ended up in very bad shape. A number of them even went out of business.

In the midst of their despair, a handful of luxury watch makers like Rolex, Longines, Ebel, and Piaget, decided to position themselves as hand-crafted, jewelry watches, and remained largely mechanical in nature. They avoided the mass production of digital and analog quartz watches. Instead, they focused the consumers' attention to the high level of Swiss craftsmanship, and created the element of exclusivity and snobbery by their limited production. Today, they have not only survived the digital threat, but have become stronger in the market as a result of an increasing demand for expensive, personalized and exclusive watches — brought about largely because of the increasing affluence of many Asian consumers.

5.4 Case Examples

To illustrate the overall impact of environmental factors on the positioning and marketing strategies, I would like to highlight three examples — property development, credit card purchases, and Australian opals.

5.4.1 Property Development

In the property development business, the developer must first decide whether he wants to focus on residential, commercial or industrial properties. Sunrise Berhad, for example, decided to focus on developing residential properties. However, there are also many kinds of residential properties such as bungalows, semi-detached houses, terrace houses, condominiums, low-cost housing, and so on. Having analysed the property market in the region during the late 1970s and 1980s, Sunrise decided to focus its attention on building mid to high-end condominiums. Then it had to decide where to build its condominiums. In fact, so long as there is a large flat piece of land, you could build condominiums. This was exactly what many Malaysian developers did, and quite a number of them failed as they were unable to differentiate their properties from one another.

In order to decide which type of condominiums and where to build them, Sunrise analysed their own corporate capabilities as well as how such capabilities could be enhanced relative to their competitors and the environment. Sunrise found that many developers avoided hills and valleys in choosing sites for building condominiums as they were considered as problems and obstacles. As a result, the prices of land with hills and valleys on them were very low, including those in prime locations in the 1980s. On the other hand, prices of lands within and near the city areas were very high.

Interestingly, the executive chairman of Sunrise, who is an architect by training, viewed hills and valleys as challenges to be met. Thus, instead of following the "herd" mentality, Sunrise went about acquiring land that had hills and valleys, at prime locations that were going at very low prices. As of early 1990s, it had a land bank of about one hundred acres in Mont Kiara alone. Such a land bank is sufficient to keep the company busy for the next fifteen to twenty years, assuming that it does not plan to increase its scope of operation significantly.

In picking hills and valleys, Sunrise was able to exploit the advantages conferred by the unique terrain for the purpose of landscaping and creating beautiful sceneries — strong features for the purpose of differentiation. In addition, the prices of the condominiums were set from RM$300,000 and upwards and targeted mainly at professional people — a deliberate market segmentation effort designed to maintain its upmarket image and to discourage speculators. At the same time, to augment its investment and rental potential, Sunrise has added an international school to cater to children of expatriate professionals at its site. It also offers a wide spectrum of supporting services ranging from interior design and furnishing, estate maintenance, rental service, supermarkets, launderette, cafeteria, and so on, aimed at augmenting the overall living ambience and image of the estate. Indeed, as of 1995, it has already turned the Mont Kiara area into one of the most prestigious and coveted residential areas in the Malaysian federal capital city.

5.4.2 Credit Card Purchases Without Signatures

In recent years, consumer purchase behaviour in Asia has undergone tremendous changes largely because of factors like the increasing affluence of consumers, the changing social trends, the advent of technology, and the availability of credit. As a result of advancements of technology, and the business and legal arrangements made between vendors and banks or credit card companies, it is even possible to make purchases with the credit card without a signature. Such a practice is already in use in many Asian economies for the purchases of tickets for theatre shows, reservations of hotel, in television shopping, and so on.

It is important to note that such transactions would not be possible if there is no consumer demand for them. Certainly the consumer's desire for convenience may be one of the many reasons accounting for the rise of such modes of purchases. However, what is more important for the marketeer to note are the new opportunities that have arisen for them to re-position their products and services to a larger target audience by using alternative marketing media. For example, television shopping is now catching on very fast in markets of Hong Kong and Singapore, and it would not be long before this way of shopping spread to the other Asian economies. In other words, the marketeer should re-examine his existing products or services to see how he may re-position them to increase his market size by adopting a different marketing strategy. Theoretically, many products can be re-positioned to reach a larger target audience through mail and television shopping. In fact, some opportunistic marketeers are already marketing products like teeth whitener, sleeping pillows, utility tools, magazines, cookwares, and many others by allowing consumers to phone in their orders and giving merely their credit card numbers (that is, making "signatureless" purchases).

5.4.3 Australian Opals

Australia produces almost 95% of the world's opal output. Yet, despite its virtual monopoly of the trade for almost one hundred years, the Australian opal industry has been unable to make its impact felt in the world of jewelry. In recent years, the Australian government and opal miners have begun to place increasing attention on how to market opals to Asian consumers. They hope to cash in on the increasing affluence of Asian consumers, and especially that of the overseas Chinese (in places like Hong Kong, Taiwan, Singapore, Malaysia, and Indonesia) who have traditionally shown a passion for precious stones.

Interestingly, despite their relative rarity, Australian opals have yet to make a strong impact on Asian consumers. This could largely be attributed to the failure of the Australian marketeers in understanding the social and cultural considerations of the Asians in their purchase of precious stones. Take the example of the black opal, reputedly the rarest and most precious stones among Australian opals. Up to date, it has yet to earn its rightful place as a jewelry item. Many Asian consumers still prefer other precious stones such as diamond, ruby, emerald, sapphire and jade. Among other reasons, the black opal, though rare, is perceived to be an ill omen. This is because black is an inauspicious colour that symbolizes bad luck and death. In addition, the Cantonese translation for opal is "loi" meaning "tear stone". As such, the black opal is associated with sadness. Altogether, the stone does very poorly with the Chinese.

Australian marketeers would have to think of better ways to position their opals to the Asian consumers if they hope to capture a good share of the precious stones market. One approach would be to shift the marketing efforts to the non-Chinese Asian consumers such as the Japanese and Koreans first, before attempting to lure the ethnic Chinese consumers. This is because the Japanese and Korean consumers are also great lovers of precious stones and are not as superstitious as the Cantonese-speaking Chinese. Once the opal is accepted as a higly desired precious stone in Japan and Korea, it would be easier to market it to the Chinese through the "trickling down" or "demonstration" effects.

Another approach may be to market equally rare, but non-black opals (such as the red and the green opals — both considered as auspicious colours) to the Chinese instead. In particular, the Australian opal marketeers may want to "dictate" the translated Chinese term for opal instead of allowing it to be called a "tear stone" in Cantonese. This would serve to correct its current poor image, and at the same time, allow the opal to seek a new position among precious stones in the mindset of the Asian consumers.

To ensure a more effective positioning strategy, the Australian opal industry may want to learn some useful lessons from De Beers in their successful marketing of diamonds to the Asian consumers. Traditionally, diamonds have been the passion of American and European women consumers. They originally did not appeal to Asians largely because their "crystal" or "glass-like" appearance lack the auspicious and rich colours of jade, ruby and sapphire — favourite precious stones among the Asians. However, with skilful marketing and heavy investment in advertising and promotion, De Beers has successfully positioned diamonds as a woman's best friend, and is today a highly desired precious stone. A key indicator of its success is that more Asian women consumers are now accepting diamonds as wedding rings (just like in the West). Presently De Beers is targetting its marketing efforts towards penetrating the China market.

5.5 Conclusion

Positioning is indeed a very challenging exercise to any marketeer. When done appropriately, it can generate fascinating results. These include generating new or additional demand for the product or service, possibilities for increasing the price and value of the product or service, and even creating new or additional benefits to the consumers. The Swatch watch, as mentioned earlier, is a very good example of what positioning can do for a product, even when competing in a very competitive market. Few marketing analysts would expect the Swatch watch to survive in a segment that is dominated by Japanese brands, more so when earlier Swiss brands competing at the lower-price range of the watch market had been literally knocked out of the competition by the Japanese watch makers. Yet, through creative marketing and positioning, Swatch watch makers have not only become a dominant player in the lower-price range market, but are giving their Japanese competitors a run for their money.

Chinese paintings and calligraphies are another good example to illustrate the power of positioning. In recent years, such works of art by Chinese masters have risen tremendously in price largely because the art dealers and auction houses had cleverly positioned them to the international market. If they had remained in China and targeted at the local collectors, their prices would still remain very low. However, as a result of positioning the Chinese paintings and calligraphies to the international world of collectors, the art dealers effectively create a bigger market and interest for such works. As a result, demand went up substantially, and inevitably prices also moved upwards.

In sum, it is important to remember that an effective marketing strategy, of which positioning is an important part, can create value in a product or service and generate benefits to the consumer. These can be achieved despite the fact that the product or service may remain fundamentally unchanged.

6

Product Design: Knowing What Features to Offer

6.1 Introduction

A company should have at least one good product if it hopes to be competitive in the market. Note that I use the word "good" and not "excellent", although the latter is something that should be pursued. This is because it is possible to have an excellent product, and still not succeed. For example, many readers will agree that it is easy to make a better hamburger than McDonald's or Burger King. Yet, many "small-time" entrepreneurs in some Asian economies who have tried to compete head-on against these western fast food chains have met with little success. They failed not because they did not make a better hamburger, but because they were unable to grasp the intricacies and complexities of the successes behind these western fast food chains. In fact, operators like McDonald's and Burger King have designed their products beyond the hamburger to include many other product attributes (such as brand name, packaging, service, and so on) and other components of the marketing function, such as promotion, advertising, pricing, and distribution.

With high economic growth rates among many Asian economies, their consumers have become more and more affluent over the past few years. Moreover, with increasing western influence (brought about by the media) and the greater availability of consumer credit, many Asian consumers are motivated by wants, not needs. In addition, they are demanding more from the products and services that they consume, and have become more conscious of the aesthetics. They are also more ostentations. In fact, there is also a significant increase in the demand for discretionary products and services. This trend is likely to continue in the future.

6.2 Marketing Hits and Misses

The changing consumption patterns and preferences among consumers are sweeping rapidly across many major cities in Asia. As shown in Table 6.1, some of the recent hits in the marketing area have been products and services that meet the increasing wants and expectations of the Asian consumers. In particular, the crave for branded goods has even prompted the Chinese government to help its local companies to hold their own against the more popular foreign brands like Mercedes Benz, Coca-Cola, McDonald's, Nikon, National, and so on. The Chinese communist party's *People's Daily* even stressed the importance of brand names in one of its editorials in October 1994. Among other things, it advocated that the government and local investors take steps to protect local brands from the threat of foreign competition. It even suggested to the local readers, "let us contribute a lot of brand names, hold high the banner of brand names and develop the grand cause of brand names!" Such "desperate" calls were obviously in response to the ceaseless onslaught of foreign brands on Chinese soils, threatening a wide array of products from consumer electronics and appliances to beer, beverages, and many others.

In many ways, the Chinese experience is not surprising. Years before, its Taiwanese and Hong Kong neighbours already had similar encounters. Beginning in the mid-1980s, the Taiwanese retail sector underwent tremendous changes and re-structuring. For example, before 1985, chain stores and shopping centres carrying foreign brands accounted for less than 5% of retail sales revenue in Taiwan. Now, ten years later, the figure has gone beyond 50%, and is still increasing rapidly. In fact, as Taiwanese income levels begin to approach income levels of the more developed economies like Australia and New Zealand, Taiwanese consumers have correspondingly developed a penchant for foreign products and brands to project their arrival as and of course to enjoy a higher standard of living. The same observations are true of Hong Kong. In fact, we are beginning to witness the increasing influence of the Hong Kong retail sector on the coastal cities of southern China. In all probability, the southern Chinese are likely to emulate the Hong Kong people in their shopping behaviour in the years to come. Similarly, the consumption behaviour of Taiwanese shoppers is most probably a good indicator of what will happen to the retail scene along the cities of eastern China.

TABLE 6.1 Some examples of marketing hits in Asia

Western fast food
Who says Asians don't like burgers and cheese? The successes of McDonald's, Burger King, and Pizza Hut in many cities have embarassed the harshest critics.

Mineral water
Marketeers have capitalized on the lack of safe drinking water from the tap by selling highly priced bottled water, the packaging of which conveys both safety and classiness.

Vitamins and food supplements
Life is becoming more precious as a result of affluence.

Designer brands and foreign brands
The Asian consumer is probably one of the most brand-conscious in the world. In China, anything that is of a foreign brand is perceived as better and more prestigious.

Karaoke
The Japanese invention that breaks down Asian inhibitions and caters to the inner desires to be a "star". A fantastic ice-breaker for social functions.

Club memberships
They appeal to the rich who, because of their newly acquired wealth, need places to socialize and show-off their wealth.

Home entertainment systems
Techonology and the abundance of laser discs, cassette discs, video cassettes, have made home entertainment affordable. These systems have allowed those living in cities such as Bangkok, Jakarta and Kuala Lumpur, to get their share of entertainment without the stress from traffic jams when going to the cinemas.

Cellular phones and pagers
This is another technologically-driven group of products that provides convenience and acts as symbols of prestige and status.

Condominiums
They appeal to an increasing number of yuppies and their families who desire a better quality of life.

Supermarkets, departmental stores, and shopping centres
The more affluent Asian consumers are demanding a more conducive and pleasant shopping environment. These shopping facilities are in line with their quest for a more gracious lifestyle.

Travel
Even the Chinese have begun to travel! The increasing number of new airlines set up in Asia, and the increased flight frequencies are all indicative of the growth of the travel industry.

Besides the changes in the shopping landscapes that are sweeping across many Asian cities, there are many other complementary developments as well. For example, resort and country clubs, condominiums and holiday bungalows, and travel packages are beginning to make their impact. If anything, marketeers will be challenged to come up with better products and services in order to cater to the new Asian consumers. However, in doing so, the marketeer must carefully study the changing needs and demands of his consumers (as discussed in the previous few articles). Otherwise, he may still not succeed. For example, despite the immense opportunities in Asia, there have been cases of marketing misses as well. Table 6.2 shows some of these misses.

Among the many reasons for failure, the main one is the inability of the marketeer to fully understand the characteristics of the Asian consumers. Take the example of the oven, and of late, the microwave oven (see Table 6.2). Despite its tremendous success in many western countries, the oven and its new cousin, the microwave oven failed to achieve the same level of penetration into the Asian market. This is because the functions and usages of the two types of ovens do not quite suit the cooking habits of Asians. Few Asian homemakers bake their food — they prefer to cook over open stoves. As a result, incredulous as it may be, those few households who have microwave ovens use them for boiling cups of water or merely to warm up food. Some even buy them just to complete their array of kitchen appliances and to impress.

It would take a long time, if at all, to change the cooking habits of Asians. Similarly, western-style dishwashers — mainly designed for the washing of plates, spoons, forks and knives — are not making much headway in the Asian market. These dishwashers are not designed to handle the woks, bowls and chopsticks of the Chinese, nor the cooking pots and pans of the Indians and Malays.

Interestingly, Corning cookware suffered a similar fate in its earlier years when it entered some Asian markets like those of Singapore and Malaysia. They were designed to be oven-safe (a feature not relevant to those who do not use the oven), and had deep but flat bases (a design unsuitable for holding soup or for displaying other dishes like pork and vegetables). As they were of very high quality, were expensive, and carried a prestigious brand name, they were bought largely as gifts, especially as wedding presents. However, few households used them as their designs were not practical for Asian

TABLE 6.2 Some examples of marketing misses in Asia

Ovens and Microwave ovens
 Do not suit the cooking habits of Asians.

Dishwashers
 Wrong configuration for Asian utensils. Besides domestic help is plentiful and cheap in Asia.

Electronic Shopping
 Too early for the Asian market as the technological infrastructure is still not in place. In addition, Asian consumers still prefer to see, feel, touch, and a smell product before deciding to buy it or not.

DIY (Do-it-yourself) products
 Too early to be introduced to the Asian market as there are plenty of cheap labour and skilled artisans around.

Generic brands
 Asian consumers want branded goods, not generic ones. Generic brands appeal more during recessions and in more matured consumer societies. With the probable exception of Japan, generic brands are unlikely to become popular in the other Asian economies for the next ten to twenty years.

Mail orders
 Many postal systems in Asian economies are not well developed enough for mail orders. Mail orders face the same problems as electronic shopping. However, there is a potential for mail orders in the marketing of some products.

---

cooking. Instead, many recipients of such Corning ware would recycle them as gifts to others when the opportunity arose! Fortunately, Corning ware discovered the problem some years later, and took actions to modify the design of their products.

The lesson to be learned is that the marketeer must be both proactive and responsive where the changing needs and demands of the consumers are concerned. Proactiveness is needed so that he can spot emerging trends and hence be able to capitalize on them. Responsiveness is required in order to fine-tune his products and services so as to suit the specific demands of a market or market segment. He should avoid replicating the same product strategy for every market.

6.3 Designing the Product

In view of the changes that are very quickly taking place among the Asian consumers, there is a need to re-evaluate the product or service that the marketeer is offering. To begin with, what is the product? Why do consumers buy it? To satisfy a basic need or for something more? For example, if shoes are merely to protect the feet, why are there so many designs, and types of shoes in the market? Why are teenagers spending more than US$100 on a pair of Reebok, Nike or Avia? Similarly, why do men and women bother to spend so much money buying different kinds of shoes to suit different occasions or purposes? Obviously, shoes no longer just serve the basic function of footwear anymore. Instead, they have become part of a person's lifestyle and more.

Similarly, if a shirt is only a piece of clothing, why then are there so many designer brands in the market? More seriously, how is it that brands like Ralph Laurent, Valentino, Christian Dior, Dunhill, and so on, can command such high premiums? Are the premiums based on quality, or are they the result of other factors? By asking questions such as these, a marketeer can obtain the most insightful analysis about what a product comprises, and how it can be packaged so as to augment its value to the increasingly affluent Asian consumers.

6.3.1 The Three Product Levels

For the purpose of analysis, a product can be viewed as consisting of three levels (see Figure 6.1). The first level is called the **core level.** This level defines what the product exists for, that is, its most fundamental function, benefit or service. For example, the basic function of a watch is to tell time; the primary usage of a pair of shoes is in protecting the feet; the fundamental benefit of a car is for transportation on land; the main purpose of a pen is for writing; and the purpose of a shirt is for covering the body. Similarly every service meets a need. For example, a hospital provides health care, an airline provides air transportation, a courier company provides speedy and on-time delivery of documents, a business consultant provides problem-solving expertise, and so on.

It is important to point out that many manufacturers in Asia are still very much operating at the core level. In other words, they tend to focus heavily on the product and its functional attributes. Their basic aim is to make a product that is cheap and acceptable to the buyer. Little attention is given to what the consumer wants. This approach is understandable, given the relatively low incomes of many Asian economies in the past. However, with increased affluence, especially over the past ten to fifteen years, it is no longer sufficient for these manufacturers to concentrate only on the functional aspects of a product and ignore the other levels or dimensional.

The second level of a product is called the **physical or tangible level.** This includes all the components or aspects that are **directly** related to the product. For example, most products come with a brand name, packaging, style, quality, and features. They form part and parcel of the product. In other words, without them, the product is not complete and is unlikely to be in a saleable condition. To a large extent, they form the aesthetic dimension of the product. Viewed from the consumer's perspective, he is unlikely to purchase the product without these tangible components.

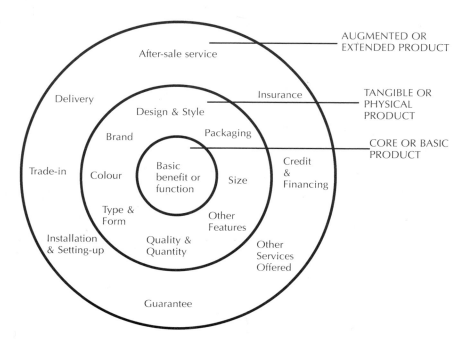

Figure 6.1 The three levels of a product

It is interesting to point out that some of the components of the tangible level may not be absolutely necessary to the product for it to be sold. However, if some of these components are missing, the consumer may expect or even demand a price discount. So, a shirt which isn't packaged properly is unlikely to be sold at its full price. In almost all instances, it would have to be sold at a discount. Similarly, few consumers would buy a television set or a hi-fi system without the packaging.

The third level of a product can be called the **augmented or extended** level. This comprises features and or services that are either **indirectly** related to the product, or at times, even deliberately added to the product. Examples of components of the augmented level include free delivery, payment by instalment, installation of the product after-sales service, warranty, free gifts, lucky draws, and so on.

6.3.2 Competing Beyond the Core Level

It is significant to note that as a result of the increasing affluence of the Asian consumers, many products can no longer compete at the core level. For example, twenty years ago, a consumer in any one of the major Asian cities, who wanted to buy a watch, would be very concerned about its accuracy in telling time — its basic function. However, any watch — and this includes even pirated watches — that cannot tell time accurately today is no longer a watch! Instead, watches today compete on a whole range of features, of designs, styles, and brands (the tangible level) that have little to do with time-telling itself. In fact, the benefits they offer are also not concentrated at telling time accurately. Instead, watches are sold as fashion items (as in the case of the Swatch brand), as technology products (as in the case of the Seiko brand), as a piece of craftsmanship the International Watch Company (IWC) brand), as a piece of jewelry (as in the case of the Piaget brand), as an investment (as in the case of the Breguet subscription set) as a status symbol (as in the case of a Rolex), as a reflection of one's personality (as in the case of designer's watches); and so on.

Similarly, twenty years ago, a consumer, say in Singapore, was concerned about whether a refrigerator will keep his food fresh in a frost-free environment. Today, if a refrigerator is not frost-free, it will probably be viewed as an ice box! The consumer is now concerned about the different features of the refrigerator: if the compartments have temperature controls; its design: if it is a two-door, three-door, four-door or even five-door refrigerator; its colour: if it will go with the colour of the kitchen tiles and walls; its brand — some models are viewed as more prestigious; and whether it has fuzzy logic, so that the temperature is automatically moderated. In addition to focussing on the tangible product level, the augmented product level also comes into play in the purchase of a refrigerator. The consumer would be concerned as to whether the refrigerator comes with warranty, after-sale service, free delivery, and in the case of higher price models, credit terms and free installation (required for those with automatic ice cubes making capability).

Clearly, for many consumer products, it is no longer sufficient to compete at the core level. This is because with improvement in technology and automation, most manufacturers are capable of turning out products comparable in quality, especially at the core level. To focus on the core level would only spell trouble as the product becomes undifferentiated, and hence favour the low cost manufacturer. By moving away from the core level, and focussing on the other two product levels, the manufacturer is not only able to differentiate and in so doing, to add value to his product. For example, marketeers of compact discs (CDs) and books in many Asian economies like Singapore, Malaysia, Taiwan, Hong Kong, and Japan, have learnt that attractive packaging, covers and designs help to sell the products.

Here, it is important to emphasize that a that product is priced higher than its competitors' needs not be owing to the core aspect. More often than not, it is the tangible components (and at other times, the augmented aspects) of the product that can add the most value. For instance, cosmetics, perfumes, colognes and many high fashion goods are marketed more at the tangible and augmented levels than at the core level. Similarly, the marketeers of designers' clothings such as Valentino, Dunhill, and Christian Dior, have cleverly used attractive and elaborate packaging, including printed description of the materials and workmanship, as ways to augment the value of their products.

On the other hand, despite the elaborate Indonesian painting and Malaysian batik shirts by hand — at times done on very high quality cotton or silk — hand-painted Batik shirts have yet to command high prices comparable to those of western brands. Similarly, the Chinese textile manufacturers have traditionally focussed only on the core level of their products. Little attention have been paid to the design and prints of their materials. As a result, many Chinese consumers today are opting to buy imported clothing materials from Japan and South Korea as they offer more choices, colours, prints and designs. Ironically, in terms of quality, these imported fabrics are inferior to Chinese silk, and yet they are able to fetch comparable or even higher prices!

Among other factors accounting for the inability of Asian manufacturers to augment the value of their products, two major factors relating to the tangible level of their products deserve special mention — branding and packaging. Branding will be discussed in great details in article 8. I will now elaborate on the issue of packaging.

6.3.3 The Need to Improve Packaging and Product Presentation

There is no lack of Asian manufacturers as far as products are concerned. Textiles, shoes, arts and crafts, handbags and related leather goods, and so on are made abundantly in many Asian economies. Unfortunately, besides paying little attention to developing and building up their brand names (which will be discussed in article 8), these Asian manufacturers have traditionally focussed on the core level, and paid very little attention to the tangible and augmented level. There is no other aspect of a product more visible than the that of packaging and product presentation. Let me cite some examples.

With more than five thousand years of history, China is rich with traditional arts and crafts, and a host of other man-made products from materials such as porcelain, enamel, semi-precious stones, copper, silk, clay, and so on. For instance, Chinese silk, enamel, teapots, ink-blocks, carving stones and many other products have been known in the world for centuries! Unfortunately, despite advances in technology and methods of production, and more importantly, changes in consumers' affluence, the Chinese manufacturers have made little attempt to improve the packaging and presentation of their products. Instead, they still use paper cardboards for packaging most of their products. Owing to this cheap packaging, the value of the product is not apparent. Being of poor quality, the packages themselves are often subjected to attacks by insects like cockroaches and silver fish. They also do not provide adequate protection to the product thus giving rise to damages during transportation.

Perhaps the way the Chinese market their paintings and calligraphies provides a good illustration of their failure to fully appreciate the value of packaging and product presentation. Currently, most Chinese paintings and calligraphies are done on rice paper. There is nothing wrong with this as it is the way and style in which such works are done. The problem is that, over the years, the Chinese have made little attempt to improve the quality of the rice paper and the scrolling. As a result, regardless of the standing and reputation of the artist or calligrapher, their works are done on a common grade of rice paper. In addition, regardless of the quality and reputation of the work, the scrolling is done using a commonly used medium. Thus, unless the collector or buyer is familiar with the reputation of the artist, it is often difficult to ascertain the quality and value of the painting or calligraphy just by looking at it. In contrast, the works of the masters are given very special treatment and handling in the western world. It is thus not surprising that the value of western paintings can command much higher prices in the international market. Certainly, among other factors, it is their packaging and presentation that help to augment the value of the works.

The Chinese are not the only ones who have fared rather poorly in the area of packaging and product presentation. Similar "mistakes" are made by manufacturers in other Asian economies like Malaysia, Indonesia, Vietnam, Thailand, India, and so on. These economies produce excellent works of art from materials like leather, ivory, wood, semi-precious and precious stones, silk, wool, silver, copper and other mediums. Unfortunately, because of their lack of attention to packaging and presentation, much of the value of these products are lost. If anything, this is one area that many Asian manufacturers and marketeers must learn from western world and their western counterparts who hve shown a marketing finesse for products like cosmetics, perfumes, clothings, shoes, watches, pens, and other high fashion items.

However, all is not lost for Asia, especially if marketeers are prepared to learn from the Japanese. Judging from the way their products are packaged and presented, the Japanese are definitely one of the gurus in the area of marketing. One only needs to note the amount of attention to detail a Japanese departmental store pays to packaging its box of candies or cookies, to realize the level of sophistication involved. Kirin beer for one, is packaged in a very attractive can; Japanese apples and other kinds of fruits are so well wrapped; and in the packaging of fragile items like hi-fi equipment, porcelain, styrofoam and polystyrene plastic are generously used.

91

6.4 Understanding Relative Strengths at the Three Levels

To develop an effective product strategy, a marketeer should carefully examine his own product and determine his strengths at all three levels. They will provide very useful clues on how to compete. For example, if his competitors are focusing more at the core level, perhaps the marketeer should then explore niches at the tangible level. When the competitors are operating at the tangible level, then the marketeer should exploit the augmented level. And when everyone moves to the tangible and the augmented levels, there may be new opportunities presented at the core level for the marketeer.

The success of western fast food in many Asian economies provides a very good example. Traditionally, many Asian fast food are sold using small hawker stalls that ply along the streets or concentrated around some corners of the cities. These hawker stalls compete only on the basis of food in satisfying hunger (that is, at the core level). Little attention was paid to the tangible and augmented levels. In contrast, the western fast food chains like McDonald's and Kentucky Fried Chicken are able to offer a whole spectrum of other benefits that include comfortable dining facilities, air-conditioning, beautiful ambience, cleanliness of the outlet, superb service, and so on. In addition, they have an internationally well-known brand name. They do not compete at the core level. Instead, they direct the consumers' attention to the tangible and augmented levels.

Similarly, when SIA first entered the world market, it found that many other airlines concentrated on providing air travel (that is, operate at the core level), and paid little attention to inflight service. This provided the opportunity for SIA to position its air travel beyond the core level, by systematically building up its inflight services (that is, operate at the tangible level). Gradually, it gained a reputation for its inflight services that even other airlines talk about. However, over the past ten years, many other Asian airlines have begun to emulate SIA inflight services. Some have even attained service standards that are equal to or even exceeding that of SIA. But on realizing that its existing inflight services no longer distinguish itself from the other airline, SIA has embarked on many other innovations such as air-telephone and fax services, video games, customized movies, amongst others. Furthermore, SIA has constantly upgraded its aircrafts so that it has become the international airline that has the youngest fleet of aircrafts. The remarkable thing about having a young fleet is that SIA has re-focussed air travellers' attention to the importance of safety and comfort (core benefits). In other words, while other airlines move towards the tangible aspects, SIA has cleverly shifted back to its core service — of course, without compromising the tangible level of its service. Here, it is important to note that while it is easier to duplicate inflight services, it is much more difficult to buy new aircrafts on a regular basis as this involves huge sums of investment. However, being one of the most profitable airlines in the world, SIA has not encountered much difficulties in buying its new planes thus far.

6.5 Examples of Marketing at the Three Product Levels

The key to success for any shrewd marketeer is to recognize that there are many dimensions to a product, though it may not be possible to fully exploit some of them for marketing purposes. What is needed is a creative mind and the willingness to explore new ways of doing business. As mentioned earlier, book publishers and CDs producers in China, Taiwan, Singapore, and Hong Kong have discovered that attractive and well-designed covers help to increase book prices and sales. Similarly, producers of cassettes and laser discs have also realized the importance of having attractive covers and packaging in the marketing of their products.

6.5.1 Private Residential Properties

Improving the offerings or benefits of the product is indeed an art for the marketeer to master. It is especially required when operating at the tangible and augmented levels. The residential property market in Singapore is a good example. Over the last ten years, as a result of intense competition as well as the effects of the 1985 and 1986 economic recession, many of the companies that are surviving today have become very bold and creative in marketing residential properties. No longer do they market properties as homes (the core benefit). Instead, they have included many other features at the tangible and augmented levels in their marketing strategies (see Figure 6.2).

At the tangible level, some property developers have concentrated on improving the quality of their products. For example, in the 1970s and 1980s, properties built by Far East Organization (FEO) were known to be of poor quality. However, since the beginning of the 1990s, FEO has embarked on a systematic programme to improve the quality of their properties. No effort has been spared as they continue to pay special attention to the quality of materials used, the features offered, the design and style of the building, the layout of the homes, and so on. The result is that they have become the first developer in Singapore to achieve the ISO 9002 quality certification in project management in 1994.

One of FEO's recently built condominiums, Dover Parkview, launched in January 1995, is certainly ahead with its many state-of-the-art features: magnetic card control lockset system, audio-video intercom, wall-mounted hairdryer, designer wardrobes, hotel-style electronic safe, gold-chrome finished sanitary fittings, video-on-demand, and cable television services, amongst others. On top of these features are other attractions: a choice location near all the major tertiary institutions and premium secondary schools, junior colleges and shopping areas; private air-conditioned bus services to the nearby MRT station and shopping area; lush tropical landscaping; a multitude of facilities which include a club house, four tennis courts, a large swimming pool with underwater music, a children's pool, a splash pool, timber sunning deck, sauna rooms, jacuzzi, family furo bath, outdoor keep-fit station, jogging track, gymnasium, barbeque pits, and ample parking lots.

The developer of Dover Parkview also boasts of its Proteq 8X computerized security and home automation system that provides security by monitoring the various entrances and rooms in the house. What's more, the system enables the owner to control lighting and air-conditioning from wherever he is, via a telephone. In sum, Dover Parkview was marketed as more than a home with its futuristic and intelligent features.

Another Singaporean company, Ban Hin Leong, has traditionally enjoyed a strong reputation as a high quality property developer. Sensing the need to build up its market presence, it embarked on an ambitious marketing and aggressive advertising programme (beginning in the 1990s) to promote a common brand name for all its residential properties – Springleaf Homes. By early 1995, it had achieved some success in establishing this brand name. The promotion of a brand name for residential properties is not unique to Singapore. In Malaysia, Sunrise Berhad has established a very strong brand name for its condominiums.

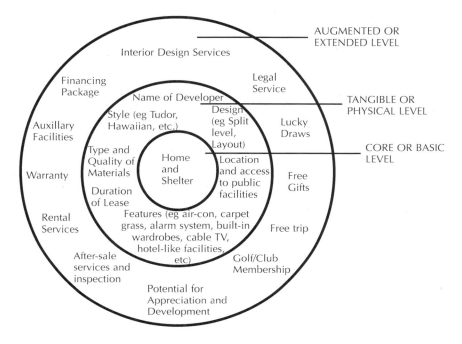

Figure 6.2 The three product levels of a residential property

At the augmented level of a product, property developers have thrown in many other features in order to provide an even more attractive package to potential buyers. Features like free valuation, free or low legal fees, 100% financing, extended repayment schemes, interior design services, warranty, lucky draws, free gifts, free seminars, rental and resale services, and so on have all been utilized by the innovative property developers.

A good example of a very innovative developer that has exploited all the three product levels has to be Sunrise Berhad of Malaysia. Besides having a strong brand name, Sunrise is well known for its attention to detail in the construction of its condominiums. Other than building in choice locations, it pays close attention to design, style, features, and the quality of materials used. More importantly, while the property is under construction, Sunrise keeps its customers posted on the progress of the project. In addition, it also sends interesting and favourable news clippings and articles pertaining to property trends and prices. These are done with the intention of assuring the buyers that they have made the right decision.

As the construction of the property is about to be completed, Sunrise offers, through one of its subsidiaries or associated companies, interior design packages and other related services. It even offers after-sales services such as organizing free seminars, talks, parties and other social gatherings for its buyers! Indeed, many of the features shown in Figure 6.2 are offered by Sunrise Berhad. It comes as no surprise that Sunrise Berhad is fast emerging as the leader in condominium development in Malaysia.

Among the various product benefits offered by Sunrise, the unique pricing strategy adopted for one of its condominiums, Kiara Palma, deserves special mention. Kiara Palma was launched in January 1992, a time when the future trend of condominium prices was unpredictable. The market was then filled with rumours of an impending glut of condominiums and a fear of falling prices were prevalent among property analysts and potential buyers. To counter such fears, Sunrise came up with its "recession-proof scheme" — to express its confidence that its properties would never depreciate in value. This it did by "guaranteeing" its properties against any impending recessions or fall in prices. The scheme worked as follows — Sunrise would reimburse the buyer, over a 36-month period, 10% of the original purchase price upon handing over of possession. This benefit was only applicable to the first buyer and would lapse should the property be sold anytime before or after possession.

The creatively designed recession-proof scheme (which is one of the aspects of the augmented level of the product) effectively locked the buyer to his purchase for a period of five years. This is because it takes about two years for the condomiunium to be built, and three years for the rebate to be completed. Empirically speaking, the probability of a property depreciating over a five year period is very low. In fact, few property slumps last that long. Moreover, in the event that the price of the property declined, the buyer was unlikely to sell out as he had a 10% price cushion. It is no wonder Sunrise boldly calls it a recession-proof scheme!

There is more to Sunrise's recession proof scheme when one analyses it carefully. First, it eliminates speculators as few of them will be prepared to hold the property for 5 years. The 10% rebate over the 36-month period is effectively a price discount which can only be gained by holding on to the property. The price would have to rise higher than the 10% for the seller to benefit as he would lose the rebate the moment he sells the property. As the new buyer cannot gain from the scheme, he is likely to push down the price anyway.

Second, Sunrise is effectively borrowing "in advance" from the buyer on an interest-free basis. This is a creative way of borrowing from the buyers to finance the whole project. Third, Sunrise is guaranteed the collection of its monthly maintenance and management fees, and sinking fund contributions for the first three years upon handing over of possession to the owners. This is because such payments can be automatically deducted from the monthly rebate. In fact, this was exactly what they did when the property was handed over to the buyers in late 1994! Finally, Sunrise is almost certain to have a large pool of long term investors from among its owners — an important factor for increasing the future value of the property.

6.5.2 Health Care

Property development is not the only example whereby the three levels of the product have been exploited for marketing purposes. The health care industry is another good example. In the 1960s and early 1970s, hospitals in countries like Singapore were only able to provide the basic services. This was largely due to the lack of financial resources to upgrade facilities and to provide better quality services. In addition, there was a general lack of qualified personnel. More importantly, the need to provide "extra" services were not as pressing as that for providing general health care.

Hospitals then were not pleasant places to be in as the facilities were inadequate. In fact, they were viewed very negatively by the general population who preferred consulting the traditional Chinese doctor and the use of Chinese herbs. The impression then was that if one were to be admitted to hospital, he or she might not come out alive. The conditions of hospitals were pathetic. In addition, the buildings were painted in black and white — colours associated with death and funerals.

Beginning in the late 1970s, the health care scene in Singapore began to undergo significant changes. The changes were necessitated by the increasing affluence of Singaporeans as well as the competition from private hospitals. To begin with, professionals were brought in. These included hospital administrators, public relations officers, and even marketing managers. Buildings and facilities were improved, expanded and upgraded. The physical environment of hospitals was also spruced up with flowers, trees, shrubs and through landscaping. Training programmes were instituted for personnel to improve the quality of service in every aspect. In addition, many other programmes were embarked upon to improve relations with the patients. In Singapore, hospital services are no longer operating at the core level. Figure 6.3 provides a useful illustration of the three product levels of hospital service.

Today, some hospitals are beginning to develop their competitive advantages at the tangible and augmented levels. Mount Elizabeth Hospital in Singapore, for example, even provides porter service for its patients. It boasts of a hotel-like lobby and reception area, and its rooms are designed very much like hotel rooms. At the same time, it offers its patients daily newspapers, in-house videos, and menus for ordering of meals! The comfort and standard of services provided are no less than those of a five-star hotel!

In other health care services like child birth, competition at the tangible and augmented levels has also begun. This is because with the advances in medical science, having a safe and easy delivery (core benefits) is no longer an issue in child birth. Instead, other benefits like the established name and reputation of the hospital, the ambience and facilities of the hospital, the type and quality of delivery

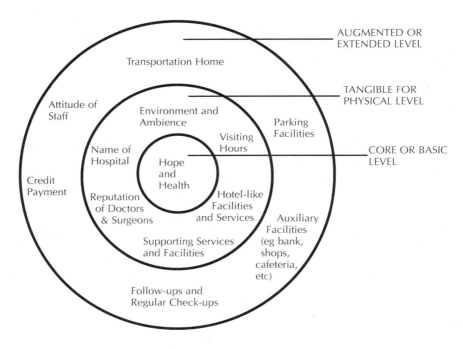

Figure 6.3 The three levels of service for a hospital

room, pre-delivery counselling classes, post-natal care (that includes home visits), free gifts upon discharge from hospitals, and so on, are being used as part of the overall marketing effort. To commemorate the auspicious occasion, some hospitals even allow photographing and video-taping of the delivery process!

Singapore's experience in health care is just at the tip of the iceberg of what can be expected in the other Asian economies in the future as their incomes continue to rise. Without doubt, they are likely to emulate the developments in Singapore. As it is, some private hospitals from Singapore have already ventured to export their "brand" of health care to the neighbouring economies, including China.

6.5.3 Funeral Services

The creative approaches adopted by many Asian marketeers to boost their products and services beyond the core level have even extended to one of the seldom talked about businesses — funerals. In the past, undertakers only provided the minimal services, and there were little efforts to coordinate the various activities needed for the wake and the funeral. This created much stress and tension for members of the bereaved family who were often lost at making decisions in their moments of loss.

However, undertakers in some Asian economies like Hong Kong, Taiwan, Japan, and Singapore, have now become very professional over the years. Gone are the days when undertakers merely provided the basic products and services like the casket, the hearse and the embalming of the corpse. Today, they offer a full range of services that includes collection of the body from the mortuary, provision of all kinds of funeral clothings and accessories, provision or booking of funeral parlours, placement of orbituary notices in the local newspapers, enlargement of the photograph of the deceased, and arrangement of types of funeral services required.

In addition, they also provide the infrastructure for the wake itself. This includes supply of flowers, wreaths, candles, jossticks, food, drinks, tidbits, tables, chairs, lightings, fans, mobile toilets, telephone lines, game sets, and so on. During the funeral itself, they provide pallbearers, transportation, and other necessary services. After the funeral, they collect the ashes from the crematorium (in the case of cremation) to put into an urn, and subsequently, placing the urn in a columbarium. Their services do not end here. If needed, they would also undertake to do the inscription and installation of the porcelain or plaque for the niche.

In sum, undertakers in many Asian cities today are able to provide a "one-stop service" that eliminates the stress which would otherwise be faced by the deceased family members if they had to look to many of the arrangements themselves. They are now able to play the role of a consultant, and at the same time provide the full range of services by exploiting all the three product levels.

6.6 Some Caution in the Product Levels

In using the three levels of product for marketing, I must caution against certain things. To begin with, not all companies can offer all three levels of the product. Thus, for the smaller competitors, there is still the need to specialize, focus and capitalize on some particular aspect from amongst the various dimensions of the product. For the larger competitors, it is also important not to be carried away with the idea that one would be more successful if all three levels of the product can be exploited. This is only true if the attributes or services offered are what consumers are looking for. Consumers do not buy products per se, they buy the **benefits** that come with the products. Thus, in designing whatever product offerings to the consumers, it is necessary to ask what are the benefits that they are looking for, not what you would like to provide! The focus should be on the consumer and the market, not your own preference!

Besides knowing what benefits to offer, the marketeer must be aware that the skills required to market the three levels of product could be very different. In particular, benefits offered at the augmented level could consist of services that are not related to the product itself! Take the case of the residential property as shown in Figure 6.2. To market the services at the augmented level requires substantial amount of coordination with other agencies like banks, valuers, interior designers, and law firms. They are complex skills that require a high level of expertise. Even at the tangible level, the property developer must ensure that his sales personnel are well-trained to handle the complexity of items like those shown in Figure 6.2.

In attempting to compete at all three levels of the product, the marketeer must also bear in mind that higher costs will be incurred. Thus, he should bear in mind the costs of providing the additional benefits, and should factor these costs into the pricing of the product. In the case of residential properties, for example, it is easy to see that the items as shown in Figure 6.2 under the tangible and augmented levels would increase the cost of the property significantly and it would be naive to assume that they are not reflected in the final price of the property. Similarly, health care cost will increase as a result of improvements made at the tangible and augmented levels. In the case of a funeral, it can be expected that the total cost for the package of services could even be significantly higher as the undertaker would definitely charge a premium for the convenience of his "one-stop" service. Moreover, in such businesses, the clients are unlikely to bargain. In fact, for some products like cosmetics and perfumes, it is the components at the tangible level that are responsible for their subsequent high prices.

Besides pricing, the marketeer must also consider the impact on the other marketing variables like distribution and promotion. For example, if a marketeer wants to provide delivery and installation, as in the case of selling air-conditioners and refrigerators, does he have the distribution network and installation capabilities to do so? Similarly, if he wants to provide after-sale servicing, he must have the manpower and resources to do so. In addition, the marketeer must factor in the costs of providing such services into the pricing of the product.

Here, it is important to note that the marketeer need not undertake the job himself. Sub-contracting could be considered. In fact, with the increasing emergence of companies that specialize in total logistics management (a topic that I will deal with in a later article), it is possible to contract the distribution task to such companies. A good example is that of Procter & Gamble. It now uses logistics companies to perform its distribution task (largely on a door-to-door basis) while it concentrates on the other aspects of its marketing . The result is that it is able to provide better service at a lower cost.

Finally, which of the three levels of the product the marketeer chooses to focus on would also determine the type of advertising and promotional strategies to be used. To begin with, he must understand which is the most important product level that he intends to focus on to develop a competitive advantage. This would allow him to decide how to execute his advertising and promotional strategy. For example, when the residential property market in Singapore moved to compete more and more at the tangible level over the last ten years, developers decided to use showflats or showhouse (in addition to the colourful brochures, models and layout plans) as key marketing tools to attract buyers. This is because the showflat is the most powerful promotional medium in showcasing the tangible product. In addition, it also allows the developer the opportunity to market the other services at the augmented level, once the potential buyer is in the showflat. However, the use of showflats demand sales personnel on the ground to be very well trained and informed. Otherwise, the investment made in such an approach would go to waste.

6.7 Conclusion

In an era of increasing competition and better educated and affluent Asian consumers, the marketeer must avoid selling his product in the way he used to twenty years ago. Rather, he must delve deeper into the make-up of the product and discover what additional benefits it can offer to the consumer. Many of these benefits do not occur at the core level. They exist at the tangible and augmented levels.

7

Managing Beyond the Product Life Cycle

7.1 Introduction

Among various concepts developed by marketing scholars, the product life cycle (PLC) is probably one of the more interesting. It is argued that a product, like any living being, goes through various phases of life. While marketing scholars have not agreed on the number of phases in the life of a product, four basic stages can, nevertheless, be identified. These four basic stages of the product life cycle (PLC) are illustrated in Figure 7.1. They are namely, the introduction stage, the growth stage, the maturity stage, and the decline stage, which eventually leads to the death of the product.

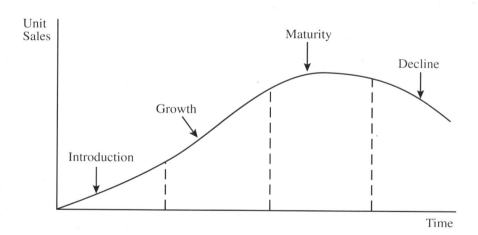

Figure 7.1 The four stages of the product life cycle

7.2 Stages of the Product Life Cycle

7.2.1 Introduction Stage

The PLC concept has allowed marketeers to focus their strategies according to the stage of the cycle. For example, at the **introduction stage**, sales are low as consumers are not fully aware of the product's features, uses and benefits. There is, therefore, an urgent need to build up demand through promotions and advertising. If the product lends itself to economies of scale, it may be necessary to price it cheaply and build up an extensive distribution network in order to achieve the necessary market penetration (that is secure a large market share). Profits are unlikely at this stage. In fact, the objective may well be to minimize losses at this stage with the objective of building up market share so as to recover investment costs and then reap profits in the longer term.

It is important to point out that when a new product or service has been introduced into the market, it has presumably gone through all the necessary steps of product and market testing. In other words, the introduction stage represents the initial phase of the commercialization of the product or service. Thus, this can be a very difficult and risky phase of the product in that there are many uncertainties and threats. These include contending with the ever changing consumer tastes and preferences, and competitive forces, amongst others. Furthermore, the ease and costs of adopting the product by the consumer may also affect the successful launch of the product.

Singapore Teleview is a good example of a service that encountered tremendous difficulties at the introduction stage. After heavy investments in research and development since the late 1980s, Singapore Telecoms (the company responsible for launching the product) found that Teleview was not making much headway in the early 1990s, despite having embarked on fairly aggressive advertising and promotional campaigns to market Teleview. While there was some noticeable increase in market share by the mid-1990s, the results weren't anything to boast about.

There are many reasons for Teleview's weak penetration of the market. One of the major factors is competition: the presence of alternative services (for example, InTV and Teletext) that are not only able to provide many basic services of Teleview more efficiently, but at lower prices as well. The technology for supporting Teleview in the late 1980s and early 1990s was still rather inadequate to provide high-end services. The end product was a rather "user-unfriendly" service with limited functions. Naturally the advent of CD-ROM and many other "stand-alone" multi-media products which can interface with the personal computer made the already bleak future of Teleview even bleaker. Essentially, Teleview is a product that suffers from a lack of focus. It has a little of everything but not enough of something to appeal to a well defined group of consumers, even though it is not altogether an unattractive product. Given its limited success thus far, it will be no surprise if Singapore Teleview does not live through the four stages of a product's life cycle.

Many communication-related products have, on the other hand, been extremely successful. For example, personal computers, CD-ROMs, fax machines, cellular handphones, and pagers have all been successfully introduced to many Asian markets. Owing to the phenomenal growth rates of many Asian economies, many of these products have already gone beyond the introduction stage and entered into the growth stage. If any product or service is to survive beyond the introduction stage, then the marketeer must pay attention to the peculiarities of its market and its consumers. He must adapt the product or service to the social, cultural and other environmental factors of that market.

Toys 'R Us initially tried to introduce their American concept of retailing toys in bulk through superstores to several Asian cities in the late 1980s. They met with very little success. There were a good many reasons for this lack of success. To begin with, their merchandising mix were largely targetted at the western consumers. For instance, it carried a fairly large percentage of self-assembled toys, which simply did not appeal to Asian consumers. Buying in bulk — which is what marketing through superstores promotes — does not go down well with the Asian consumers, even today. The typical Asian consumer wants to buy his or her toys from a specialist or department store where services include gift-wrapping. Finally, the distribution structure for toys in many Asian cities is not a tight-knitted one and unlike America, toys can easily be purchased at many retail and convenient stores. It was only after modifying its concept, and in particular its merchandizing mix and location, that Toys 'R Us managed to have some impact on the Asian retail toy market.

In the same way, some overly enthusiastic marketeers have also tried to introduce DIY products into the Asian market. In the early 1980s, DIY products and stores began to emerge in Singapore, Hong Kong, and other Asian cities. Unfortunately, after more than a decade, they have yet to enter into the growth stage. This is because unlike the West, labour costs in Asia are still very affordable and there is no strong motivation for one to do the job himself. Moreover, while there is little difference between blue and white collar labour costs in the West (in some instances, blue collar jobs like plumbing and construction command even higher premiums than white collar jobs), there is a great disparity in earnings between white and blue collar jobs in many Asian economies. A professional lawyer, doctor, banker or accountant would earn many times more than an electrician, plumber, carpenter, or mechanic. This is particularly so when there is no shortage of workers in the latter types of jobs. Finally, with relatively smaller living space in most Asian cities, there is very little scope for DIY activities!

7.2.2 The Growth Stage

At the **growth stage**, the product begins to gain market acceptance, so that there is rapid growth in sales and profits. This is a critical stage for most products in that when sales and profits become large and visible, they invite competitors. Aggressive advertising and promotion ensue and possibly price cutting as well as attempts to grab market share hot up. There are plenty of such examples happening in the Asian market.

When the IBM personal computer was first introduced into the markets of Singapore and Hong Kong in the early 1980s, it commanded a very high price. However, as the product gained acceptance, it attracted a stream of new and competitive products. Over the years, competition has become more and more intense as the different brands of personal computers began to fight for market shares not just in Singapore and Hong Kong, but in many other Asian cities as well. These competitive products include American brands like Hewlett Packard, Compaq, Dec, and the AST; European brands like Philip; Japanese brands like NEC, Fujitsu, and Toshiba; and other Asian brands like Hyundai (of South Korea), Acer (of Taiwan), and IPC (of Singapore). Today, the personal computer industry in many Asian cities is characterized by aggressive marketing and promotional gimmicks, bold price-cuttings, and constant product innovations and improvements.

Competition at the growth stage can also be triggered off by regulators or the local government. The telecommunication industry is a good case in point. Many Asian governments like Singapore, Hong Kong, Malaysia, the Philippines and Indonesia have not only begun to privatize their telecommunications industry, but have also actively encouraged new competitors to enter the industry. For example, on 9 May 1995, the Telecommunication Authority of Singapore awarded the second license for cellular handphone operation, and three new licenses for radio paging. These new competitors will enter the Singapore market in 1997. What is significant to note is that the Singapore government has deliberately introduced competition at a time when the handphone and pager markets are at a very healthy growth stage — the handphone penetration rate reached 8% of the population while that of paging reached 25% as at the end of 1994.

During the growth stage, it is important for the marketeer to strengthen and enlarge his market share by emphasizing the unique features of his product and thereby, establishing a niche. Besides focusing on building market share, there is a need to establish brand loyalty as well. As the product matures in due course, and as competition gets more intense, the replacement market becomes important. Loyal customers will ensure that the marketeer retains his market share and profits.

Unfortunately, during the growth stage, many marketeers tend to ignore the importance of building up their products and brands in the minds and hearts of consumers. They are contented since the market is expanding very fast. The expanding pie seems to be sufficient for every marketeer. This is the area where many Asian marketeers and producers are most vulnerable when compared to their western and Japanese counterparts who are established market players skilled in the art of brand building through intensive advertising and promotion. In fact, the local producers in China are beginning to feel the aggressive onslaught of these established foreign players. Many Chinese producers of food and beverages, clothings and other products are fast losing out. They now resort to playing on nationalistic sentiments, urging consumers to support "national" brands.

The vulnerability to foreign competition is of a greater degree in many other Asian markets that are expanding very fast but have very weak local producers. Economies like Vietnam, Indonesia, Myanmar, India, and even Malaysia are examples of such economies. The danger of not investing in brand and market share building can be illustrated with the case of Asian manufacturers of personal computers.

Beginning from the mid-1980s, there has been a tremendous growth in the demand for computers. The market growth seems limitless — and it appears that this will to be the case for the foreseeable future. As a result, Asian computer manufacturers like Acer from Taiwan, and IPC from Singapore grew tremendously with relatively little investments in marketing. These manufacturers paid little attention to building up their brand names. If these manufacturers remain local or regional players, those issues can remain of small concern. However, as these manufacturers expand and attempt to compete in the world market, they now have to face world class competitors who not only excel in production and innovation, but are gurus in the art of marketing as well. Moreover, many of the competitors of Acer and IPC — such as IBM, HP, AST, Philips, NEC, and so on — have invested heavily over the years to build up their current world class brands, product image and position. Acer and IPC have also begun to pay more efforts in marketing, advertising and promotions. Unfortunately, many other smaller Asian manufacturers of personal computers did not survive the intense competition.

It is a pity that many Asian marketeers have yet to fully appreciate the need to invest more on marketing efforts during the growth stage of the product life cycle. The temptation for not doing so is further compounded by the very rosy market conditions in Asian markets. They should never forget that at the tail end of the growth stage for any product or brand, profit margins will begin to fall significantly (largely due to competitive forces), and sales volume can become very important for sustaining profits. Without a larger pool of loyal consumers, the marginal supplier will be squeezed out of the market faster.

The urgency for focusing more on the marketing front is all the more critical in the light of many foreign and well established products and brands that have entered the markets of many Asian economies over the past few years. As it is, many Asian consumers are beginning to show strong preferences for foreign products and brands. While it is true that many of these foreign products and brands are of better quality, their strong appeals are also largely attributed to their huge investments in advertising and promoting their products and brands — something which the local producers are still reluctant to do, or fail to see the long term benefits of. As a result, the foreign brands are fast becoming better known and are able to capture large market shares within relatively short periods of time. Good examples of such trends are in the apparel, textile, and even beverage businesses where foreign brands have overwhelmed the local producers in economies like China and Vietnam.

The growth stage of the product life cycle therefore presents a great challenge to the Asian marketeer. Owing to the tremendous current market demand and high growth rates in many Asian markets, it is very tempting not to do much on the marketing front, especially on brand building. This is because in a situation where demand greatly exceeds supply, the product sells itself. A long term perspective to sustain profits calls for a proactive stance in marketing.

7.2.3 Maturity Stage

At the **maturity** stage, the industry sales curve reaches its peak. This is the stage where the replacement market — where consumers purchase a product to replace his old or broken-down one becomes important to the company. Profits continue to decline as severe competition among multiple brands tend to erode profit margins even further. This is the stage where product differentiation is rife and weaker competitors are eliminated. The maturity stage presents the biggest challenge to any marketeer. It is the stage where dealer-oriented promotions, fresh promotional and distribution efforts are needed in order to maintain market share. This is because at the maturity stage, consumers have become very familiar with the product characteristics. They are no longer novices, but have become experts in evaluating the pros and cons of various competitive products. As a result of competitive offers and increased consumer's knowledge of the product, profit margins are squeezed. It takes the very creative marketeer to survive and win in this market.

Many household products like colour television sets, refrigerators, and washing machines are at such a stage in the more advanced Asian economies like Japan, Singapore and Hong Kong. It would be true to say that the sale of such products are largely made in the replacement market. New sales at this stage are more difficult in view of the low birth rate and late marriages that are prevalent in these economies. Given that the typical family size is relatively small and the homes are not large either, there are limits for the typical Asian consumer in these more advanced economies to purchase the second or third unit of the same product even if he can afford to do it. It is almost impossible — from a practical standpoint — for the typical

Japanese or Singaporean or the home of to accommodate a second refrigerator.

At the maturity stage, some marketeers often use a strategy called "planned obsolescence" as a way to phase out the old models of the product, and entice the consumer to replace his old model with a new model. In planned obsolescence, the old model is still working well. However, as a result of a new and improved model in the market, the existing model is made to look inefficient, out-of-date, and of lower value. In fact, the Japanese manufacturers have cleverly used planned obsolescence to replace many of its products in matured markets. These products include cameras, refrigerators, hi-fi systems, video cassette players, television sets, washing machines, cars, and so on. It is not as if the basic technology engaged in these products has changed drastically. The Japanese manufacturers would, however, constantly come up with new features, new materials, new designs, new functions, amongst others as attractions to get the owners of old models to upgrade to the latest models.

One of the most glaring examples of planned obsolescence must be that of the personal computers. While it is true that this industry is largely driven by technology, a phenomenon capable of fantastic progress, nevertheless, it is startling that barely has an existing model reached its maturity state, a new model is already being launched in the market. What is even more startling is how the new model can make the existing model appear very inefficient and outdated. In fact, the product life cycle of personal computers has become shorter and shorter over the last decade as a result of the quantum leaps in the realm of technology.

Figure 7.2 shows the stages of the life cycles of different models of the personal computers as they evolved over time in economies like Japan, Singapore and Hong Kong. Note how barely ten years ago — some time in the 1980s — the 286 was the state-of-the-art. Within a decade, the 286 had been superceded by the 386, 486 and the 586 Pentium models consecutively by 1995. In fact, the life cycle of each new model of the personal computer is also getting shorter and shorter. Note also that what helps to accelerate the departure of the older PC models is the parallel advancement in software development. Many of these new computer softwares require more powerful storage and processing capacities which the older models do not possess. As these new softwares are very sophisticated, they also need faster processing speed, and hence better micro-chips.

Interestingly, despite their sophistication, new computer softwares have also become more user-friendly, and this has motivated existing users to upgrade. Thus, the market for PCs in economies like Japan, Hong Kong and Singapore has been driven by both push and pull factors.

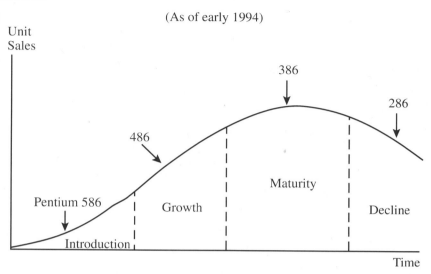

Figure 7.2 Product life cycle of the personal computers in Japan, Hong Kong and Singapore

7.2.4 Decline stage

At the decline stage (which may include death of the product), industry sales fall rapidly owing to changes in social trends, consumer incomes, tastes and preferences. At times, the emergence of a new technology may also make the existing products obsolete. Thus, the marketeer may be forced to phase out products at this stage if they are no longer profitable. Take the case of the 286. In the early 1980s, the 286 was the state-of-the-art personal computer in markets like Japan, Hong Kong and Singapore. However, it was considered obsolete by 1995 with the advent of the pentium (586). Similarly, black and white television sets were highly demanded in the 1960s in economies like Japan and the four Asian NIEs. Today, black and white colour television sets are being phased out in many Asian economies, including China, as they are overtaken by colour television sets.

Sometimes, it may not be possible to phase out a product so easily. If this is the case, then the marketeer should engage in cost cutting measures such as reducing promotional expenses and eliminating marginal distributors. Consider Gillette single blades. They are still being sold in the market despite the advent of twin blades (like the Atra and Swivel models) and electric shavers. This is because there is still some demand for such products in many Asian markets. For goodwill purposes, Gillette company has to continue to produce the single blades although they may not be profitable. It has, however, stopped promoting the single blades.

Many products will inevitably enter the stage of decline. This is because new products with better technology and operating features are constantly being introduced into the market. The marketeer can try his best to delay a product from entering the decline stage. However, this is only possible if he can improve on his existing product, find new consumers, or new uses for his product. In essence, he can try to manage the life cycle of the product.

7.3 Managing the Product Life Cycle

7.3.1 Balanced Portfolio of Products

What is interesting about the PLC concept is that it has provided marketeers a better understanding on how to manage a company's portfolio of products. To begin with, as each product has a life cycle, it is most essential that a company should have a **basket of products** that not only have different life spans, but are at different stages of the cycle. Having a balanced portfolio of products will enable the company to be in a better position to maintain sales and profitability. A company which relies only on a single product, lends itself to being vulnerable to market forces. A good example is Creative Technology, a Singapore-based company listed on the New York Stock Exchange. In 1994, it was still a single-product company that relied heavily on its Sound Blaster family of sound cards. With increased competition and narrowing profit margins, Creative Technology's shares began to lose favour with investors in mid-1995. Its share price began to drop.

To move away from its single-product strategy, Creative Technology began to actively look for new products. In 1994, it launched the Sharevision hardware and software solutions for video conferencing, followed by the Vibra sound chip, a chip that squeezes all the function of its cards into a single chip, in June 1995. The PhoneBlaster, an all-in-one card that combines the functions of a fax, modem and answering machine, and the Creative Quadratic Modulation (CQM), the music synthesis chip for its sound cards, were also launched in 1995. Unfortunately, these were relatively minor achievements as compared to its original Sound Blaster. They had little impact on sales and profits. It was not until its successful launch of its 3-D Blaster graphics card in September 1995, which offers graphic features, that the market responded favourably with a strong rebound in its share price — by over 33%. Creative Technology's situation goes to show the vulnerability of a company that relies heavily on a major product for success. Despite having a new successful product in its 3-D card, Creative Technology must increase its portfolio of products in order to sustain its growth. As it is, barely after launching the 3-D card, its US multimedia competitors like Nvidia and Diamond Multimedia System also announced their versions of 3-D cards.

The need to break away from relying on a single major product has led IPC, another Singapore company that produces personal computers, to actively look for new product opportunities and business ventures. In March 1995, it entered a joint venture with French computer giant, Bull, to develop smartcard technology. This was a good move, considering the fact that IPC has begun to build another line of products — point-of-sales devices like cash registers. The smartcard technology will allow IPC to integrate it with its point-of-sales products to provide value-added network systems and services. IPC has also planned to market its computer network business in Shanghai (China) by the end of 1995 in another move to reduce its reliance on the personal computers business alone.

Having a balanced portfolio does not necessarily mean that the marketeer must carry different types of products. He could very well be carrying the same type of products. Take the case of a retail shop that is engaged in the sale and rental of videos and laser discs. To attract customers, the operator must ensure that he carries a wide variety of titles. This is because the life cycle of each movie may be very short, and new titles must be brought in constantly in order to attract more customers. Of course, there will always be some titles — the Sound of Music, for one, — that have long lasting appeal. Nonetheless, to sustain sales and profits, the portfolio of movie titles run into hundreds and thousands in a typical video and laser disc shop. Typically, "outdated" titles — products in the decline stage — are sold at great discounts.

The need to have a balanced portfolio of products is in many retail businesses. For them, the life cycles of products are determined largely by the changing consumer tastes and preferences, including emerging fads and trends that may be set by fashion houses in the western world. As such, retailers have to respond very quickly in order not to be left with products that have been accelerated into the stage of decline as a result of changing market conditions.

7.3.2 Different Shapes of PLC Curves

The shape of the PLC curve differs from product to product. Each of its phase differs in duration. Each of these phases differs from product to product as well.

When the Cabbage Patch doll hit the North American market in the early 1980s, it had a very short introduction phase, a steep growth phase, a short maturity phase, and a sharp and quick decline phase — the product was as good as dead by the end of the decade. Similarly, many fad items that are by-products of popular movies or television shows also do not last long. Good examples of such products that have enjoyed short product life cycles in many Southeast Asian markets include Care Bears, Teenage Mutant Ninja Turtles, Smurfs, and Mr. T, amongst others. Most fad and fashion items tend to have short and "violent" life cycles.

In contrast, there are products in the market that have reached the maturity stage long ago, but have maintained their positions because their sales are affected more by demographic rather than lifestyle factors. Good examples include refrigerators, television sets, air-conditioners, toasters, and many other household appliances. True, these products have, over the years, undergone much improvements. However, they have yet to be replaced by entirely new types of products.

There are other products that may experience very low growth rates even after successful introduction. The microwave ovens and dishwashers in many Asian markets are good examples. Owing to the different cooking and washing habits of Asians, these two products have yet to have strong impact on consumers in Asia. Their market penetration rates have not been significant when compared to those of other household appliances.

The failure to understand consumption habits has caused other products to meet similar fate. The United States, as part of its efforts to redress its trade imbalance with Japan, has been trying very hard to export more American rice to the Japanese market. In 1994 and 1995, the Japanese government even actively encouraged the Japanese consumers to switch to the cheaper American rice. Unfortunately, the typical Japanese consumer prefers the short-grain, sticky rice as opposed to the long-grain, non-sticky American rice.

Similarly several years ago, the Singapore government tried to promote the consumption of wheat in a national effort to reduce dependence on rice. After a strong introduction, it failed to take off. Today, rice remains the staple diet of the average Singaporean, and wheat remains basically a supplementary item.

7.3.3 Extending the PLC

While it is true that most products go through the four stages as mentioned, the marketeer should attempt to extend the lifecycle whenever possible through product improvement, differentiation, and even finding new markets or uses. Take Gillette razor, for example. When the first Gillette razor blade was introduced in 1903, the company made many attempts to extend the life cycle of the blades over the years through various product improvement such as the thin blade, stainless steel blade, platinum-plus blade, twin blade, adjustable twin blade, swivel twin blade, sensor twin blade, and so on. In this way, for almost ninety years, Gillette has still managed to hold its ground even against the modern electric shavers.

The Japanese manufacturers of hi-fi systems did not allow the home radio to die a natural death. When the Americans decided not to innovate any further beyond the transistor radio, the Japanese manufacturers took it upon themselves to extend the life cyle of the radio through numerous product innovations and improvement. Over the years, they evolved the transistor radio into radio cassette, stereo radio cassette, ultra-thin radio, walkman with radio, stereo micro cassette components, radio-in-television, digital clock-radio, radio-in-pocket calculator, earphone radio, . . . the list goes on.

Besides radio, the Japanese have similarly done wonders to the wrist watch and the calculator by introducing various product innovations and improvements. The Japanese wrist watch has gone beyond attributes like accuracy and quality. Over the years, new features in the form of water-resistance, day or date indicators, luminous hands, a second hand being battery operated, a slim look and design, resin casing, ultra-slim styling, microcomputer games, calculator cum memory functions, dual or multiple time telling, stop watch facilities, melody cum alarm clock, quartz or digitally operated, and so on, have been added incrementally. The Japanese have rejuvenated what would otherwise be matured but dull products, with new features that themselves provide exciting dimensions for product differentiation. Here's something to watch out for: Seiko has been actively promoting its kinetic energy model in recent years as the watch that would distinguish itself from all other watches in the future.

Finding new markets is another way to extend the life cycle of a product since the stage of the product life cycle will more probably than not, differ from country to country. The desk-top 286 personal computers is at the stage of decline in the PLC in Singapore and Hong Kong as shown in Table 7.1. But in many places like Vietnam, Myanmar and Cambodia, it is at its introduction stage. The shrewd marketeer should therefore plan to capitalize on the "timing" difference of such products in selecting his product strategies for the various markets. His 286 and 386 PC may not sell at all in Singapore and Hong Kong markets, but he will find ready buyers in the new emerging markets of Vietnam, Myanmar, and Cambodia. The dial phone is another product in a similar situation.

In essence, while the demand for a product in one market may be bottoming out and reaching the decline stage of its life cycle, it may be just be picking up in a different market. The job of the marketeer

TABLE 7.1 Example of product and services at various stages of the product life cycle in Singapore and Hong Kong as of 1995

Introduction	Growth	Maturity	Decline
Video-on-Demand (VOD)	CD-ROM	Videos	Cassettes
Pentium (586)	486 PC	386 PC	286 PC
GSM (digital) handphone	Pagers	ETAC (analog) handphone	Dial-phone
Multi-media systems	Integrated Hi-fi systems	Colour TV sets	Black & White TV sets
Home movie system	Laser discs	Refrigerators	Redifussion

is to identify such markets, and exploit the opportunities accordingly. Of course, in doing so, he may want to ensure that the gap in the life cycle between two markets is not too large so as to limit the application of similar marketing strategies to exploit the business opportunities.

Figure 7.3 illustrates what the PLC gap means. The marketing strategy needed for the marketing of a product at a stage of decline in its home country is likely to be applicable to Country C where the product is at the maturity stage. If the company chooses to market the product in Country A where the product is only at the introduction stage, then it must be aware that the marketing strategy would have to be changed drastically. This is because market conditions and consumer factors differ greatly between the two markets. In other words, owing to the wide gap between the PLC of these two markets, similar marketing strategies cannot be used. It is for this reason that many companies prefer to introduce their products into markets that are at similar stage of the PLC, for example, between the United States and Canada, and among many west European countries so as to synergize their marketing efforts.

This is where the "step-ladder" grouping of economies in Asia becomes useful for marketing planning purposes. To recapitulate, at

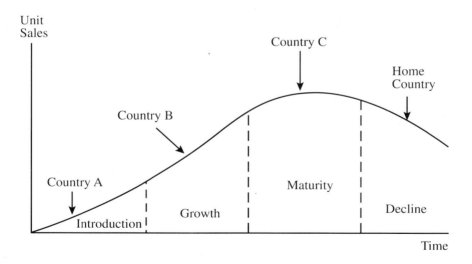

Figure 7.3 Life cycle of a product across countries

the top of the ladder is Japan followed by the four Asian NIEs of Singapore, Hong Kong, Taiwan and South Korea; then the semi-NIEs of Malaysia, Thailand, and Philippines, and, the LDEs of China, India, and Indonesia, and finally the newly opened economies of Vietnam, Myanmar, and Cambodia. As a general guide, the marketeer can phase his products gradually from the highest step of the economic ladder (Japan), to the next step (the four NIEs), and the next (the semi-NIEs), and so on. It would not make sense to market the pentium 586 to economies like China, Vietnam and Myanmar at the moment. The 386 would be more than adequate.

7.3.4 Don't Ignore Costs of Investments

When using the PLC for planning purposes, the costs of investment for the creation, manufacture, marketing and distribution of the product must not be forgotten in the midst of analyzing sales and marketing share data. Profits are only realized after the investment costs are fully recovered. Often times, this happens only in the long run. Therefore, the time frame needed to recover investments must be scrutinized very carefully. The advent of a new technology could, overnight, make existing products obsolete.

Consider Singapore Teleview again. Since the mid-1980s, Singapore Telecoms has invested substantially to develop this service. However, over the years, more and better competitive services entered the Singapore market. Hence, despite modest success in the 1990s, it is unlikely that Singapore Telecoms will ever be able to recover the full cost of its investments.

Costs of investments become more important when going overseas. In the case of Asia, the costs of entering a new market can be considerable. It may involve building up the marketing infrastructure from scratch. This would include developing the distribution networks and systems, including the setting up and training of dealerships and agencies. Unfortunately, having invested heavily in opening up a market, the distribution and marketing networks may be piggybacked upon by the latecomers, including the local producers. At the same time, given the political uncertainties in some of these Asian economies, there is also no guarantee that the marketeer can operate there forever. A case in point is Giordano, a fashion brand from Hong Kong. At its peak of operations in China, and when its full range of products were just beginning to enter into the growth stage, it was almost forced to shut down in 1995.

7.3.5 Impact of Technology

In today's high technology environment, product life cycles can be very short, and even suffer violent "deaths". The personal computer industry fits this description to a "T". Within a few decades, and in particular over the last ten years, the technology that went into the micro-chip is indeed mind-boggling. The personal computer is not only getting smaller — the most compact being notebooks — but more powerful and efficient. From the 286 in the early 1980s, it has moved up to the pentium as of early 1995. And as we have seen, the life span of each new model of personal computer is getting shorter and shorter!

Fast changing technologies can be very disruptive. On 18 September 1995, the market leader, Compaq Computer Asia, announced price cuts of up to 21% on several models of its personal computers, following a similar move in the United States. Besides aiming at gaining market share, the drastic slashing of prices is a typical move to get rid of less efficient models that are in stock so as to prepare the market for the launch of newer and better models. Compaq's price slash of models powered by pentium chips that run at the slower 75 megahertz and 90 megahertz — the market was already filled with machines running at greater speeds of 100 megahertz and 133 megahertz — sparked a price war. Several of Compaq's competitors followed suit with similar price cuts, with some vowing to maintain their price advantages (that is, lower prices) over Compaq. Such moves are not surprising, considering the fact that many of these competitors rely heavily on the personal computers as their main line of business. They cannot afford to lose market shares, which are greatly needed for the replacement and upgrading markets.

In the telecommunications industry, when the first analog cellular handphone made its entry into many Asian markets during the late 1980s, it was priced very high. In Singapore, one model of the Motorola handphone retailed for over S$5,000! Similar high prices were observed in other Asian markets like Hong Kong. During this period, significant improvements in the analog technology were made to improve the reception and transmission capabilities of the cellular handphone. Undoubtedly, with competition, there were also improvements in the product design and prices also began to drop gradually. However, the advent of digital technology in the early 1990s brought about a full range of GSM cellular handphones that literally made the old analog phones obsolete. Almost overnight, many retailers of the analog cellular handphones slashed their prices significantly, some by as much as 50%, so as to get rid of existing stock. As an added measure to protect their market shares, many retailers also allowed consumers to trade in existing analog models for the newer digital handphones.

The computer and telecommunications industries are not the only ones affected by the fast development of technology. In the wrist watch industry, when the Japanese introduced quartz and digital technology in the 1970s and early 1980s, many Swiss watch makers did not pay much attention to the impending threat. The result — many non-jewellery Swiss watch makers were wiped out by Japanese brands like Seiko, Citizen, and Casio as they were cheaper, of better quality, and more accurate. It was only in mid-1980s that the Swiss, through the efforts of the Swatch watch, managed to make a dramatic comeback, ironically, using quartz and digital technologies.

There is no doubt that technology is fast becoming an important competitive factor in the 21st century. Many products are going to be revolutionalized by each wave of new and improved technology. Obsolete products are likely to increase. Unlike fashion goods and outdated models or designs (as in the case of cars, shoes, watches, amongst others), products that are made obsolete by technology will have difficulty finding buyers within the same market. On the other hand, they are still functioning and in good working conditions. Thus, the search for new and less developed markets where these products will suit the needs of these markets, will become a more important consideration in the mindset of marketeers. It is an issue that marketeers must pay increasing attention to.

7.4 Conclusion

The booming economies of Asia is going to make the era a very challenging one for marketeers. As mentioned, it presents abundant opportunities for the strategic marketeer to exploit fully the life cycle of any generic product by positioning and targetting it appropriately to the different Asian economies that are at various stages of economic dvelopment. This is the time in which the shrewd and innovative marketeer will stand to be richly rewarded.

8
Branding Strategies: Ensuring and Enhancing Competitiveness

8.1 Introduction

A brand name can play multiple roles. To begin with, it provides the consumer with a symbol to identify a product and thus facilitates the purchasing process. A symbol makes it easy to create the top-of-mind awareness among consumers and hence helps to sustain sales, and encourages repeat buying. In addition, there are many intangible benefits that come with a brand that has built up a strong equity and image. For example, it is commonly known that consumers are willing to pay a little more for a product if it has a well-known brand. This is because an established brand is often equated with reliability, creditability, and quality. As such, they can be trusted for performance and hence helps in risk reduction.

It is interesting to note that for many consumer products, the consumers remember them by their brand names rather than by the names of the companies that manufacture or distribute them. For example, few consumers would know the manufacturers behind brands like Lux soap, Fab detergent, Tiger Beer, Tiger Balm, Pampers disposable baby diapers, and Swatch watches. Thus, it is not surprising to find that consumer advertising is heavily oriented towards brand development and image building.

A brand can also provide a distinctive identity for a company. This is especially felt when the company deliberately abbreviates its corporate initials into a brand name (for example, IBM for International Business Machines, HP for Hewlett Packard, SIA for Singapore

* Note: The contents of this chapter are taken mainly from Chow Hou Wee (1994), National Branding Strategies and Economic Development: Implications for NIEs and LDCs, The International Executive, U.S.A., Vol. 36, No. 2, pp. 119–145.

Airlines and GM for General Motors) or uses the corporate name as the brand itself (for example, Toyota, Hyundai, and Sony).

When a brand is well established, it can even project many other attributes that have significant marketing mileage. For example, brands can become symbols of quality (as in the cases of Mercedes cars and Rolex watches), of craftsmanship (as in the case of Steinway pianos), of service and efficiency (as with Federal Express and McDonald's), of innovation (as exemplified by IBM), of fantasy and imaginations (as with Walt Disney World), of economy and fair price (as is the case with NTUC supermarkets in Singapore), of designs (as exemplified by Ikea furniture), of social status (as is the case with Rolls Royce), and fashion (as with Swatch watches), and so on. In fact, an established brand can become a very valuable asset for a company and forms part of its equity value. As such, no one else can own or market it. This means the brand name itself communicates goodwill that can command a high market value in terms of franchising and licensing possibilities.

The usefulness of establishing strong brands extends to services as well. For example, SIA is not just synonymous with top quality service, but its brand name is becoming legendary as well. In the same way, DHL is fast establishing a world-wide reputation for itself in the area of courier service.

8.2 Japanese Experience in Brand Development

The important roles played by brands can be felt even at the macro and strategic level of a nation. Here, the best example can be illustrated by the way many Japanese companies had developed their brands into brands of world class standing.

8.2.1 Starting from a Position of Weakness

When Japan started its post World War II industrialization policy, it did not have any notable brands of international standing. In fact, it produced and sold many of its products through American and European distributors, very often under the latter's brand names as well. In the initial phase of the Japanese industrialization programme, Japanese products could not even stand on their own brand names in the international market. They had to be "camouflaged" by using American and European brands. However,

Japanese companies did not give up, despite starting from a position of weakness.

Owing to their large domestic market (Japan had a population of 123.5 million as of 1990), and the strong support of their government, they were able to improve the quality of their product over time and develop their own brand names. Even so, when the first Japanese brands hit the shores of overseas markets, they were known to be cheap products of inferior quality. For example, when Datsun (now called Nissan) cars were first sold in Singapore in the 1960s, their quality was poor. They had to rely on very cheap prices in those days (it was priced around US$2,000) in order to attract buyers.

As Japanese products improved in quality and gained market acceptance in the 1970s, Japanese companies began to embark systematically and relentlessly on brand development and image building. Japanese investments in brand development over the last forty to fifty years are now paying handsome dividends. In fact, Japanese brands of a wide range of products have distinguished themselves from their competitors. Brands like Sharp, National, Matsushita, Sony, and Hitachi are well-known for products like hi-fi systems, television sets, radios, washing machines, refrigerators, vacuum cleaners, and other household appliances. Nikon, Canon, Yashica, Olympus, and Ricoh are established brands for Japanese cameras. In watches, Japanese brands like Seiko, Citizen and Casio are worn on the wrists of many consumers. For cars, the number of Japanese brands are even more — Nissan, Honda, Toyota, Mazda, Mitsubishi, Daihatsu, Subaru, and Suzuki. For business or office products, Canon, Toshiba, NEC and Sharp are known for their high quality photocopying machines, personal computers, calculators, printers, fax machines, and computer peripherals.

It is amazing to note that many Japanese brand names, like those highlighted above, are familiar names in households and corporate boardrooms in most countries of the world today. In fact, it would be no exaggeration to state that the average consumer and corporate buyers are probably more familiar with Japanese brands than with the brands from any other country. Yet forty years ago, many of these Japanese brands were probably unheard of!

8.2.2 Benefits of Brand Proprietorship

In creating their own brand names successfully in the world market, Japanese companies are beginning to exploit this to greater advantage.

For example, their established brand names ensure **proprietary claims**, and give them the added opportunity to manufacture overseas when needed. In fact, this was exactly what they did from the mid-1970s when many Japanese companies of consumer electronics began to shift their operations to lower cost countries in Southeast Asia and the Far East. In doing so, they did not suffer any drop in demand for their products. Instead, they continued to dominate the world market. How was this possible? To begin with, since the late 1970s, Japanese brands have become symbols of high quality. As a result, the average consumer has become less conscious of where the product is manufactured, so long as it carries a Japanese brand. This, indeed, is the acid test of the success of branding — the brand itself has become more important to the consumer than the country of manufacture. When this happens, the potential for market exploitation increases tremendously.

As a result of establishing strong brand names, Japanese companies have also created tremendous economic leverages for themselves. For example, faced with increasing pressures from the United States against the predominance of Japanese products, especially in the automobile industry, the Japanese car makers were able to shift some of their production into the US as a means of protecting their market share. Interestingly, as events unfolded in the late 1980s and early 1990s, American-made Japanese cars continued to enjoy wide acceptance with the result that their total market share — vis-a-vis those of American and European cars — continue to climb in the US market. Thus, not only did the Japanese car makers successfully protect their American market share, but they managed to increase it as well.

Beginning in the mid-1980s, Japanese companies began to consciously exploit another leverage garnered as a result of their strong brand presence – establishing corporate alliances with their western partners. Indeed, with the emergence of a more united Europe (from the collapse of the Berlin Wall) and from the fallout of the Warsaw Pact countries (including the breakout of the former Soviet Union) in favour of free market economies, the opening up of China, the trends toward regional trade blocs (for example, the United States, Canada and Mexico have formed the world's largest trading bloc, NAFTA, in August 1992), new challenges have been created. In particular, many MNCs have found that the amount of investments, technologies, management and marketing skills needed to develop these new markets are normally beyond the expertise of a single MNC.

124

Instead, there is a need to integrate the expertise and resources among various MNCs in order to overcome such challenges.

In the process, those MNCs which have strong international brands, are likely to develop alliances among themselves in order to create greater competitive synergy. Japanese companies are fully aware of their unique strengths, and are beginning to reap handsome dividends in the field of corporate alliances. For example, Japanese companies like Canon has established partnerships and joint ventures with Texas Instruments, Hewlett Packard, Apple, Eastman Kodak, Motorola, Olivetti, NeXT, and Cray Research. Toshiba entered into a strategic partnership with Motorola. Its memory technology was traded for Motorola's advanced microprocessor technology. Sanyo has entered into alliances with LSI Logic of the United States to develop a new generation of semiconductors for use in high-definition television (HDTV), and with General Electric to develop environmentally safe, highly efficient compressors for Sanyo air-conditioners. Other Japanese companies like Hitachi, Toray, Minolta, C. Itoh, Olympus, NEC, Brother, ANA (All Nippon Airways Company), and so on are all fast developing alliances with foreign companies. In doing so, not only have Japanese companies managed to ward off criticisms against its "economic dominance" policy, but have successfully developed new strategies to protect their market shares in various products. More importantly, they have now won many corporate allies to further exploit new markets and business opportunities in Eastern Europe, America, and the rest of the world.

Figure 8.1 provides a summary of how Japanese companies went about developing their brands in the world market. It is clear to see that the Japanese branding strategy is indeed a well thought out processs.

8.3 Brand Names Can be Created and Developed

The Japanese have clearly shown that brand names can be created. In particular, they have shown that even if the brand names may sound somewhat alien or unfamiliar, they can still be successfully built up over time. For example, few people could pronounce Fujitsu, Matsushita, Nikon, Nakamichi, and Mitsubishi when these names first appeared. Yet, these names are now easily remembered and pronounced — even among western consumers — because they are associated with products of high quality. What is important to note is that a reputable brand name does not appear overnight. It takes **time**, and often many years, to establish a brand name.

In the case of Japanese companies, it took them about forty to fifty years to achieve their present world class standings. As can be seen in Figure 8.1, Japanese companies made great efforts to build their brands systematically over time. It was only when they had learned the necessary marketing skills that Japanese companies began to invest heavily in brand development. Today, they are in a position to milk returns from their efforts.

Of course, there are many other successful examples besides those of the Japanese. For example, brands like IBM, General Food, General Motors (GM), Philips, Hewlett Packard, Coca-Cola, Gillette and McDonald's are the results of years of investments in advertising and marketing, besides improvements made to the product or service. In addition, many western countries are also adept at brand creation and development. The French, Italians and Americans, for example, have developed very strong brands in the areas of cosmetics, perfumes, and fashion goods. Interestingly, some of these brand names are also difficult to pronounce, yet they have become acceptable: Loius Viutton, Etienne Aigner, Christian Dior, Guy Laroche, and so on.

Perhaps one of the most noticeable examples of brand creation in recent years can be found in the aerospace industry — the success of

STAGE ONE (1940s–1950s)	SELLING THROUGH OTHER PEOPLE'S BRANDS (Gaining access to distribution)
STAGE TWO (1950s–1960s)	DEVELOPING ONE'S OWN BRANDS (Acquiring marketing skills)
STAGE THREE (1960s–1970s)	INVESTING AND BUILDING BRANDS (Cultivating relationships and bonds)
STAGE FOUR (1970s–1980s) foreign	DIRECT EXPORTING OF JAPANESE BRANDS (Milking equity value of brands through direct investments)
STAGE FIVE (1980s–1990s) equity	CREATION OF ALLIED OR GLOBAL BRANDS (Protecting world market shares and increasing value of brands through alliances)

Figure 8.1 Japanese Brand Development Strategy

Airbus. In the market for large commercial aircrafts, Boeing and McDonnell Douglas had virtually wiped out all potential competitors in the field. Undaunted, the French, German, Dutch, Belgian, British, and Spanish aircraft companies joined forces to build a commerical aircraft to rival that of the American giants. After some initial hiccups, the European consortium began to pose a serious threat to Boeing and McDonnell Douglas. For example, as of June 1992, it has succeeded to fill 30% of new orders for commercial aircrafts. By offering leading-edge technology and a full complement of aircraft, Airbus is now on the order list of fourteen of the seventeen largest airlines in the world. More importantly, it has sucessfully penetrated the North American market — a terrain traditionally dominated by the big American manufacturers like Boeing and McDonnell Douglas. Indeed, Airbus has become a model for the future. Companies may increasingly consider forming alliances to produce products that they can not manage if they continue to operate individually. Branding, in its new form, will ideally suit such mega projects and high risk ventures.

Another interesting example is that of the creation of the Swatch watch. When Japanese watches like Seiko, Citizen, and Casio took the world by storm in the 1970s and early 1980s with their cheap prices and reliability, the traditional Swiss-made wrist watches that once dominated the mass market, suddenly found themselves things of the past. In an attempt to follow the Japanese by using digitized technology, many Swiss watch makers were almost threatened with extinction. Only the high-end, jewelry-type watch makers managed to ward off the Japanese challenge — largely because the Japanese did not go after the higher price range watches.

After several years in the doldrums, the Swiss watch makers managed to pull their act together by capitalizing on mass production technology (which they already had to) and individual creativity and distinctiveness (which are the hallmarks of their jewelry-type watches) to produce the Swatch watch. It became an instant success because not only was it priced competitively against the Japanese watches, each batch of watches was designed differently with an unique appeal. What's more, it could not have chosen a better name! Today, Swatch watches have become collectible items, and Swatch clubs have even emerged in many parts of the world. In fact, some of the earlier models have even appreciated significantly in value!

Brand development is equally applicable to the service industry. A very good example is that of SIA. When it first started, SIA was plagued with many problems. More seriously, its domestic market was simply too small to support an airline. The area of the country is only 626.4 square kilometres and the population was only three million as of 1994. Undaunted, SIA embarked on a concerted effort to develop itself into an international airline. It chose to focus on its inflight service in its earlier years of development – an area ignored by many other airlines – and concentrated on creating the "Singapore Girl" image. Today, after about thirty years of hard work, it is consistently rated as the top airline in the world with an inflight service that even other airlines talk about. More importantly, it is also the most profitable airline in the world today.

The success stories of how companies have managed to create and develop brands of world class standing suggest that there are some factors that need to be considered. These factors may not be exhaustive, but they represent areas in which companies should pay close attention to.

8.3.1 Product Attributes and Characteristics

A brand acts as a surrogate to project the various attributes of the product or service. Among other attributes, the quality of a product or service ranks high in helping to develop the brand image. As such, there is a need to focus on this and to ensure that it is consistently maintained and improved upon over time. For this reason, it is not surprising to note that most Japanese manufacturers are very obsessed with product quality and improvement. In fact, it is no exaggeration to state that Japanese brands have become very successful today largely because of the efforts put in by Japanese manufacturers to ensure that they consistently improved upon quality. For many consumer durables, Japanese brands have become symbolic of high quality, credibility and reliability.

For a brand to compete effectively, there is also a need for it to have unique product characteristics. Marketeers call this unique selling propositions (USPs) or features that differentiate it from those offered by competing brands. If there are tangible benefits or attributes about the product or service, highlight them clearly to the consumers. For example, in the early years of competition, Japanese cars were differentiated from American cars in some very obvious ways — they were smaller, cheaper, more economical to operate, and came fully equipped with accessories and had superior dealer services. Even today, after having upgraded their cars gradually to compete in the luxury market, Japanese car makers have not forgotten to differentiate their brands from those of their competitors. For example, Lexus (from Toyota) still prides itself on its legendary dealer service, and has focused heavily on its high-technology and engineering features.

In the same way, European cars like the BMW are deliberately projected as classy, reliable, expensive, well-made, and sporty — all adding up to a unique reputation. In fact, BMW has chosen to position itself as lighter, less teutonic, and more exciting as compared to the Mercedes. It has also targetted itself at the younger and more fashionable professionals who see themselves as sleek, well-groomed, prosperous and successful.

In the case of IBM, the world's best architects and designers are engaged to create a strong, individual visual style for its buildings. The aim is to depict IBM as the most thoughtful and thorough company in its field. This is in turn supported by strong advertising and promotion campaigns, and well-developed distribution outlets. The idea is to simply dominate the minds of its consumers so much so that they would not even consider other alternatives in their choice of business machines. As a result of such a successful differentiation strategy, IBM has been able to position itself as the market leader over its competitors, and at the same time, command a premium on its products.

Similarly, SIA engaged the best advertisers and designers to project the ultimate image in airline travel and service. Its differentiation strategy even include details like remembering the names of all its business and first class travellers, careful selection of on-board menu and wines, chinaware, reading materials, and so on. Most importantly, it has successfully marketed the "Singapore Girl" image that symbolizes the ultimate inflight service in air travel. More recently, it has also deliberately upgraded and modernized its fleet of aircraft. All these constitute a very unique and complex differentiaion strategy that few other airlines can copy.

8.3.2 Ease of Recognition and Remembering

A brand is meant to facilitate identification of a product and to promote its sales. Thus, the brand name must be **easy to remember**. In this regard, names that are shorter and easier to pronounce would be beneficial. A good example is the choice of the name **Swatch**. It is a very creative yet practical name in that it is very, a simple, catchy and apt name.

To facilitate ease of recognition and recall, a brand name should, to the extent possible, be accompanied by a logo. For example, Coke is a very strong brand name, characterized by a distinctive logo. This logo, including the colour, does not change no matter where the product is sold or manufactured. Only the brand name of Coke is translated if necessary. The same can be said about McDonald's. Kids all over the world never fail to recognize its yellow and big "M" displayed prominently outside each of its restaurants. Its brand is further augmented by having a character (Ronald McDonald) as its corporate mascot. In the case of IBM, its three letters have been used both as the brand name and the logo.

It is important to note that Japanese branding strategy does not depart from the practice of having a logo either as part of the brand name or as the brand itself. For example, all Japanese car makers make full use of their corporate names as brands and use logos as well. Obviously, they have recognized the value of the logo, especially in international marketing. This is because a logo is, in a sense, a universal language.

What is perhaps more interesting is that the Japanese have also shown that there is no magic in picking the right brand name. In fact, as mentioned earlier, many Japanese brand names were not easy to pronounce nor were they easy to remember when they first appeared. It was through sheer efforts of brand building and investment that they have become familiar names today. Note that Japanese brand names were first established in Japan where those seemingly unfamiliar sounding words were definitely not difficult to pronounce or remember to the Japanese consumers. It was in the international market that Japanese brand names encountered some initial problems.

8.3.3 Meaningful and Commercially Valuable

As mentioned earlier, choosing brand names that are easy to remember would mean avoidance of words that are strange or difficult to pronounce. However, as illustrated in the case of the Japanese, brand names can be built over time. Even the most difficult or peculiar names can be made familiar so long as the company has a good product, and is willing to invest in brand development. But, the process will be sped up if the brand names are meaningful as well. For example, IBM, SIA, Burger King, Kentucky Fried Chicken, Toys 'R Us,

Pizza Hut, Swatch, and Federal Express are not just brand names, they portray their businesses as well. Without doubt, a brand with strong meaning is also likely to generate **commercial value**. In fact, the commercial value attached to established brands cannot be discounted easily. In the case of Coke, the company found that it was almost impossible to replace it with a new brand, New Coke in 1985. The subsequent overwhelming protests from brand loyal customers forced the company to reinstate the old Coke as Classic Coke. The result was incredible: the company not only regained their lost market share from Pepsi, but even expanded its share and successfully introduced a new brand!

Commercial value would naturally be accumulated as a company invest time, effort and money into developing the brand. However, the proper choice of names would facilitate the process. In Singapore, for example, the National Trade Union Congress (NTUC) has cleverly chosen **Fairprice** for its supermarket business, **Comfort** for its taxi business, and **Income** for its insurance business. These names are not only meaningful, but project attributes that have strong commerical value. Similarly, the name **Hour Glass** has been appropriately chosen by a retailer to stand for her watch company.

8.3.4 Culturally Non-Offensive

Another point to note about the choice of brand names is the need to take into account the **cultural effects** that may arise as a result of translation. This is especially important when marketing to other cultures or countries. The translated brand name must, to the extent possible, be meaningful. For example, in Singapore, the brand Kotex (a brand of lady's sanitary pads) has been translated phonetically in Chinese. As a result, the words have no meaning in themselves. In contrast, the same brand has been cleverly translated into words which mean "reliable" in Taiwan. The name thus become not only meaningful, but also contains high commercial value. Similarly, while Datsun (now known as Nissan) was translated phonetically in Singapore but not in a meaningful way, it was translated as "victory" in Hong Kong. Pizza Hut is also interestingly translated, as "surely win customers" in Hong Kong.

On phonetics, it is also important to take note of local interpretations and jargons. For example, in Singapore, the brand Suzuki, sounds like "losing all the way" in Hokkien, a local dialect, Concerto (a Honda car) has been shunned by Chinese businessmen as it sounds like "company going bankrupt"; and "Subaru" sounds like "just lost" in Hokkien and Malay. In Hong Kong and Singapore, Alpha 164, supposedly a very well-built Italian car that offers great value for money, found few buyers because the numbers one, six and four, in Cantonese mean "dying all the way!" The Hong Kong agent finally took the initiative to change the numbers to 168, which means "prospering all the way" in Cantonese, in order to boost sales.

In sum, there is no magic formula in picking the right brand name. However, attention to the various factors highlighted will hopefully provide some direction. More importantly, a company should never hesitate to invest in brand research when in doubt.

8.4 Brand Extension Strategy

Another of their skills which the Japanese have put to maximum effect that of extending an already well-received brand name of one product category, to other kinds of related products. Canon, for instance, extended its established brand image in cameras to other products like photocopiers and calulators; Sharp used its successful brand name in consumer electronics to other products like personal computers and fax machines; Sony extended its products in consumer electronics to include telephones and related equipment; Ricoh is now known not just for cameras, but for photocopiers and other office equipment; the list goes on. What is interesting to note is that in extending their brand names to other products, the Japanese have shown that it is possible to use the same brand beyond the "immediate family" of products. In other words, they have successfully used the same brand name for different categories of products in the consumer, commercial, and industrial markets.

In addition, they have even stretched the power of branding to completely unrelated products. For example, Mitsubishi places its brand name on products ranging from canned food (for example, canned tuna, salmon and crab meat), to cars and trucks, banks and financial institutions, aircraft and heavy industries, home appliances and hi-fi equipment, and so on.

8.4.1 Choice of Monolithic Identity

Another thing noteworthy of the Japanese's brand extension strategy is that their companies, in general, subscribe to the notion that using one name on all products and services would lend more credibility and strength to the entire conglomerate. This would in turn help to develop a **monolithic identity** and promote corporate culture. In addition, by extending the same brand name across a cross section of products, the Japanese have ensured that the brand has become relevant and meaningful to a significant number of consumers. It also provides the element of **consistency** in that the positive attributes of the brand are imputed to the new products. In particular, advertising and marketing become easier in that one simple message repeated a dozen times is louder and clearer than a dozen different messages broadcasted only once each. To some extent, a monolithic approach will help to promote sale of the new product as the brand is associated with the previously dominant and established brand. In fact, acceptance of the new product may even be sped up. Such an approach also means that the costs, that would otherwise have been incurred in the creation of new brands, can be avoided. By using one brand, the unnecessary fragmentation of the market is avoided and so too, the proliferation of brands that confuse the consumers. Indirectly, it serves to deter potential competitors from entering the product category.

However, there are some important prerequisites to the success of the monolithic approach. First, to have the same brand across all products (related and unrelated) would require that a high standard of performance and quality be maintained at all times and under all circumstances. This is because any sub-standard performance on the part of any product within the same brand name can severely affect the whole group of products. Second, attention to detail is necessary to ensure that the consistency in high standards and other requirements of the brand are met. Third, products or services that tend to vary significantly in quality and performance are not suitable for the monolithic approach. In other words, the products and services must lend themselves to automation and standardization to ensure uniformity in quality. Finally, the monolithic-type of brand strategy requires frequent monitoring and evaluation of the whole system — something that could create great stress, friction, and tension if not properly managed. In sum, it requires a highly integrated team approach with unselfish sharing of information for it to work.

Japanese monolithic brand extension strategy therefore, tends to focus on manufactured goods that are produced for the mass market. This applies to both the consumer and the office or commercial markets. This is for the obvious reason that manufactured products lend themselves to automation, and for which it is easier to establish performance and quality standards. Consequently, it is not surprising to know that Japanese manufacturers are very obsessed with quality control and production technology. At the same time, they generally stay away from customized products and services, although some efforts are now being made to address these areas.

8.4.2 The Western Experience

Like brand creation and development, the use of one brand across different products is not unique to Japanese companies. Many European and American firms have used the same brand on a family of products long before the Japanese. For example, Campbell cleverly exploited its success in its mushroom soup by producing a whole range of other soups. Texas Instruments has stamped its brand name on its whole range of products, including its now defunct watch. Similarly, Philips has used the same brand name on products like vacuum cleaners, television sets, radios, hi-fi systems, coffee makers, microwave ovens, computers, irons, and many other household and office products. Dunhill has also capitalized on its established brand image in the traditional cigarette business. Under this brand, it has successfully diversified into designers' products like belts, ties, wallets, handbags, shoes, and other costume jewellery and accessories. And for Walt Disney World, its spinoffs are even greater. Not only its brand, but many of its characters — like Mickey Mouse and Donald Duck — are even used in many licensing businesses.

What is important to note is that while many western companies practise brand extension strategy, they do not favour the monolithic approach that is commonly adopted by the Japanese. If anything, the use of the monolithic type of brand strategy tends to be more of an exception with western companies. In other words, monolithic identity is not pursued **proactively** as an integral part of the corporate strategy. In the case of Dunhill and other tobacco companies, for instance, brand extension was used primarily as a **reactive** attempt to move out of the declining tobacco industry and diversify into other areas. In fact, the lack of adopting a proactive stance has caused many other tobacco companies to fail in moving out of and diversifying from their traditional business. This is despite the fact that most tobacco companies have very strong brand images. Dunhill is one of the few fortunate cases of success.

In general, western companies prefer to develop different brands for different products. This could be largely attributed to their culture of individualism, and their inability to fulfil the conditions necessary for the highly integrated team system that is so essential for the monolithic brand strategy to work. In sum, their basic branding philosophy is different from that of the Japanese.

8.5 Economic Power of Established Brands

The Japanese have demonstrated that strong brand names can translate into economic domination as well. This is evident in the number of Japanese brands that dominate both the consumer and commercial or business markets. As pointed out earlier, the ability to create brands of world class standing has enabled Japanese companies not only to build larger market shares for their products, but also allow them to shift their production overseas without suffering any loss of product quality or brand image.

Of course, the Japanese are not the only ones who know the economic power of strong brand names. The Americans and Europeans, too, have understood the commercial value attached to an established brand name. In the case of Coke — a beverage with very low technology requirement — the company has built a worldwide network of bottling plants. Similarly, many American fast food chains like McDonald's, Burger King, and Pizza Hut have cleverly capitalized on their established brand names by granting **franchises** of their businesses to overseas markets. In so doing, they pass the risks of investment, and, at the same time, collect a fee for the use of their brand names — a double-win situation.

A strong brand also facilitates the establishment of joint venture partnerships and the formation of strategic alliances. A good example is the strategic alliance formed by SIA, Delta and Swiss Air which effectively increases the overall value of all three airlines. What is interesting about the SIA story is that it has also capitalized on its strong brand image and goodwill to develop another airline. Recognizing that it is not possible to replicate its successful "Singapore Girl" story outside its current carrier, and facing increasing regional and international competition, SIA decided to create a new subsidiary airline — Silk Air. Today, barely two years after its operation, Silk Air is fast establishing a strong image for itself in the airline business.

The economic power of established brand names extend beyond the ability to shift production overseas and international franchising. For brands like IBM, HP, BMW, Mercedes, SIA and Rolex, their companies have found that it is possible to consistently put a premium on their products and services. In fact, some Japanese cars and consumer electronics are beginning to enjoy premiums on their products as a result of their brand gaining prominence.

It is interesting to note that premiums resulting from strong brands even extend to the area of education. Many of the top American Universities like Stanford, Harvard, Yale, Michigan, Wharton, MIT, and Chicago, for instance, are able to charge very high tuition fees because of their excellent brand images. The strong images enjoyed by universities from the western countries have also enabled some American, British and Australian institutions to cleverly exploit the Asian market by exporting their degrees. Having realized the tremendous demand for education among Asian economies, and faced with severe cuts in funding at home, these universities have begun to offer a whole spectrum of distant learning programmes and degrees. Indeed, one cannot help but notice the increasing number of advertisements placed in the papers almost weekly in countries like Hong Kong, Singapore, Malaysia, Indonesia, and Thailand.

Some well-known American universities have even gone a step further by offering high level executive programmes. Examples of such are University of California, Berkeley; University of California, Los Angeles; New York University, Harvard, Stanford, Michigan, Cornell, Wharton and Chicago are now tapping heavily into the lucrative market for executive education in the Asian region. It is very likely that more western universities will follow suit. INSEAD of France, for instance, is beginning to compete head-on against the American institutions.

The possibility of commanding a premium as a result of having a strong brand name has led many marketeers to put a lot of effort into brand development and image building. In fact, this can be commonly found in products like cosmetics, writing instruments, designer clothings and accessories (like belts, ties, wallets, and handbags), watches, and of course cars. For such "ego" products, marketeers have successfully developed the "snob appeal" that attract consumers who are very conscious of their social status. The result is that many of such consumers are willing to pay high prices for branded goods — at times ridiculously high premiums — for the more exclusive brands. Indeed, no shrewd marketeer will ignore the tremendous marketing mileage that can be "milked" from a brand that has become legendary.

Without doubt, branding is one of the most powerful ways of promoting a product. The greatest strength of a brand is that it is created deliberately in great detail and care with the intention of appealing to a targetted segment of people at a particular point in time. As such, the brand can become a powerful symbol that contains very complex and personal attributes to the individual consumer that may even extend beyond the rationality of the human mind. How else can one explain the highly emotional outbursts and widespread appeals against the dropping of the old brand name, Coke, in 1985?

The economic power of a brand suggests that when properly managed, it can be a very effective marketing tool for a company. It is therefore of little wonder that many companies are prepared to spend millions of dollars in brand building. At the same time, there are also many other companies — British Airways for one — which are prepared to spend an equally large amount of money trying to re-position a brand that is declining in popularity.

8.6 Experiences of the Four Asian NIEs

The experience of Japan in brand development can be contrasted with that of the NIEs. When Taiwan, Hong Kong, South Korea and Singapore started their industrialization efforts, they concentrated heavily on making other countries' products like shoes, textiles, and electronics. This was done in several ways such as direct foreign investments, joint ventures, or even licensing. In many instances, products were made and marketed through using foreign brand names. Even today, these four Asian NIEs still relied heavily on making products that are sold under the brand names of the large MNCs. Take South Korea and Taiwan for example. They are well-known for making products for brands like Arrow, Nike, Puma, Yamaha, Dunlop, amongst others. In the case of Singapore, its products basically carry the brand names of MNCs that use the island as an overseas production base — Sony, Matsushita, Hewlett Packard, IBM and Texas Instrument are some of these MNCs. It is also the case for Hong Kong.

There is nothing wrong with producing and marketing one's products under the established brand names of others. Unfortunately, such a strategy means that there is **no claim of the proprietorship** of the products. When the costs of production go up, the foreign investors — who are driven by profit maximization or cost minimization — will not hesitate to shift their operations to lower cost countries. This is precisely what is happening in Taiwan, South Korea, and Hong Kong where most of their electronics, textiles and shoes industries are losing out to countries like China, Indonesia and Thailand. Similarly, many international firms have moved out from Singapore to Johore in Malaysia and Batam in Indonesia in search of cheaper factors of production. Without doubt, MNCs are mercenary in their orientation, and they will not hesitate to move out to seek greater cost or profit-advantage.

8.6.1 South Korea

Compared to the other Asian NIEs, the South Koreans are probably the most successful in the area of brand development. The South Korean *chaebol* or conglomerates are not only the driving force behind the country's export-oriented strategy, but have been instrumental in creating world class brands like Daewo, Hyundai, Samsung, and Goldstar. They are basically trying to replicate the success stories of the Japanese corporations by extending the same brand name across different categories of products, that is, by adopting the monolithic brand strategy. For example, Samsung, the largest South Korean conglomerate, capitalized on its strengths in consumer electronics and extended its brand name across a wide spectrum of products in industries as diverse as semiconductors, aerospace, food, machinery, apparel and clothings, trading, insurance and advertising. Similarly, Hyundai capitalized on its successes in the heavy industries by using the same brand name on products like cars, consumer electronics, appliances, computers, and telecommunication equipment. Likewise, Daewo and Goldstar have pursued similar strategies in branding.

In pursuing the monolithic branding strategy, like the Japanese, the South Koreans have demonstrated that they too can be successful in the world market. What is more remarkable about the South Koreans is that they are able to achieve world class brand standing within a shorter period of time than the Japanese — in about 25 years which is half the time of that taken by the Japanese. Without doubt, they have benefitted by learning from the Japanese.

One reason that the South Koreans are able to build up their own brand names is because of their large domestic market. South Korea has a population of 43.8 million as of 1994. While this is less than half the population of Japan, it compares very favourably against the estimated 3.0 million for Singapore, 5.8 million for Hong Kong, and 20.8 million for Taiwan (see Table 8.1). The large local market allows them to build up domestic credibility before launching into the international arena. This approach of the South Koreans, again, is copied from the Japanese — the huge domestic market is used as an incubator for the "world conquerors" of the future.

8.6.2 Taiwan

Among the NIEs, Taiwan is likely to feel the effects most in the future. Over the years, it has made little attempt to develop its own brands. Instead, it has chosen to copy and borrow technology from other countries to produce cheaper products for the domestic market. This strategy was possible owing to the relatively closed Taiwanese market and the rather relaxed copyright laws. Many consumer products like shoes, textiles, electronic equipment, appliances were produced with little attention paid to developing national brands. Interestingly, even the automobile industry became a victim of such a policy.

The Taiwan automobile industry probably never lagged behind that of the South Koreans in the 1960s and 1970s. It was known to produce many variants of Japanese models. In fact, it had the best opportunity, among the four Asian NIEs, to develop a national car for the world market. Unfortunately, the lack of government support and cooperation among members in the automobile industry resulted in a lack of concerted efforts so necessary for the development of a national car. Today, not only have the Taiwanese lagged behind the South Koreans in the automobile industry, but they, also, do not have a car of the same international standing as Proton, the national car manufactured by Malaysia.

Despite its heavy manufacturing base, there are few international brands of Taiwanese origin in the world market today. For example, brands like Kennex (tennis rackets and balls) and Giant (bicycles) can hardly be considered as world class although they do have some international standing. Fortunately, some Taiwanese companies like Formosa Plastics, Evergreen and yet others (Acer, for instance) in the computer industry, are beginning to realize the importance of branding. More efforts are now being invested in brand development. In fact, this renewed thrust to develop world class brands has led industrialists like YF Chang to set up Taiwan's first private commercial international airline, EVA Air, in 1990. Today, EVA Air is increasing its destinations not only in Asia, but in Europe as well.

8.6.3 Hong Kong

In the case of Hong Kong, the lack of a sense of nationhood and its relatively small population (5.8 million as of 1994), have greatly hampered its brand development. Hong Kong's economic development has largely been a result of its free trade and capitalistic society which continuously throw up entrepreneurs who do not hesitate to capitalize on any available business opportunity. Governmental guidelines and macro economic policy have been almost absent. As such, while Hong Kong may be the base of many regional headquarters of MNCs, it has never been able to groom brands that are of world class standing. True, there are huge conglomerates like Cheung Kong Holdings, Hutchison Whampoa, and Sun Hung Kai. However, they are mainly in trading, services, and real estate rather than in manufacturing.

To be fair to Hong Kong, there are also some successful cases. Names like the Hong Kong Bank, Cathay Pacific Airlines, Satchi, Giordano, and Goldlion do have some international standing. Nevertheless, considering the economic dynamism of Hong Kong, these achievements cannot be considered as outstanding. Interestingly, as an economy, Hong Kong has one of the highest number of billionaires in Asia. Yet, it has hardly any world class brands in the same league South Korean brands like Samsung, Daewoo, Goldstar and Hyundai.

With Hong Kong reverting to China by 1997, it is even harder to expect businessmen to take a long term perspective which is very essential for the development of brands. If anything, with 1997 drawing closer and closer each day, it is likely that Hong Kong's businessmen will adopt an even shorter term perspective in their business dealings and investments. This will inevitably be detrimental to the creation of strong brand names. To some extent, this is somewhat unfortunate. This is because in the case of Hong Kong, there is actually no shortage of entrepreneurs and creative talents. It has, for instance, a fairly big pool of creative talents in the movie, television, fine arts, and advertising industries. It also has good designers and a fairly well-developed fashion industry. Unfortuntately, political realism has undermined the blossoming of such talents for the development of world class brands.

8.6.4 Singapore

In trying to develop world-class brand names, Singapore faces the most difficult problem. Among the four Asian NIEs, it has the smallest population: estimated 3.0 million as of 1994. Its small population means that the domestic market cannot be used as an incubator in the development of brands. To be successful, it has to be successful in its export markets from the very beginning. It is this lack of a domestic market that has, perhaps, prompted its policy makers to pick the "reliance on MNCs" as a strategy to spearhead its industrialization programme.

There are definite advantages in relying on MNCs as engines of economic growth. MNCs not only bring along investments, technology, and management skills, but also create jobs and provide opportunities for the upgrading of skills. More importantly, they come with **established brand names** for their products that are known in markets the world over. This advantage has definitely been recognized by the policy makers in Singapore. In addition, the MNCs help to stimulate the growth of local industries. For example, YCH, a local transport and freight forwarding company has been growing by leaps and bounds over the past ten years as a result of providing support services to the MNCs. Today, YCH has reached such a level of growth that it is ready to go regional or international. In the same way, Pico Art International, which is in exhibition services, has been able to reach its present world class standing as a result of servicing MNCs.

In order to cushion the "withdrawal syndrome" by the MNCs as a result of increasing costs of production over the years, conscious efforts have to be made to attract higher value investments. At the same time, industries that are no longer competitive have to be phased out. For those that are competitive, they are encouraged to upgrade to higher value-added products. Indirectly, "old brands" are replaced by "new brands," but they are all established brands! In pursuing such a strategy — reliance on MNCs — Singapore would have to constantly keep itself ahead of its competitors. It has to constantly seek out new technologies and products and services to replace existing ones that are losing their competitiveness. Not surprisingly, this task is getting increasingly difficult, especially when the competition for foreign investments is now very intense among countries.

Recognizing the greater challenges ahead, and the importance of developing world class brands, the Singapore government is now paying greater attention to grooming its own MNCs (and hence building world class brands) as a means for long term growth. To this end, it has appropriately established a Brand Assistance Scheme (BRANDAS) in February 1991 to help Singapore companies and products to make a name in the world market. Today, only SIA and perhaps Tiger Beer and Tiger Balm are brand names of international standing. Others like Risis (in gold-plated orchids and ornaments) and Bonia (in leather goods), while enjoying some regional reputation, are yet to make any major impact internationally.

Perhaps one of the recent success stories by a Singapore company that has made some impact on the world scene is in the high technology area. Creative Technology managed to get itself listed in the American Nasdaq in August 1992. It is well-known for its popular Sound Blaster range of personal computer (PC) sound cards — devices that enable IBM-compatible PCs to generate stereo-quality sound. As of 1991, it has captured close to 75% of the world PC sound market with a turnover of US$100 million. Owing to its success, it has also successfully entered into strategic alliances with other companies. In early 1992, it obtained a licence to use US-based Emu's technology to develop a new product called Midi Blaster. This new product is intended for use in making multi-media presentations in business and education as well as for music composition. Hopefully, Creative Technology will be able to build a strong brand image in its corporate logo.

8.7 Experiences of the Other Asian Economies

Among the other countries in the Asia-Pacific region, Malaysia deserves special mention for its success in developing its automobile industry. In particular, its efforts in creating and developing its national car — Proton — reflects the great foresight its government had, especially that of its Prime Minister, Dr. Mahathir Mohamed. It must be noted that when the Proton was first conceived by Dr. Mahathir, it was the brunt of criticisms and sarcastic jokes. This was because the typical route of economic development was that of starting from light industries before any medium and heavy industries could be considered. Dr. Mahathir opted for the reverse; to let the automobile industry lead the development of the light and medium industries. In doing so, it was hoped economic leapfrogging might be achieved.

Today, Malaysia has successfully developed its automobile and supporting industries. The Proton has not only become Malaysia's pride, but it has also captured a respectable share in the world's small-size car market. It has also successfully introduced a wider range of models targetted at the European market. Besides the Proton, Malaysia also has a century-old reputation in Selangor Pewter, a brand well-known for its range of tin-related products. It is a name synonymous with quality and distinction, and rivals well-known brands in silverware. In an effort to reflect its diversified business, Selangor Pewter changed its name to Royal Selangor in August 1992. In recent years, Malaysia has also established two fairly credible brand names in the clothing or fashion industry — Padini and John Master.

China, in fact, produced some very respectable brands in the 1950s and 1960s, that were marketed to Southeast Asia and even to the other parts of the world. For example, brands like Seagull (a brand of camera), Chung (a brand of leather shoes), Warrior (a brand of canvass shoes, especially basketball shoes), Aeroplane (a brand of shuttlecocks), Double Happiness (a brand of table-tennis rackets, balls, and nets), Swan and Pagoda (brands of singlets and underwears), Hero (a brand of fountain pen), Tsingtao (a brand of beer), and Great Wall (a brand of pencils) were familiar household brands. The demands for such products then were strong, especially in Southeast Asia. Some of the brands like Aeroplane, Swan, Tsingtao, Warrior, and Double Happiness could even be considered as world class in terms of product quality at that time. Unfortunately, the Chinese never quite knew how to build up their brands. Today, these brands are seriously being threatened by many foreign brands to the extent that many Chinese officials have begun to advocate the need to support and develop the local Chinese brands. Otherwise, it would be a matter of time that these Chinese brands become bygones.

8.8 Increased Emphasis on Brand Development and Creation

Without doubt, there is a renewed and increased sense of urgency among many Asian economies to develop their own national brands. This is a result of economic affluence; the preference for well-known brands is a trend that has become irreversable. Thus, unless these Asian economies are able to create and develop their own national brands, they are likely to lose substantial market shares to foreign brands. These losses will be aggravated over time as more consumers possess greater discretionary purchasing power.

8.8.1 Favourable Factors

Despite the limited successes in the area of brand development, there are several factors in the favour of the NIEs and semi-NIEs in the Asian region. First, these countries have fairly large populations. With the exception of Singapore and Hong Kong (see Table 8.1), the rest have fairly large population bases to support the development of national brands. For example, with a population of about 18.9 million, Malaysia has been able to support the development of its national car, Proton. Thus, there is no reason why the other countries like Taiwan and Indonesia which have even larger population bases cannot do likewise. In fact, there are several other industrialized countries (see Table 8.1) with much smaller population bases — Belgium with 10 million, Switzerland with 6.9 million, Finland with 5.0 million, Norway with 4.3 million, and Sweden with 8.7 million — that have well-known international brands to their credit. Sweden has world class brands in luxury cars (Volvo and Saab), telephone (Ericsson) and furniture (Ikea); Switzerland is well-known for its countless number of brands of watches, including the latest Swatch watchs; Norway is known for its Nokia telephone; and Denmark is reputed for its Danish cookies, butter and tableware.

Second, many of these Asian economies are already making various products under licensing from well-established brands. The kinds of products that these countries make include shoes, rackets, clothings, appliances, consumer electronics, and so on. What this suggests is that these countries already have the necessary expertise and production capabilities to generate high and consistent quality products. Otherwise, the MNCs would not have located their production facilities in this region anyway. What is perhaps lacking are marketing skills and creative talents which are required for the development of world class brand names. In particular, these countries have to develop its creative industry if they hope to achieve world class standing in branding.

Third, the economies in the Asian region are now experiencing very healthy economic growth rates. With the increasing affluence is a corresponding rise in the demand for branded goods. If carefully managed, this demand can in itself be very useful for the development of brands in these countries, especially if the brands have a national appeal and the government is willing to lend some support. A case in point is the success of the Indonesians in badminton in the 1992 Barcelona Olympics. This could be capitalized upon by, say, creating a brand name using the popular player's name, Susanti. In particular, many economies in the Asian region have also in recent years become more nationalistic and, to some extent, have also adopted a more cautious and skeptical attitude towards accepting western values. In some instances, there have even been attempts

TABLE 8.1 Population and GNP per capita (1994) of selected economies

Economy	Population	Per Capita GNP (US$)
Asian LDEs		
India	883.6	350
China	1162.7	470
Vietnam	73.7	220
Myanmar	45.8	450
Cambodia	9.3	216
Sri Lanka	17.8	530
Asian Semi-NIEs		
Indonesia	185.6	670
Philippines	64.5	850
Thailand	58.8	2085
Malaysia	18.9	3230
Asian NIEs		
South Korea	43.8	7290
Taiwan	20.8	11240
Singapore	3.0	18025
Hong Kong	5.8	18360
Developed Economies		
Spain	39.1	13970
Belgium	10.0	20880
Netherlands	15.2	20480
France	57.4	22960
Denmark	5.2	26520
Norway	4.3	25820
Sweden	8.7	25010
Japan	124.5	31460
Finland	5.0	20970
Switzerland	6.9	36480
Italy	58.0	19600
Britain	58.4	17990

Source: Various sources

made to reject the western value system and lifestyle. This inevitably creates a vacuum for the development of indigenous brands. Moreover, the Asian region is reputedly highlighted as the growth area for the 21st century. This provides yet greater impetus for companies in this region to start developing brands that cater to this greater market and demand.

Fourth, there are many rich traditions in this part of the world owing to its long history and many established cultures. These cultures and traditions provide a lot of symbols and identities that can be exploited for branding purposes. For example, when one thinks of China, two world class symbols come to mind: the Great Wall and the Panda. Yet, these two symbols, despite their high commercial value, have yet to be fully exploited for branding. In fact, some years ago, when I was consulting in China, I highlighted these two national symbols to the Chinese factory managers. They were able to tell me all the attributes associated with the Great Wall: strength against the elements, cultural and historical richness, collective efforts, determination and perseverance, hard work and sacrifice, dignity and courage, greatness and heroic achievement. Interestingly, the Great Wall has been used to brand products like thermo flasks, pencils, cars, and clothings. Obviously, these products (with the probable exception of cars) bear little relation to the attributes associated with the Great Wall.

Similarly, the Chinese managers were able to list the attributes related to the panda: affection, high value, rarity, gentleness, obedience and softness. However, the panda has been used to brand products like radio, television, sewing machines, bicycles, arts and crafts, and clothings. Again, those attributes associated with the panda do not relate to the nature and characteristics of the products. A "soft" symbol like panda is obviously not suitable for "rugged" products like sewing machines! In fact, the Chinese tend to use these two symbols more as trademarks rather than for brands. The equity value and commercial potential of two symbols have never been fully exploited. On the other hand, some marketeers have cleverly exploited some seemingly less significant symbols like the frog for Giordano products, and the crocodile for designer clothings. Depending on which direction the reptile is facing, the crocodile stand for the brand Lacoste or Crocodile!

Fifth, there are already some emerging consumer brands in this part of the world. Bonia is fast developing a niche for itself in the fashion goods leather industry in Southeast Asia. Malaysian brands of clothing like Padini and John Master are also beginning to make some regional impact. Similarly, Batik Keris of batik clothings and Tens of tennis balls from Indonesia. Kennis of tennis rackets and tennis balls, Giant of bicycles from Taiwan, and Goldlion of clothings from Hong Kong are beginning to gain attention. What is needed is for these companies to continue to invest in building up their brand images in the Asian region, and then gradually extend to the world market. With the increasing affluence of the region, the demand for branded goods is likely to increase as well, thus presenting tremendous opportunites for companies in this part of the world to invest in brand creation and development.

Finally, many countries in this part of the world have a lot of strengths in services. For example, other than SIA, the other countries in the region also have airlines that are of respectable standards. These include Cathay Pacific, Malaysian Airlines, and China Airlines. Furthermore, these countries are also well-known for their hotel, shipping, and other related services. While services cannot be exported in the same intensity and scope as manufactured products (as they are harder to control in terms of quality), the knowledge and experiences gained in the production and marketing of these service can, nonetheless, be useful. For example, some of the skills on brand creation and development in services may be transferable to the manufacturing sector. At the same time, management systems for services could be developed and exported. This is precisely what SIA and Shangri-la (which provide hotel services) have begun to do. There are also possibilities to develop franchise businesses in services like advertising, accounting, consulting and legal practices along the same lines as world renown companies like Arthur D. Little, Ernst and Young, Arthur Anderson, Batey, Hill and Knowlton, amongst others.

8.8.2 Government Support and Encouragement

To be successful, some level of government support and encouragement is necessary. Industry collaboration would also be useful. Here, the Airbus is a classic case of how the pooling of resources among a group of smaller players can, in fact, create a serious challenge to the major players. Strategic alliances, partnerships and joint ventures can and should be explored.

One possibility of collaboraton in the industry is to allow an established company to gain a strong foothold in a foreign market, and allow the smaller local companies to piggy-back on the brand name of the parent company. For example, in the case of Singapore, if Keppel Corporation (a highly diversified company that has various business activities in the Asia-Pacific region) manages to create a strong image for itself, it is conceivable that the smaller companies can market their products under the Keppel name. Similarly, the smaller computer companies may wish to consider marketing their products under the umbrella of Creative Technology. In doing so, not only is there pooling of resources, resources are also not wasted in trying to re-invent the wheel. Afterall, the investment needed for building up a brand name in a foreign market can be quite substantial and beyond the means of the smaller companies. By using this piggy-back approach, speedy penetration of a market is possible. This is applying the monolithic approach used by the Japanese and Koreans.

It should really be thought of as a strategic alliance approach. The smaller companies should not worry about losing their identities and control. In reality, such an approach is not new. Many local companies in Singapore and other NIEs and semi-NIEs in the Asia-Pacific region are currently serving the MNCs anyway, and have rarely sold their products under their own brand names! What is needed is a change in orientation and mindset. To use such an approach effectively, government support and encouragement may be necessary, especially in promoting industrial cooperation, and strategic alliances — a concept that is now increasingly being accepted in corporate boardrooms.

8.9 Conclusion

Countries that have done well in the world are known to produce brands of world class standing. In fact, the economic strengths of nations may be assessed even by the number and quality of established brand names that they have in the world market. Japan, West Germany, the United States, Switzerland, and France are good examples.

The use of brand names to create strategic advantages is likely to become more and more important in the future. This is because as the nature of competition shifts from production orientation to a marketing orientation, as society becomes more affluent and status conscious, and as competition becomes keener, there will be pressing needs to fight for the share of the consumer minds through the use of brands. A good brand will act as a surrogate for a whole range of product attributes. Besides, it is still the best way to differentiate one product from another. It is fast becoming a competitive tool that will be exploited not only by corporate boardroom strategists, but by policy makers of countries as well.

9

Understanding Relevant Costs: The Key to Innovative Pricing

9.1 Introduction

One of the most important aspects in the development of an effective pricing strategy is a clear understanding of various cost concepts. Concepts like fixed cost, semi-fixed cost, variable cost, and marginal cost are all very well defined concepts in the literature on pricing. Over the years, these concepts have influenced marketeers substantially in their understanding of costs and the setting of prices. However, besides having a good understanding of costs, there are additional concepts that the marketeer needs to grapple with if he hopes to develop more effective pricing strategies for the Asian region.

9.2 Understanding Relevant Costs

One of the challenging tasks facing the marketeer operating in the Asian region must be that of understanding what to include or exclude in his calculation of costs. Unlike the more developed economies where clear outlines exist with regard to the treatment of costs, investment, and expenditures, such guidelines are lacking in many Asian economies so that some expenses like purchases of gifts are in a grey area. Yet, these are costs that cannot be ignored.

One way to assist the marketeer to have a better grasp of what to include or exclude in his calculation of costs is an understanding of the concept of **relevant cost.** Simply put, the marketeer should include only costs that are relevant, that is, costs that have a **direct impact** on the pricing decision. Costs that are irrelevant or do not directly impact on the pricing decision should be excluded. Of course, it is in the interest of any company that all costs, including a desired rate of return, be recovered by a certain period of time. However, strict adherence to full cost recovery at all time result in missing market opportunities. Rather, the marketeer must be given more flexibility in his treatment or application of costs in order to exploit every market opportunity, especially when the Asian region is so dynamic and fast changing. The following are some examples to illustrate the concept of relevant cost.

9.2.1 Historical versus Future Costs

A pricing decision made today, is in anticipation of events — such as sales — of the future. Yet, very often, managers make their pricing decisions based on cost information, such as accounting records, of the past. This tendency to rely on historical data arises largely because they are readily available and are well documented. Moreover, it is a practice that has been adopted by many companies for umpteen years and there is no apparent reason why it should be changed.

There is nothing wrong with using historical cost data so long as the future business conditions are similar to those of the past, and the competitive environment remains relatively stable. In other words, using historical data is valid when there is little change in the operating business environment. Unfortunately, this is a very naive stance to take. Many economies in the Asian region are growing rapidly. Change is the order of the day! These dynamic conditions cause the costs of doing business to fluctuate greatly. In many instances, the costs of doing business — rentals, wages and salaries, land and building costs, marketing and distribution, and so on — are rising rapidly. These, plus fairly high inflation rates (for example, in China, the inflation rate was 20% in 1994) and fluctuating currency exchange rates (for example, the Chinese renminbi which was higher than the Singapore dollar in the early 1980s, was only worth S$0.17 September 1995). Thus, planning on the basis of "last year's figures" would make little business sense, especially in the fast changing Asian region.

Historical costs are meaningful to the extent that they apply to the acquisition or purchase of the products. In most instances, to dispose or sell the products, there are many more costs that have to be incurred, such as expenses for distribution, advertising and promotion, commissions for salesmen, margins for dealers, wages and salaries, amongst others. These costs occur only in the future, and can best be estimated upon the sale of the product. Unlike manufacturing where stockpiling of materials, supplies, and inventories may cushion the volatility of costs (especially against cost increases), it is not possible to inventorize future marketing costs. In addition, the amount to be spent would depend on many other factors such as the general business outlook, the nature and intensity of competition, the difficulty of marketing the product, and so on.

If such marketing expenses are substantially higher than the cost of the product itself, as is the case for cosmetics and fashion goods, it becomes more important to focus on **future** costs. In a rising cost situation, any pricing based on historical costs will significantly reduce or even wipe out any profit margin. Similarly, in a declining cost situation, the company can lose its competitiveness owing to high pricing based on past data.

Yet despite the need to be future-oriented in developing pricing strategies, many companies still rely heavily on historical data. I can think of at least two reasons for this. First, as mentioned earlier, historical data are easily available, especially from accounting records. Little effort is needed to obtain the information. In contrast, it is difficult to forecast future costs, and many managers may not even have the skills and resources to do it. Moreover, to be future-oriented requires a **proactive mindset** and a willingness to take **risks,** both highly unattainable for most managers without strong support from their companies. These managers would require additional commitment of manpower and resources to scan, study, analyze and evaluate future business conditions — investments that few companies are willing or capable of undertaking.

Second, most managers' mindsets are cast by their training in accounting and economics — disciplines that rely heavily on historical data for analysis and which were well established before the advent of marketing. Moreover, in the past, business conditions were relatively stable in that competition was not rife and technological changes were not sudden or rapid. Such conditions no longer exist today. Any cost advantage enjoyed currently for any product can easily be wiped out by new technology or cheaper and better foreign imports. Strict reliance on the past, therefore, courts disaster for the future.

In the area of strategic pricing, it is crucial to note that the experience cost curve is a good illustration of how pricing can be done on the basis of future costs. Under experience curve pricing, the company fixes the price of its products on the basis of future lower cost as a result of economies of scale generated from expected large scale production. Using such a pricing strategy, a company may even price its products below the current cost of production and attempt to use a lower price to penetrate the market faster. This is because by capturing an increasingly larger market share, the company would be able to realize economies of scale sooner. In this way, the cost of production would be pushed down faster, and profits will still be realized in the longer run.

Many Japanese companies are reputedly using the experience cost curve concept in their pricing strategies, especially in their penetration of overseas markets. They tend to pursue market shares relentlessly in order to justify their low pricing strategies, and to achieve economies of scale through large volume production. The result is that Japanese companies have often been accused by their western counterparts of dumping and subsidizing their exports. While there may be some truth to such accusations in the earlier years of Japan's export drive, the reality may be the failure on the part of western competitors to appreciate the subtlety of the Japanese approach to the treatment of costs.

Pricing based on future costs as in the case of experience curve pricing is not without dangers. To begin with, there must be a good understanding of the market, especially with regards to the demand for the product. This is because the success of using experience curve pricing is based on expected future demand that must be realized. Otherwise, the expected fall in costs will not materialize! Second, production and manufacturing facilities must be in place so as to meet the expected high demand. Third, extensive distribution channels must be set up to cover as large a market area as possible. Fourth, marketing and other related promotional activities to sustain the expected large scale operations must be well coordinated. Finally, the right kind of sales personnel and organizational structure must be in place. It must be remembered that the success of experience curve pricing depends largely on how fast the company can bring future costs down through large volume of production. Sales must materialize, which means that the forecasts have to be as accurate as possible!

Historical costs are not likely to be very meaningful when there are tremendous changes in the environment. This is especially the case for many economies in the Asian region. For instance, operating and marketing costs have been going up tremendously in China since it opened up in the late 1970s. It also experienced high inflation rates, and its currency has undergone severe "depreciation" over the same period. And therefore using historical costs as the basis for computation makes little sense in the case of China. In fact, its recent experiences of high inflation rates, depreciation of currency, and general increasing costs may also not hold for the future: the Chinese government has begun, since 1994, to take drastic steps to curb its inflation rate, stabilize the exchange rate of its currency, and curtail cost increases. Obviously the past will not serve to project the future.

9.2.2 Incremental Costs

Another aspect of relevant costs relates to **increments.** By this, I mean the types of costs that may increase as a result of taking a particular course of action to expand one's business or increase sales. Those costs that would increase are relevant, while those costs that will not increase as a result of that action should not be considered at all. So variable costs like direct labour and sales commission are incremental costs, and are to be taken into consideration as they would increase if the marketeer should decide to increase his sales or business operations. On the other hand, most fixed costs like rentals and the salaries of executives do not increase proportionately as a result of increasing sales. They cannot be considered as incremental costs and hence are not relevant to deciding pricing strategies for the additional sales to be generated.

Bear in mind that we are referring to the need to distinguish between incremental costs and non-incremental costs in the context of pricing for additional market share or sales volume. Incremental costs should also be clearly distinguished from **investment** decisions. It is business folly if one cannot recover the full cost of investment and enjoy favourable returns on it. The objective of any profit-oriented business is to maximize returns on their investment. And it is this quest to maximize returns that makes the concept of incremental costs all the more relevant to the marketeer exploiting every viable option and making pragmatic decisions. Let me illustrate.

A company has invested S$10 million in a production line that is designed to produce two million units a year, but is currently operating at 50% capacity owing to limited local demand. The variable cost for producing each unit is S$7. If the company receives an overseas order to supply five hundred thousand units, what would be an appropriate pricing strategy, assuming that there is no threat of parallel importing back into the home country?

155

Clearly, it is to the company's advantage to negotiate for as high a price as possible. However, in arriving at an acceptable price, the company should not be distracted by the fixed cost of S$10 million, or the local price. This is because the S$10 million is already a sunk cost, and it is irrelevant whether or not the company decides to export. In other words, even if the company chooses to sell only to the domestic market, it would still have to incur the S$10 million. Similarly, if there had been no possibility for exports, the local price would not be changed anyway. The fixed cost and the local price should not be the factors in deciding on exporting the product.

Rather, the relevant cost to be considered is the variable cost of S$7 per unit. Any unit price above S$7 should be seriously considered. This is because the company is currently operating way below capacity, and any additional revenue resulting from selling the product above the S$7 per unit would contribute toward defraying the fixed cost of S$10 million. If the company is already operating above break-even point in the domestic market, then the incremental revenue would contribute directly to profits! Let's say that the company is able to sell the product at S$17 per unit in the domestic market, it would already be breaking even at 50% capacity. There is, therefore, no reason for it to reject, say an offer price of S$10 per unit for the overseas demand of five hundred thousand units. By selling at S$10 per unit, it stands to make S$1.5 million gross profits!

The concept of incremental costs is very useful in pricing products for export. It is incremental costs that should be the determinant in deciding if an overseas order is worthwhile accepting, and not the domestic price of the product. This is because in exporting, it is often not possible to sell at the domestic price. While the conventional maxim is that export prices have to be higher as they involve seemingly more efforts and costs in getting the products overseas, many Japanese companies have proven that this is not so. The reason — they are able to differentiate the relevant from the irrelevant costs involved in export marketing. Similarly, McDonald's does not have a uniform price for their hamburgers that are sold in its numerous fast food outlets in Asian cities. Instead, it adopts a differential pricing strategy that takes into account the relevant costs and the purchasing power of the consumers.

The application of the concept of incremental costs has also allowed the Malaysians to sell their national cars, Proton Saga and Proton Wira, to the international market. The Malaysian domestic market is fairly large, and this allows the bulk of the fixed costs to be absorbed at home. In so doing, it allows the export price to be set at a very competitive level, so as to gain market share and to use up the excess capacity of the production facilities. This approach has allowed Proton not only to minimize its losses in its initial years, but also enable it to build up its competitive advantages, especially in the area of pricing. Today, it has become a very viable venture, and makers are even looking forward to setting up overseas joint ventures!

9.2.3 Avoidable Costs

Another useful concept for the purpose of decision making is that of avoidable costs. As its name implies, it refers to those costs which may be avoidable or need not be incurred. If a cost is avoidable, then it would be relevant to pricing. Take for instance the case of a company. There are many types of costs that are not avoidable in the running of a business. These would include costs like rental, maintenance, payments to the government for services provided, salaries of top management, and so on. Generally, such costs have to be paid regardless of the volume of business. If they cannot be avoided at all, they should **not** be considered as relevant costs for pricing decisions! This may seem rather confusing, but it will become clear with the case shown in Table 9.1.

TABLE 9.1 Renting out your property

> You have just bought an apartment in a condominium estate for S$1 million with the sole intention of renting it out so as to generate extra income. The apartment is paid for with cash and a bank loan of $600,000 at 7% interest per annum. Besides paying bank interest charges on the loan, you would also have to pay monthly condominium maintenance charges of $350, and other related charges to government agencies (for example, to the Public Utilities Board for waterborne fees, and so on) amounting to $50 a month. If the apartment is rented out, the additional miscellaneous expenses relating to maintaining and upkeeping the unit would be about $750 per month. This amount includes any additional property taxes as well. Of course, this $750 would not be incurred if the apartment was not rented out. What is the minimum rent that you are prepared to accept?

When confronted with the problem as formulated in Table 9.1, many people would be tempted to calculate the full cost of investment in making their decision. As a result, they may end up with a fairly high rental figure, depending on their desired rate of return as well. I have tested this problem with a great number of executives in my training, and over 95% of them quoted an expected minimum rent in excess of S$6,000 per month. There is nothing wrong with wanting to obtain the highest rental possible. The important part is how do they arrive at that number. In other words, what criteria are used? If the full cost as outlined above is used, many rental opportunities may be lost, especially when the market cannot pay the rental desired. For instance, if the minimum rental needed is S$6,000 per month, would the owner consider letting it out for S$5,000 or even S$4,000 per month if that is the prevailing market rate?

Interestingly, when presented with the situation outlined, many executives do opt to rent out the apartment at S$4,000 per month. Why is this so? This is where understanding the concept of relevant costs comes in. In reality, whether the aparment is rented out or not, the owner still has to pay the mortgage on his S$600,000 loan, the monthly condominium maintenance fee of S$350, and the government-related charges of S$50 per month (regardless of whether he flushes the toilet or turn on the tap or not!). These are costs that **cannot be avoided**, and they must be paid regardless of whether the apartment is rented out. Indeed, the relevant cost here — which represents the minimum rent — is any amount above S$750 per month! This is because any amount above $750 per month — though the landlord should ask for as much as he possibly — would help to defray all the unavoidable costs. One hopes of course, to get a good return when the market is strong. However, given a weak market, a rental of even S$3,500 isn't a bad proposition at all. Afterall, S$750 is your avoidable cost.

It is precisely the application of the concept of avoidable costs that enables shrewd developers to opt for renting out their properties instead of outright sale during weak market situations. What they do is to ensure that the rental incomes are comfortably above the avoidable costs, and then ride through the leases in anticipation of an upturn so as to reap their returns from both higher rental returns and capital gains. In fact, many Asian investors have bought properties in Australia and New Zealand during the period 1990 to 1995 precisely for capital appreciation. Based on rental returns, they are very low, with almost all cases not even breaking-even with mortgage interest payments.

The understanding of avoidable costs is most relevant and useful in the context of many Asian markets. This is because there are many "hidden costs" in doing business in Asia. These hidden costs, when properly managed, can be avoided. Such "hidden costs" may range from little gifts and souvenirs to expensive free trips and even outright bribery. In the case of marketing, channel members may have to be bought over, and favours may have to be secured from local government officials. Yet, when properly managed, many of these costs can be avoided. The problem with many companies operating in the region is that they do not bother to do their homework and investigate. Instead, they take the easy way out by simply paying, which in turn compounds the problem. What is even worse is that they may be breeding internal corruption within the company! Instead of following the herd mentality of "pay and pay", they should ask, "why pay?" With thorough investigation, careful analysis, and proper management, much of these costs can be avoided and other alternatives explored.

Let me reiterate that understanding what constitutes relevant costs can help the marketeer to manage costs in a more strategic manner. To begin with, he will be able to know what would be the lowest price that he can set for his product, the level of contribution margin that he should get, and the likely profits to be realized. Moreover, by freeing his mind from the constraints of "full" costing, he will be able to develop more innovative pricing strategies.

9.3 Pricing Considerations

In developing a pricing strategy, several factors must be taken into account. Relevant costs, as discussed previously, are obviously important. However, using costs solely for the purpose of pricing is not sufficient. This is because costs is only one important input to the determination of a suitable price. There are other equally important factors to be considered in price setting.

9.4 Consumer and Demand Factors

To begin with, price is very much affected by consumer demand. If the demand for a product is high, there is no reason why the price should be set at a low level. Imagine if someone in Asia were to discover some drugs that can cure cancer, AIDs, and other terminal diseases, the demand for such drugs would, I imagine, be tremendous and the prices astronomical as well. Afterall, any shrewd marketeer will capitalize on such opportunities. Of course, there are situations in which moral and ethical standards dictate that one should not over-price to exploit desperate or ignorant consumers. Thus, in the case of the drugs for curing terminal diseases, moral considerations would moderate the temptation to set exorbitant prices for them.

I believe that the moral issue in business is not how much money you can make, but rather how you go about making it. If you are straight and honest, by all means, make all the money you can. On the other hand, if you are crooked, even making the smallest sum of money can lend you in trouble with the law. In other words, the crux of the moral debate in business is the means, and not the ends. If you have a high quality product and there is great demand for it, there is no reason why you should not sell it at a very high price — this, in essence, is what market forces are all about.

In recent years, owing to the high growth rates in many Asian countries and increasing affluence of their consumers, the prices of some products have been pushed up by strong demand. Property is one such example. Property prices have literally skyrocketed in many Asian cities like Kuala Lumpur, Bangkok, Jakarta, Shanghai, Hong Kong, Singapore and Taipei, amongst others largely because of tremendous consumer demand. In some of these countries, property prices have more than doubled within three to five years! Other luxury items like cars, paintings, and antiques have also witnessed increasing prices.

Probably the best example to illustrate how consumer demand can impact prices is that of the bidding for certificates of entitlement (COEs) for the purchase of cars in Singapore. In Singapore, before a consumer can purchase a car, he has to bid for a COE from the quota released each month by the government for the various categories of cars. As the monthly quota is fixed (that is, there is a limited supply of COEs each month) but the demand for cars are very high in Singapore, the inevitable result is high COE prices. In fact, the prices of COEs in some categories of cars are equal to the price of the car itself in many other countries! When added to the price of the car, it is therefore not surprising that car prices in Singapore are probably the highest in the world. Given the strong consumer demand and the healthy economic conditions, it is unlikely that prices of COEs in Singapore will drop significantly at all. Since its implementation about ten years ago, there has only been one occasion in which prices of COEs dropped significantly — the Gulf War.

Besides the general demand for a product, seasonal demand should be taken into consideration too. During the festive seasons of Christmas, Hari Raya Puasa, Deepavali, and Chinese New Year, the demand for some products push prices to ridiculously high levels. During the Chinese New Year period, the prices of Mandarin oranges, flowers, potted plants, and many Chinese delicacies would go up rather significantly in many Asian cities like Hong Kong, Kuala Lumpur, Singapore, and Taipei, where large ethnic Chinese communities still celebrate the lunar new year in a big way.

9.5 Competition

The effects of competition should not be ignored either. Other than a pure monopoly situation whereby the supplier can ignore both the consumers and competitors in setting the price for his product, most market situations are characterized by various degrees of competition. In any market filled with products or services that are perfect or near subsitutes to one another (so that there is limited scope for product differentiation), no single supplier can push up his price without suffering a drop in demand. At the same time, any attempt to reduce price would be swiftly followed by the competitors. Good examples of such products or services include the gasoline and banking services industries. For these two industries, most players would avoid competing on price to the extent possible. Instead, they would rely on the other three Ps of marketing — product or service offering, distribution and promotion — to create competitive advantages. In fact, many of them attempt to use services offered as the basis for differentiating themselves from the competitors.

The package tour industry in many Asian markets is a another good example of a service where, despite increasing demand for tour or travel services (owing to the increasing affluence of consumers, and the availability of leisure time), the prices have remain very competitive. This is precisely the case in markets like Singapore, Malaysia, and Hong Kong. Without doubt, the presence of countless tour agencies are largely responsible for the low prices. These agencies compete very aggressively, with many of them even forgoing their commissions from the airlines, in order to secure a larger market share. Price-cutting in this industry is very common in markets like Singapore, Malaysia, and Hong Kong. Besides intense competition created by too many operators, many agencies also offer similar product offerings in terms of transportation, itinerary, hotel accommodation, sightseeing and food. Information pertaining to these are normally advertised in their brochures. The consumer shopping for the best tour package knows he has the pick.

In general, as a product and its technology mature, more brands and models will proliferate the market and competition really hots up. A number of household products in Hong Kong, Singapore, and Japan fall under this category. There is intense competition in Singapore among the countless retailers of many brands of television sets, hi-fi systems and refrigerators. The profit margins for these products have been eroded substantially. In contrast, retailers of similar products in China and Vietnam today are enjoying very healthy profit margins. They have less competition and their markets are growing.

The retail industries in Hong Kong and Singapore faced severe competition in 1994 and 1995. Too many retailers, declining tourist spending, and increasing costs have all contributed to the woes of the retailers in these two economies. As a result, sales promotion and drastic price reductions are common events. So intense is the competition that some big names like Lane Crawford and Metro in Singapore were forced to scale down their operations. On the other hand, large departmental stores are only beginning to make their entries into markets like China and Vietnam in the 1990s. For these new markets, the retail scene looks very bright indeed for the next few years.

No sensible marketeer can ignore the effects of competition. However, taking into account the prices of competitors does not mean that the marketeer has to set the same price as those of his competitors. The marketeer can still set a lower or higher price than his competitors, depending on the package of benefits and product attributes that he can offer to consumers. Take the examples of IBM and HP. Despite having high quality products and adopting very strong consumer orientation, they still have to lower prices (at times, significantly) periodically in order to cushion any erosion of market share. Similarly, while SIA has been very successful in pricing its tickets higher than other airlines as a result of its first rate services, its premium is set in a way that takes into account the prices set by competitors. When competition gets tough, SIA is also known to respond with attractive promotions. For one, it has gone into strategic alliances with Swiss Air and Delta Air, and is a partner to Passages — the Asian version of the frequent flyers' programme.

9.6 Corporate Objectives

Naturally, corporate objectives play a part in the price setting process: what is the required return on investment, and over what time period should the investment be recovered? Does the company have the financial resources to sustain a longer recovery period? What is its cost structure like? How much of it consists of fixed versus variable costs, relevant versus irrelevant costs? Are there any other objectives that the company may have besides seeking the highest profits possible? Does the company want to be a price leader or price follower? Is its policy generally to price its products higher or lower than those of its competitors? What about issues like discounts, rebates and commissions? These are but some possible corporate objectives that have to be considered.

There are circumstances in which pricing for survival may be particularly important in the decision-making process. This may mean that the company will have to take short term losses if necessary. In a recession, for instance, the shrewd marketeer may be forced to shift his pricing objective to that of survival, accepting low margins or even absorbing losses in order to keep the business going.

Without doubt, there are many corporate objectives that would influence the price to be decided upon. For the purpose of illustration, there are two diametrically opposite pricing strategies that are worth discussing — market skimming versus market penetration. In market skimming, the marketeer would set his price very high so as to go after the high yield customers. The marketeer would only lower his price gradually over time so as to capture the next level of consumers, or when faced with serious competitive threats. Market skimming allows the marketeer to generate additional profits as the high-end consumers are prepared to pay a price premium for the product. By easing itself gradually into the market, the marketeer can reduce the amount of outright investment needed, allow time to improve the production and marketing of the product, and allow room for downward price correction if the expected demand does not materialize. More importantly, by pricing the product high in the first instance, the marketeer can also hope to foster. This is precisely the pricing strategy adopted for the marketing of luxury brands like Mercedes cars, Rolex watches, Mont Blanc pens, Cartier spectacle frames, Steinway pianos, Dunhill ties, amongst others.

Market skimming through high pricing is particularly useful when the marketeer enjoys strong competitive advantages (like in the case of the branded goods mentioned earlier) or when he is in a monopolistic position. For example, before the Singaporean and Malaysian governments liberalized their telecommunications industries, the prices of many telecommunications products like the cellular handphones, pagers, fax machines, and so on were rather high as they were sold only by the government agencies. Today, the prices of such products have dropped substantially largely because of the presence of competitors into the market.

Market penetration on the other hand involves using a very low price strategy that is designed to gain maximum market share in the shortest possible time. The basic objective is to deter competitors from entering the market owing to the low price — and hence, low profit margins. By pricing the product low, the marketeer is targetting at the marginal consumer. The idea is to build up sales quickly so as to allow him to gain economies of scale. This in turn would contribute to lower costs, resulting in higher total profits through a large volume of sales. Interestingly, by pricing low, the marketeer is trying to create higher entry barriers against his competitors, while at the same time, attempting to build customer loyalty quickly. Of course, to be effective, the marketeer has to ensure that he has the available resources — manpower, production facilities, and distribution networks — to support the penetration strategy.

Market penetration strategy has been widely practised by Japanese companies in the marketing of their products since they entered the world market in the 1950s and 1960s. Through a consistent use of the strategy of low pricing over the years, the Japanese companies were able to use price as a way to differentiate their products from those of the competitors and at the same time, capturing large market shares very quickly. Today, many Japanese companies have dominated the Asian market with their wide array of products and brands. With some products like cameras and household appliances, the competition is practically among Japanese brands themselves! Note that Japanese products in the 1990s are no longer cheap, neither are they of an inferior quality. Despite the higher prices, they have held their grounds very well against competitive products. The reason — their large market shares, and hence economies of scale, have allowed them to compete effectively against their competitors. Effectively, Japanese companies have created very strong barriers against their competitors.

The success of the Japanese marketers in using low pricing have inspired many other Asian developing economies like South Korea, Taiwan, Malaysia and China to do likewise. Indeed, the "threats" posed by these Asian economies in terms of their export to the developed economies in Europe and America have caused much unhappiness and tensions among policy makers in the latter group of economies. Trade disputes, and often with agenda extending beyond trade matters, have escalated substantially in the 1990s. In September 1995, the U.S. threatened to impose punitive taxes on South Korean cars if the latter did not exercise self-restraint on their exports. This was because the cheap Korean cars had began to make an impact on the American car industry, something that the U.S. could ill afford. As the various Asian economies began to grow and prosper, and as they continue with their export-driven policies, more trade frictions, tensions, and disputes are likely to arise in the years ahead.

9.7 Regulatory Constraints

Regulatory constraints on pricing are widely practised by many Asian governments for various reasons, but especially the need to protect the welfare and interests of their citizens. Thus, the prices of utilities like water, gas, and electricity are regulated. Many Asian governments also regulate the prices of public transport (such as bus, taxi and train fares), telecommunications services (such as telephone, fax, and telex charges), postal rates, and other essential services. In the case of Singapore, the government goes a step further. It plays an active role in moderating the prices of essential commodities like rice and sugar through the stockpiling of such products. This is done intentionally to curb inflation and excessive profiteering by unscrupulous businessmen as was in fact, the case in late 1960s and early 1970s.

In the same way, the Singapore government, through the HDB, plays an active role in influencing the prices of properties. This is because the HDB builds the bulk of homes in Singapore — about 85% by the end of 1995. In so doing, the government ensures that the average Singaporean can own his own home because of an affordable price. The result is telling — Singapore has the highest home ownership in the world! Its success in ensuring affordable homes to its citizens has become a model that many other Asian countries like China and Vietnam aspire to follow.

The government of a country may also intervene to influence the prices of some products that are deemed to be undesirable. Good examples include duties and taxes imposed on cigarettes and liquor. The result is that the prices of such products are relatively higher in many Asian countries. At other times, the government may use taxes and duties to increase the prices of certain imported products that it wants to develop or produce locally. For instance, in order to develop the local car industry, the South Korean and Malaysian governments imposed hefty duties on imported cars. Both South Korea and Malaysia have very automobile industries owing to high local demand for the relatively cheap local cars. Several brands of their national cars are also gaining world attention and market share.

For purpose of economic development and the promotion of local industries, many governments intervene to "distort" prices when necessary. This was the case in the early years of economic development in Japan, Taiwan and South Korea, where many of their industries were protected from foreign competition. This phenomenon is not confined to Asian economies. Even in the United States, there are regulations and laws that prohibit companies from price fixing, price collusion, deceptive pricing, and discriminatory pricing against competitors and consumers. Furthermore, in industries that are of national strategic importance, protection against foreign competition is also necessary. Defence-related industries are usually heavily protected in most countries fall into this category. In some countries, even the telecommunications industry is shielded from foreign competition.

No marketeer can therefore ignore the strong arms of the law in influencing the way in which prices can be affected. To be effective, he must be vigilant about the latest changes in government policies and regulations. Any changes may create new pricing challenges or opportunities to the marketeer.

9.8 Other Environmental Influences

Besides regulatory constraints, there are other environmental factors that can affect pricing. The first of these is the general economic conditions of the country and its region. If economic conditions are favourable, and consumers are optimistic about their future they are then generally willing to pay high prices for their products and services. Conversely, if economic conditions are poor, then consumers are reluctant to pay high prices. Such observations were made of the tender prices of COEs for the purchase of new cars in Singapore. In March 1991, when the Gulf War was at its most intense, the average price for all five categories of cars (from the small to the open category) was only S$755. However, the average price went up to S$11,274 in the August 1991 bidding when the war was clearly over. A pent-up demand coupled with better economic prospects and expectations were responsible for the big increase. Such favourable conditions continued and COE prices exceeded S$32,000 by September 1993, and by 1995, it averaged in excess of S$45,000!

The favourable economic conditions in many Asian economies are likely to affect the attitudes and spending patterns of the Asian consumers in the years ahead. To begin with, as a result of governments liberalizing central planning and moving towards a more market-oriented economy (as was the case with China and Vietnam), and encouraging privatization (as was the case with Indonesia, Thailand and Malaysia), the demand for many products and services in these Asian economies have literally exploded, creating unbelievable increases in prices and inflation rates. For instance, property prices in many Asian cities have skyrocketed over the past five to ten years largely because of over-zealous businessmen who are all out to profiteer from the new market opportunities provided. Owing to the healthy economic growth of the Asian region which creates excessive demand, and the short term supply constraint, it is likely that prices of many products will continue on their upward trend for some time.

While it is true that the general economic outlook for many Asian economies is very rosy, the marketeer must not overlook the **level of income** of the country that he is operating in. The demand for goods and services in economies with low levels of income are different from those with high income levels. For example, while the average Singaporean consumer may be craving for his car and condominium unit, the average Sri Lankan consumer may be very contented with just a simple television set. Obviously, the difference in income levels not only affect the type and quality of products and services to be offered, but the pricing as well. An alternative to marketing to low income countries is to downscale the product — called "backward innovation" — so that the price can be slashed to an affordable level. Many Japanese companies adopt such a strategy in their overseas market penetration strategies in countries like China, India and Sri Lanka. One cannot help but be impressed by how the Japanese car makers can "downgrade" their vehicles so that they are within the means of the importing countries.

Pricing can also be the purchasing power of the consumers, especially if components or supplies can be sourced locally. A good example is the way in which McDonald's price its hamburger in the various Asian economies. There is no doubt that the price of the hamburger in Beijing is much higher than the local food, but it is definitely within the purchasing power of the local residents. However, when compared to the price in Hong Kong or Singapore, a McDonald's hamburger in Beijing is very cheap. In view of the great disparity income among the Asian economies, pricing to make the product affordable to the locals or downscaling the product or service offerings are strategies that marketeers should seriously consider.

The physical environment, which includes climatic conditions, natural disasters, and the country's infrastructure, is something that the marketeer should also pay attention to. Unlike the developed economies of the West where technology is very advanced for cultivation, protection, preservation and storage of food and related supplies, many Asian economies are more vulnerable to both calamities caused by man and natural calamities like floods, typhoons, droughts, earthquakes, soil erosion, deforestation and fire. Consider how each time there is a flood or drought in China or India, prices of commodities would escalate. Similarly, the great speed at which the Chinese farmers sold out their arable land for industrial and commercial uses in recent years has caused food prices to escalate, causing much alarm and concern to the Chinese government.

The severe under-development of infrastructure and land transport system in many Asian economies also create price distortions. The difficulty of getting to many areas means higher transportation costs, and hence putting upward pressure on prices. Next, water and energy supplies may be inadequate, which in turn would push up the costs of operations. For this reason it has not been surprising to find that much of the marketing activities in Asian economies are largely confined to the major cities where the infrastructures are well-developed.

Finally, cultural and social factors can also affect the way prices are set. However, their effects are more psychological than economic. We will examine this in the next article.

9.9 Conclusion

By distinguishing relevant costs from the irrelevant costs, the marketeer would be in a better position to develop an effective pricing strategy. However, this strategy is not driven by costs alone. It has to be decided in the context of the overall corporate objectives which, of course, are themselves subjected to review from time to time. At the same time, the shrewd marketeer must keep track of the changes among consumers, the competitive forces and the environment These factors can impact both his costs and pricing as well.

10

Pricing: Consumer's Perspective

10.1 Introduction

Besides understanding pricing from the viewpoint of the seller, it is equally important to know how the consumer perceives pricing — an area that is more an art than a science since the average consumer may not be as rational nor knowledgeable as the marketeer wishes him to be. More importantly, in Asia, many ethnic groups attach a lot of significance to the meanings of numbers (which are used to reflect prices). Their cultural and social backgrounds have significant impact on how they value certain possessions, and the extent to which they are prepared to pay for them. Such behaviours are especially manifested by the Chinese consumers, although other Asian ethnic groups may also display similar dispositions. Thus, it is worthwhile to examine how the Asian consumer's perspective on pricing is influenced by their cultural and psychological factors.

10.2 How Consumers Formulate Prices

Each of us has some idea about the price to pay for a product or service. For example, if we were buying a pair of working shoes, there is a limit as to what we are prepared to pay. In other words, there are some **reference points** which a consumer will use as the basis to benchmark the price of the product or service that he is prepared to pay. In general, the way a consumer formulates his reference price is dependent on the degree of his awareness of competitive prices, the frequency, and the context in which the product or service is purchased.

10.2.1 Awareness of Competitive Prices

How a consumer formulates the price for a product or service will depend how readily he can find out about **competitive prices**. Undoubtedly, competitive prices act as points of reference to the consumer. This is why in a highly competitive market situation, prices tend to be pushed downwards (or at least face the difficulty of moving upwards). Consumers can easily avail themselves of the prices of alternative suppliers. In many Asian cities, the emergence of many shopping centres that are stocked with a great variety of similar products (such as shoes, clothings, toys, and so on) have greatly facilitated price comparisons. Thus, it is not uncommon to find an increasing number of urban Asian consumers who are "educated" shoppers as a result of the availability of competitive products and prices.

In a market where products are becoming more similar in features and quality because of improved technology and standardized production systems, the consumer can become a semi-expert in seeking out the best deal. This is true of products like refrigerators, fans, computer diskettes, pocket calculators, cameras, and television sets where the products are fast becoming very reliable in terms of quality. It is becoming increasingly difficult even to differentiate the quality of one brand from another. This has enabled many consumers to favour several brands at any one time. The final brand purchased will depend on the price or some promotional offers (tantamount to a price reduction).

In air travel, a top airline like SIA has traditionally differentiated their services as a means to justify higher ticket prices. These differentiating features include frequency of flights, convenience of departure and arrival times, number and duration of stopovers, inflight services, type and safety of aircraft, speed of check-in and ground services, availability of airport lounges, and inflight services. However, these service offerings are increasingly being copied and matched by its competitors, especially those from Asia. As a result, the competitive edge of SIA, and hence the premium it commands, have been eroded gradually over the years. Indeed, the airline industry is very competitive today. The problem is further compounded by many travellers who are prepared to sacrifice some services and convenience for cheaper prices. Thus, it is not uncommon to find many ticketing agencies who heavily advertise cheaper airfares.

In the travel industry, the sale of package tours has, because of competition, become like that of products. This is because the destinations and attractions offered by the various tour companies are very similar. In addition, many of them also use the same hotels and restaurants. As a result, product or service differentiation has become increasingly difficult. It is thus not surprising that when consumers cannot perceive differences in the services offered, they would rely on price as the basis for decision making. Most tour agencies in Asia, therefore, feature price and sales promotion heavily in all their advertisements. This has allowed the consumers to do even more price comparisons!

In essence, the knowledge of prices of other brands of a product will place the consumer in a more advantageous position as much as it puts the seller in a difficult position. To justify any price difference, the seller must be able to demonstrate product or service features that are not only distinguished from others, but also worth paying for. Of course, to be able to compare the prices of products or services, the search costs (in terms of the time, money and effort needed) must not be too high. If search costs are high — as in the case of a consumer who values his time and effort highly — then the consumer may be contented with paying a higher price, regardless of alternative products or services that may be available at cheaper prices.

Using prices of one's competitors to formulate the reference price need not be confined to the same market. At times, the consumer may extend his comparison beyond one market. Owing to the escalating prices of properties in Singapore over the past ten years (1986 to 1995), some foreign developers (especially those from Australia) have cleverly exploited the situation by offering their properties for sale in Singapore. With the depreciating Australian dollar vis-a-vis the Singapore dollar, and the abundant supply of land, many Australian properties appear cheaper to the average Singaporean buyer than local properties. For example, in 1995, for A$350,000 (which is about the same amount in Singapore dollars, given that the exchange rate was almost equal), one can get a huge bungalow (say, of 3,500 square feet of built-in space that is sited on a 15,000 square feet of land) in a very posh new housing area like Caringdale, Brisbane. A house of similar quality would cost between S$6 million and S$8 million in Singapore! For A$350,000, one could hardly buy a government HDB five-room flat in Singapore! It is no wonder that many Singaporeans are snapping up Australian properties, besides those in Malaysia, New Zealand, China, and Britain, like hot cakes!

Similarly, shopping across national boundaries is also becoming a common phenomenon among the well travelled urban Asian consumers. Take the case of the "Scribe" shoes made by Bally of Switzerland. The hand-made leather shoes were marketed in Singapore for about S$1,100 a pair. When it was found out that the same pair could be bought for about S$600 in London, England, a great deal of price comparisons of luxury goods between various cities began. They made local news in early 1995.

In general, as the Asian consumer gets more educated and travels more, he is likely to become an "expert" in the art of shopping, especially in terms of price comparison. Such comparisons will be augmented further with the advances made in computer technology whereby the latest information can easily be obtained through subscription networks like the Internet, World Wide Web and others.

10.2.2 Recency Effects

A consumer's perception of price can also be affected by the prices that he has been exposed to **over time.** Depending on his ability to recall, he will then form in his mind the idea of a fair price. One good example of this recency effect in affecting price formulation was the pricing of transferable certificates of entitlement (COE) for the purchase of new cars in Singapore. Since the end of the Gulf war, coupled with an expected economic growth rate of 7% to 8% for 1991, prices of COEs had been increasing since March 1991. This caused much unhappiness and resentment among prospective new car buyers. They were suffering from recency effects of an increasing price trend, as they tended to make references to lower COE prices in the past.

In the same way, many Asian consumers had difficulty reconciling the higher prices of Japanese cars in the mid-1980s with its past low prices, especially after the Japanese yen appreciated substantially. Japanese cars were known to be cheap since they entered the Southeast Asian market in the 1960s. This image of being an economical car continued into the 1970s as compared with those of European and American cars. Despite the vast improvement in the build, quality, comfort, performance, technology, and equipment levels of Japanese cars over the years, the Japanese car makers kept their prices very competitive right up to the early 1980s. Many Asian consumers therefore had difficulty accepting the higher prices of Japanese cars as a result of the upward appreciation of the Japanese yen. It took the Japanese car makers several years of marketing efforts to convince the consumers that Japanese cars deserve to command higher prices, and to shake off their cheap price image.

Interestingly, the "hangover" effects of cheap Japanese cars have created new challenges for Japanese luxury car models like Cima (Nissan) and Lexus (Toyota) in the Southeast Asian market. Japanese cars have been marketed as cheaper alternatives to European and American cars in the Southeast Asian market for over thirty years and Japanese car makers have focussed on the mass car market (that is, on small and medium-sized cars). As a result, when the Japanese car makers introduced luxury cars to the Southeast Asian market in the early 1990s, they encountered problems in trying to position their cars against the established European models like the Mercedes, the BMW, and the Jaguar. This difficulty was compounded by the fact that the prices of these Japanese models are comparable to those of their competitors. The recency effects created by their lower prices and quality still linger on today to the extent that Lexus and Cima are not making significant inroads into the market shares of Mercedes and BMW.

The problem of recency effects are not confined to cars alone. Over the past ten years, property prices in many Asian cities have skyrocketed dramatically. An upmarket condominium unit in Kuala Lumpur, Malaysia, which cost less than RM100,000 in 1989, was worth RM300,000 to RM400,000 in 1995. A semi-detached house in good location in Singapore could be bought for S$800,000 in 1988. This same house was worth about S$3 millions in 1995! This trend is seen in many other Asian cities. As a result, many Asian consumers, especially the yuppies, are having problems reconciling the escalating property prices in recent years to those of the past. Such recency effects have prompted very extreme responses and behaviour. One group, still using immediate past prices as benchmarks, would consistently hesitate to enter the market to buy their properties, only to be frustrated time and again for missing the boat. The other group, fearing further escalation of prices, would simply plunge into the property market and buy without much consideration of any likely downturn. It is this group of consumers who is responsible for the entry of speculators who add more "fuel" to the already over-heated property market.

Unfortunately, strong recency effects may cloud the judgement of these buyers and speculators. This is because property prices in Hong Kong and Japan also escalated in the late 1980s and early 1990s, to the extent that the buyers were blinded to the possibility of downward price movement. This downward movement in price came in late 1994 and 1995 when prices dropped by 30% to 50% in the case of Hong Kong, and by up to 70% in the case of Japan. In both cases, many speculators, investors and genuine buyers were "burnt" severely. Thus, even among the high growth economies of Asia, there are instances in which there are downward price movements.

Without doubt, recency effects can significantly affect a consumer in his formulation of the reference price. This is particularly true of products that are purchased frequently or of high ticket value like cars and houses. On the other hand, if a product is not purchased often and is not of very high value, recency effects would not come into play in the decision-making process of the consumer. For example, one does not instal an air conditioning system or a burglar alarm system in the home frequently. Thus, what would affect the formulation of the consumer's reference price are likely to be the prices of competitors' products that are available and not the price that he paid for his last purchase.

10.2.3 Context

The third factor that influences how a consumer formulates his price is the **context.** By this, I mean that the consumer's perception of price is affected by the situation and environment that he is in. If a consumer shops in a supermarket in Singapore for a can of Coke, he would probably be willing to pay no more than S$0.60 for it. However, if he were in the midst of watching an exciting soccer game, he may be prepared to pay S$1.00 for the same can of Coke. When the context is changed to that of a coffee house in a five-star hotel, he might even be willing to pay up to S$3.00.

Contextual effects have given marketeers plenty of opportunities to create premiums in their pricing strategies. By improving layout, decor, design, and services — like in the case of a restaurant — the prices of the products could be increased substantially. Boutiques, special stores, upmarket departmental stores, and even restaurants have never failed to exploit the contextual effects on pricing.

At times, drastic changes are not even necessary. Take the case of the shrewd drink seller at a soccer match or a festive carnival. He is able to price his drinks much higher with the minimal service because of his ability to capitalize on the **urgency of the situation** and the **convenience of the service** that he is providing. Similarly, in times of frequent rainfall, sellers of umbrellas often charge higher prices than the usual for their products. In many Asian cities which are often flood-prone during rainy seasons, boat operators are often known to exploit the situation and change exorbitant sums for their serivces.

Buying a gift is an interesting context. More often than not, a consumer may be more particular about the price that he is paying for his own product than when it comes to gifts where his point of reference may not be every exact. Rather, he would probably have a benchmark value of the gift that he is prepared to pay, and would be less fussy about the exact price that he is paying, especially when he is not constrained by budget. On the other hand, if he has a budget constraint, he will probably buy something within the budget, and not be particular about the exact price that he is paying for the product. In other words, he forms his reference price differently in this instance.

10.3 Psychological Perception of Price Change

Besides understanding how a consumer formulates prices, it is equally important to know how he views **price changes**. Here, I would like to address two major pyschological concepts that have bearing on the marketeer.

10.3.1 Just Noticeable Difference

The first concept is called "just noticeable difference" or JND in short. What this means is that a consumer will not be sensitive to price changes if the amount of increase is small since it is barely noticeable. On the other hand, if the amount of increase is large, it becomes very noticeable. For instance, when China began to adopt a more market-oriented economy and to liberalize its central planning control in the early 1980s, the prices of many essential products rose significantly overnight. These increases were substantial. As a result, there was severe outcry and unhappiness among the Chinese consumers. The Chinese government has since adopted inflation control as its top priority. This is because inflation rates and prices were increasing at about 20% per annum for some years. Fortunately, the situation as of 1995 was very much under control, with inflation rate at a single-digit level.

Many potential car owners were very unhappy with the car quota bidding system in Singapore from May to August of 1991. They were unhappy with the significant increases of COE prices after February 1991. The prices of COEs for the small, medium, big, luxury and open categories of cars were S$652, S$909, S$210, S$1,004 and S$998 respectively in March 1991. However, within five months (by August 1991), they rose to S$9,660, S$9,040, S$12,558, S$12,742 and S$12,368 respectively. Thus, not only there was **recency effects**, but the increases were simply overwhelmingly significant to be ignored. In fact, the outcry was so strong that the Singapore government decided to make the COE non-transferable. However, since then, COE prices had increased steadily over the months and years that the car buyers in Singapore have gradually grown to accept the high prices.

The JND concept is very useful to the marketeer in deciding price increases. If a marketeer wants to increase price, he should ensure that it is not significant so that the increase will not be noticeable to the consumers. Conversely, if he wants to reduce price, he must ensure that the discount is significant enough in order to attract the attention of the consumers. Of course, the extent of price increase or discount that would be deemed noticeable or not would depend on the product or service concerned. In the case of many consumer products such as shoes, clothings, and fashion items, the discounts would have to be very large for them to be noticeable. This is because the mark-ups for such products are very high. On the other hand, for many industrial or commercial products, a price increase of 3% to 5% may be deemed very significant. Similarly, for some high ticket consumer items like cars and houses, any price increase of 3% to 5% would also be considered as very significant.

The JND principle was aptly applied by the relevant authority in Singapore in deciding on taxi price increases after the bad experience in April 1985 — then, the significant increase of taxi fares caused the market to react very unfavourably. Since then, each round of taxi fare increase was kept below the JND level. As of October 1991, the taxi fares in Singapore were approximately the levels that the government had intended for them to be in April 1985. However, it took the authority more than five years to achieve its original objective. In adhering to the JND principle in implementing taxi fare increases, the commuters had learned to accept small price increases as inevitable to offset inflation and other cost increases incurred by taxi operators. By 1995, taxi fares in Singapore had further increased compared to those of 1991, and way above that what was intended to be achieved in 1985. This was accomplished despite increasing the supply of taxis on the roads.

Let's now look at JND and promotions through discounts. No consumer will be ecstatic with a discount of 10%. However, if the discount is 30% to 70% on a store-wide basis, the impact is likely to be tremendous. Many departmental stores are aware of this and have now cleverly applied the JND principle in their promotional strategies. Conversely, if a marketeer wants to reduce benefits to consumers, he must ensure that they are not noticeable by reducing them a little at a time. The impact will be further cushioned if the reduction takes place over a longer period of time. Consumers will hardly feel the pinch of the loss.

Based on the JND principle, it would be better to plan for small and predictable price increases rather than large and unpredictable ones. There are good reasons for this. By increasing prices in small quantities and more frequently, consumers would be conditioned to accept the need for price adjustments owing to inflation and other cost factors. The increase would also be perceived as fairer and easier to absorb into the operating expenses of the consumers. On the other hand, if price increases are sudden and in large quantums, consumers are likely be caught off-guard and thus react strongly. Big ticket items like cars and housing could find themselves priced out of the market if their prices are increased very substantially. This could then generate much consumer unhappiness. Many Asian cities are facing such situations today, largely due to the sudden asset inflation over the past few years.

10.3.2 Threshold Effects

Besides the principle of JND, the "threshold effects" is also relevant in pricing a product. By this, I mean the upper limit of any absolute price that a consumer is willing to pay for a product or service. In his mind, a consumer would have formulated what constitutes the "maximum" price for a product or service. This maximum price may take the form of a price range. For example, when going out for dinner with his family, the consumer would have a rough idea of what he is prepared to pay if his family were to dine at a hawker centre. Similarly, if he were to buy a pair of working shoes, a shirt or a pair of trousers, there is a limit to what he is prepared to fork out.

The threshold level is understandably affected by a consumer's budget and his level of income. It changes over time as his income increases. So what he considers to be expensive a few years ago may now appear cheap as his purchasing power increases. His idea for what constitutes a fair price may also be affected by the context of his purchase. Whatever it is, every consumer has a threshold price that he is prepared to pay. Beyond this threshold, he will either switch to another product or service or even boycott the purchase. At times, the extent of the boycott or switch can be quite significant and sudden. Take the case of taxi fare increase in Singapore on 1 April 1985. The fare increase not only violated the JND principle, but the total fare structure also hit the threshold level of what commuters were prepared to pay. The combined effects of these two factors caused the market to over-react to the new fare structure at that time. However, as a result of rising income over the last ten years (which inevitably raised the threshold level) and subsequent careful management of fare increases, commuters did not feel the effects in a significant way. Obviously the need to consider the "feelings" of the consumer cannot be ignored.

The threshold concept may be getting more relevant to Asian consumers. As a result of rapid economic growth in many Asian economies over the past ten to fifteen years, the prices of many consumer products have risen by leaps and bounds. Asset inflation, is especially a serious concern. Big ticket items like cars and properties are becoming extremely expensive (relative to the earning powers of consumers) and beyond the reach of many local consumers. In the case of properties, the high prices present another form of challenge to the local authorities in these Asian cities. More and more of these prime properties are snapped up by rich foreign buyers who push up the prices even higher. In fact, local consumers in Malaysia and China are beginning to blame the rich Hong Kong people, Taiwanese, and Singaporeans for their high property prices — a sign that should not be ignored by both marketeers and policy makers.

10.3.3 Perception of Gains and Losses

Consumers do not perceive the gain and loss of the same amount equally. Generally, they perceive that paying is psychologically more painful than foregoing the gain of the same amount. In other words, a consumer feels the pinch more if he has to pay, say S$10, for a product or service than if he has to forgo receiving the same benefit. This is because the consumer tends to value more highly the certainty of loss than the uncertainty of the gain.

This unequal perception of gains and losses has been cleverly exploited by companies in their marketing strategies. For instance, it is still a fairly wide and common practice amongst many small retailers in Asia to insist on charging 2% to 5% more on the prices of goods purchased should the consumer opt to pay by credit card. Very often with this practice, they succeed in making the consumer pay cash.

Compare this to the case of many supermarket retailers who generously use cut-out discount coupons (commonly advertised in newspapers and magazines) to entice shoppers to buy more products. The discounts are only valid if the consumer produces the cut-out coupon. Interestingly, the rate of redemption is typically not very high. This is because even if a consumer does not have the coupon, he is only forgoing a potential gain (which is psychologically less painful) than experiencing a loss.

The market is filled with examples of how consumers can fall "victim" to their own perception. **Product and service bundlings** are perhaps classic illustrations. Basically, a product or service bundle is one in which the total price is less than the sum of the individual items. Package tours, set lunches and dinners, personal (priority) banking services are examples of product or service bundles, whereby the price of each individual product or service item when totalled up, would exceed the price of the bundle. In the case of gift hampers, marketeers like Noel Hampers of Singapore even highlight the detailed breakdown of the price of each individual item in the hamper so as to bring home the message that the hamper is worth more than it costs.

The effects of a bundled price on consumers are very interesting. Take the case of a set lunch. Assuming you are planning to spend, say only S$15 on lunch in a restaurant. On arrival, you notice that there is a set lunch menu consisting of salad (your own choice), soup (two choices), main course (three choices), dessert (two choices), and coffee or tea. These items, as reflected in the menu, may cost S$5, S$4, S$12, S$4, S$3 respectively or a total price of S$28. However, when ordered as a set lunch, they would cost only S$18 altogether. How would you, as a consumer, react?

Many consumers, when confronted with such a situation would go for the set lunch. The logic for such a behaviour is not difficult to see. By having items priced individually, the restaurant operator has shifted the reference price of the consumer to the sum of the total price, which is S$28. Thus, S$18 becomes a very attractive offer for the set lunch. Such a creative pricing strategy has several interesting implications and results. First, the consumer is prompted to spend more than he plans to (S$18 as opposed to S$15). Second, the restaurant operator is able to sell more set lunches and hence achieve greater sales volume. This is where relevant costing becomes useful in deciding on the pricing strategy. Third, the consumer himself, may even be prepared to forgo consuming one or two items in the bundle (for example, forgoing coffee or tea) without feeling the pinch. In contrast, having to pay for the cup of coffee or tea, would be psychologically more painful. Finally, the consumer may even be prepared to pay for items in the bundle that he may not need! This is why, as in the set lunch example, he is prepared to forgo the consumption of one or two items in the bundle.

Product or service bundling has been exploited greatly by marketeers. Very often, it is used to make the product or service package appear more attractive than it actually is. A consumer may, in fact, forgo parts of the bundle without feeling the "pain" of doing so. For instance, after paying for a tour package, the consumer may not mind not visiting certain tour sites or attractions even though he has already paid for them. To him, the overall price is still cheap even if he doesn't consume all that is the package. In the same way, it is not uncommon to find passenger forgoing meals on board the plane, a subscriber of cable television not tuning in to every programme, a car owner not capitalizing on all the "free" maintenance services that come with purchase of the car, and so on.

As products get more sophisticated, they are sold more and more as bundles. Yet, after paying so much for the complete product bundle, many consumers do not fully use all the benefits or features offered with the bundle. It isn't surprising to find that the owner of a fully-loaded luxury car rarely uses the cruise control; that the full capabilities of a personal computer are hardly exploited; the various sophisticated features in a Canon EOS 1N camera has been put to use; and that the fanciful features of a home-video cum karaoke set hardly tried out. Yet, all these added features are paid for in the bundle. The interesting point to note is that the consumer does not perceive the non-usage of these features as losses (which would be painful) but rather as gains forgone.

Bundling is widely used by Japanese manufacturers of many products such as cars, consumer electronics, watches, appliances, amongst others. They bundle up all the conceivable product options of a product itself and price it very attractively. In fact, Japanese car makers have been using this approach very successfully in their market penetration of Europe and America since the late 1960s. Then, car makers in Europe and America tended to sell only the basic car with other options sold separately. The result was that these options could add up to 50% more to the price of the car! In contrast, Japanese cars were sold as a bundle, with all the options included as standard items. By pricing them attractively below the European and American cars, Japanese cars managed to gain very strong footholds in these markets, especially in America. Today, the Japanese strategy in product bundling has been copied not only by other car makers, but by many other product manufacturers as well.

10.3.4 Evaluation of Price Difference

A consumer, really, has great difficulty in judging a number on absolute terms. He evaluates price changes relative to the base price. When the base price is low, any price difference would appear greater than it really is. On the other hand, when the base price is high, any price change would be perceived as smaller than it actually is. To illustrate, the average consumer would have no difficulty in recognizing the difference in prices between a shirt that costs S$30 versus another shirt that costs S$40. This is because S$10 difference appears to be very large relative to the base price of S$30. However, many consumers would have difficulty seeing the magnitude of difference, say between a home video system that costs S$12,000 versus another one that costs S$11,000. In this instance, S$1,000 difference between the two systems is a fairly large sum of money. However, it would not be surprising to find many consumers willing to pay for the S$12,000 system as they perceive that paying S$1,000 more may not be too significant, especially if it is of a brand that he is more confident of.

This weakness in appreciating price changes in absolute terms has enabled many marketeers to sell a lot more items to the consumer than what he set out to purchase. This is because as the sum of expenditure gets bigger, the percentage of increase seems smaller, although in absolute terms, it can be fairly large. To some consumers, it may even cause them to develop the "penny-wise, pound-foolish" mentality in price bargaining. Thus, it would not be surprising to find a consumer bargaining aggressively for a discount of just a few hundred dollars when purchasing a car that costs S$100,000, and yet would not negotiate for an additional thousand dollars off when the car costs S$300,000!

Similarly, a consumer can be tempted to spend more than he needs when the original expenditure is large. Again, this is due to the fact that any increase from an already large sum appears to be small. For example, when one has already planned to spend S$300,000 on home renovation, it is very easy to be lured (by the contractors and designers) to spend an additional S$30,000 to "make the house look even better". Similarly, having spent, say, S$35,000 on a home video system, it is not surprising to find the same consumer parting with another S$5,000 on accessories. Even the shrewd retailer of luxury consumer products would know how to make the vulnerable consumer part with more cash when his initial purchase is large. For example, after convincing the consumer to spend S$1,100 on a pair of Scribe shoes from Bally, the retailer can easily tempt him to buy the appropriate set of shoe-trees, polish, and even socks.

As the Asian consumer becomes more affluent, he is likely to spend more, often unwisely and as a result of his own psychological weakness. As he moves from the stage of "needs" (which tend to be governed more by rational decisions) to that of "wants" (which tend to be governed more by emotions), his purchase decisions are likely to be affected more by the heart than the mind. This is where attempts must be made by the relevant authorities to educate the consumer. Indeed, consumer education is very lacking in Asia. Many Asian consumers have socially undesirable spending behaviour.

10.4 Cultural Influences

On 27 July 1994, a Hong Konger offered to sell a car licence plate, HK 1997 for HK$5 million or about S$990,000! Ten years earlier, the same owner had bought it for only HK$21,000. This may seem very ridiculous to the western consumers, but is perfectly understandable to many Asian Chinese. This is not an isolated incident. In 1993, an official car number plate "2" of the Hong Kong government was sold to a businessman for HK$9.5 million (or about S$1.98 million then). To the Cantonese-speaking Hong Kongers, "2" is a very auspicious number. It sounds like "easy" and hence, they believe, brings good luck and fortune. At the same time, the shape of "2" resembles a rooster. According to Chinese astrologers, the rooster symbolizes decisiveness, alertness, and adaptability. Thus, to the superstitious Hong Kong business community, it is a number that is worth a fortune! The interesting thing to note is that HK$9.5 million is not the highest price paid for a car number plate. On 19 March 1994, the car number plate "9" (which sounds like "forever" in Mandarin or "surely" in Cantonese) was bought at a record price of HK$13 million (S$2.7 million) by Hong Kong businessman Albert Yeung Sau-ching.

The crave, and hence the record prices paid, for auspicious numbers are not confined to car number plates. In the southern Chinese city of Shenzhen on 21 April 1994, a telephone number, "908-8888" was auctioned off for RMB655,000 or about S$120,000. The number sounds like "surely prosper forever" in Cantonese. Other high prices at the same auction included RMB39,800 (about S$7,300) for number "908-9168" and RMB67,000 (about S$12,275) for "908-8999." It is amazing that even businessmen in China are prepared to pay big bucks for sheer numbers! Apart from the cultural preference for auspicious numbers, there is one other main reason for the high prices paid. Chinese businessmen are generally very "face-conscious," and they would not want to be seen as losing out to their competitors in a social setting. This has fuelled the bidding process, with prices being pushed up very quickly to ridiculously high levels — all for the sake of gaining social recognition. It was certainly the case with Shenzhen's auction of telephone numbers.

This demand for auspicious telephone numbers are not confined to Cantonese-speaking businessmen. In Hong Kong, large and well established companies also vie for auspicious telephone numbers. These include Hong Kong Telecom (its telephone number is 888-2888), Jardine Fleming Securities (its telephone number: 843-8888), Vickers Ballas Securities (its telephone number is 878-8888), Cathay Pacific Airways (its telephone number is 747-1888) amongst others.

The same fixation for "lucky" numbers is also found in Singapore. Singapore Telecoms cleverly exploits it when it allows public bidding of telephone numbers which it calls "Golden Numbers." Similarly, the Singapore's Registry of Vehicles also allows public bidding of car numbers plate numbers with a minimum bid of S$1,000. Thus far, while the prices paid for auspicious numbers have not reached the levels in Hong Kong, they are nonetheless no petty sums.

The effects of culture on pricing are probably felt more among some races in Asia than in other parts of the world. The Chinese generally favour some numbers over others as they contain hidden meanings and implications. This has led to the use of even numbers like "2", "6", and "8" for the pricing of auspicious products and services like wedding gifts and dinners (price of a table), rental charges for bridal gowns, bridal cars and honeymoon tour packages. The pricing of cars, cellular phones, hi-fi systems, furniture, and many other high-ticket items tend to be of auspicious numbers. This is because the auspicious numbers tend to complement the relatively large sums of money spent on such items, especially when these numbers signify prosperity and good fortune. They form part of the product package.

On the other hand, with events of loss like funerals, the prices of goods and services related to them are normally stated in odd numbers. In fact, a superstitious Chinese family would often state the age of the deceased as an odd number. They believe that if an even number is used, the deceased may want another person to accompany him or her in death.

Then there are also unlucky numbers to be avoided. Generally, numbers ending with "4" are to be avoided because "4" sounds like "death" in Chinese. Interestingly, an auspicious number ending with "8", when preceded with the number "5", as in the case of "58" becomes a number to be avoided: "58" sounds like "will not prosper"! Thus, "5" as a preceding number must be avoided.

The impact of culture can perhaps be best illustrated in the pricing of residential properties in markets like Hong Kong and Singapore. Similar properties located on the same street can command different prices owing to the difference in house numbers. A house number like "12" (which sounds like "surely easy"), "18" (which sounds like "surely prosper"), or "26" (which sounds like "easy to do") would easily command a price premium over "14" (which sounds like "surely die"). In fact, a number like "28" (which sounds like "easily prosper") would fetch an even higher price. So prevalent is this fixation with auspicious numbers that even non-superstitious Chinese consumers like Christians and the other non-Chinese races in Hong Kong and Singapore (who belong to the minority of the population) are also influenced by it. The reason being that while they themselves do not have connotations with numbers, when they decide to sell their properties, the majority of buyers do bother about numbers!

The lesson about auspicious numbers for residential properties was something that many Australian, New Zealander, Canadian, and British developers failed to understand when they first tried to market their properties in the Asian market. Many of them failed to understand why the Asian ethnic Chinese paid so much attention to a house number when they should be concerned about other details! They were further puzzled as to why some land plots and houses were quickly snapped up when they were obviously in inferior locations. It took these westerners some time to figure out the intricacies. However, once they mastered the meanings of numbers, these western developers began to price their properties with auspicious numbers as well.

Actually, the cultural influence on numbers is not unique to Asians or the Chinese. The westerners have always frowned on the number "13" as it is considered an unlucky number (which interestingly, to the Cantonese Chinese, is not a bad number — it actually sounds like "surely multiply"). In the same way "666", the number of the Anti-Christ is to be eschewed in the west. So, idiosyncrasies where numbers are concerned are not confined to any one society, except that in Asia, they probably take on more prominence.

10.5 Price-Quality Relationship

When consumers are unable to assess the product or service or when the quality is based on very intangible attributes, marketeers are known to put a high premium on the product or service. You can see this with cosmetic products, designer clothings and jewellery. This has misled some practitioners to believe that by setting a high price, consumers would associate it with high quality. This is a fallacy. They do not. At times, it has also given rise to the issue of ethical pricing. Some businessmen in the newly emerging economies of China, Vietnam and India, are pricing products of inferior quality highly in the hope that they would conjure an image of high quality. Such practices will come to be exposed. They will not stand the test of time.

What is not a fallacy is that a high price is the **result** of high quality. Many established products that we know today like IBM computers, Mercedes and BMW cars, Mont Blanc pens, Rolex watches, and services like that of SIA command premiums because they have developed excellent and reliable quality over the years. The same is true of many Japanese products like cars, hi-fi systems, cameras, home appliances, and computers. These were only able to command higher prices from the late 1970s onwards after they had improved significantly in quality. When they first started in the 1950s and 1960s, Japanese products were priced very cheaply because they were of inferior quality compared to those made in the West. Today, some Japanese products such as Nikon cameras, Seiko lenses, Nakamichi sound systems, and Lexus cars are even enjoying premiums as a result of their superior quality that has been achieved over time. Similar products produced by Taiwan and South Korea, on the other hand, are priced much lower because they have yet to reach the level of quality of the Japanese.

But how much premium should an established product or service command? This question deserves close scrutiny. Consumers may not have the expertise to determine the size of the price premium for a higher quality product or service. Take the case of air ticket pricing. Everyone knows that the services provided in the business and first class cabins are definitely better than those in the economy section. However, whether the better services deserve the hefty premiums that are currently levied on prices of business and first class air tickets is an issue that few consumers can rationalize.

Similarly, many consumers know that Rolex watches, Mercedes cars, Bally's Scribe shoes, Mont Blanc pens, Steinway pianos, and Motorola handphones are products of excellent quality. So they are prepared to pay hefty premiums in order to own them. Herein lies very precious lessons for the manufacturer and/or marketeer. If he is able to pay close attention to improving the quality of his product, including building up the brand name, the long term financial payoffs are tremendous. When the quality and brand names of products become firmly established, they can become legendary. Such has been the path to success for well-established quality brands like Mercedes, Steinway, SIA, and Motorola.

10.6 Conclusion

Understanding how consumers view prices is never an easy subject of study. Without doubt, as the Asian economies get more developed and as they move more and more into consumer-driven societies, the consumer will be the focus of many marketing decisions. In particular, marketeers will learn to price based on the needs, wants, and expectations of the consumers. Thus, consumer research, and in particular studies that attempt to unravel the mindsets of the Asian consumer, are likely to become increasingly important. Hopefully, the experiences of the western world in the 1970s and 1980s will provide useful insights for the Asian marketing scholars and practitioners.

11
Distribution: Moving Towards Total Logistics Management

11.1 Introduction

Among the four P's of the marketing mix, distribution is probably the least understood. Often, it is the other three Ps — product, pricing, and promotion — that get greater attention. This is reflected in the fact that distribution is usually given little attention by top management. Yet, it is ironical that the history of marketing actually began with physical distribution. However, over the past ten years, the distribution function has undergone tremendous transformation, and it is unlikely that it will take on a secondary role again. In Asia, there are many factors which account for the ever increasing emphasis on distribution.

11.2 The Distribution Function has Arrived

With the increased volume of trade in the Asian region, distribution becomes critical in ensuring the timely arrival and departure of the products. It is therefore not surprising to find that at the macro level, many Asian economies are stepping up the development of their air and sea ports. China, for example, has enlarged and built new air and sea ports in all their major cities, including Shanghai, Beijing, Shenzen, and Pudong. Taiwan has ambitious plans to develop Kaoshiong into a major sea port. Thailand has decided to expand its Laem Chabang port so that by 1997, its container capacity will increase by four times its capacity in 1994. Hong Kong, owing to its proximity to China, has always been an important transhipment centre. In fact, it has overtaken Singapore as the largest container port in the world by 1995. The Malaysian government has, in late 1995, announced strong measures to develop its Senai airport in Johore and its port at Klang so as to handle more air and sea cargo, as well as to reduce their reliance on Singapore's facilities.

It is significant to note that from Singapore to China, many Asian economies are overhauling and expanding their sea ports to meet the increasing demand for international shipping lines. These Asian economies are increasing the capacities and improving the facilities of their ports and increasing the types of services offered. With increased trade and business among these Asian economies and with the rest of the world, money is not made from the ports alone. Rather, there is whole array of related businesses to be made in warehousing, financial services, telecommunications, and so on.

Among the top ten container ports in the world in 1995, six are located in Asia. They are Hong Kong (the first), Singapore (the second), Kaoshiung, Taiwan (the third), Pusan, South Korea (the fifth), Kobe, Japan (the sixth), Yokohama, Japan (the tenth). With the heavy investments in port expansion, it is likely that more Asian ports will make it to the top ten list within the next five to ten years.

Besides the growth in sea transportation, air shipment has also grown tremendously in Asia. Air cargo and freight is such a very fast growing industry that many Asian airlines are acquiring planes specifically to perform this function. All these trends are posing new challenges to the respective local governments, especially in the area of infrastructural development. Asia is expected to invest up to US$150 billion on new and/or upgraded airports by the year 2000. Many airports in Asia have ambitious plans to become regional air hubs for passengers and air cargo. Besides developments at the macro level, there are several factors that account for the arrrival of the distribution function in Asia.

11.2.1 Distribution as a Viable Business by Itself

With economic growth, competition among companies operating in Asia has become more intense and rife, especially with the arrival of increasing number of foreign firms. In particular, marketeers have found that competitive edges need to be established and exploited in all the four Ps of the marketing mix. As such, distribution is no longer viewed as the mere physical movement of the product. Just like using the product concept, marketeers find that it is possible to extend the distribution function beyond its "core" service to include the tangible and "augmented" dimensions. In other words, many other value-added activities can be created beyond the physical movement of the product alone. Take the example of YCH Group in Singapore (formerly known as Yap Chwee Hock Transport Company). When it first started in 1955, it was a local transport company which rented out lorries for the transportation of goods, including for house moving. By 1995, forty years later, the YCH Group has emerged as a total logistics company that provides a full range of services to its clients. These services include door-to-door shipment using all modes of transportation, documentation and customs clearance, warehousing, packaging, re-routing, and so on.

The YCH Group is not alone in moving beyond their core service. DHL, a courier company that is well-known in Asia, also provides a full range of services on a door-to-door basis. What is more interesting is that DHL no longer confines its delivery service to documents alone. Today, it can even deliver blood samples, antiques and other delicate items where speed, safety, and confidentiality are important considerations. Other courier companies like Federal Express, TNT and UPS are doing likewise.

Even at the consumer level, distribution has taken new dimensions. Take the case of house-moving services in Singapore. In the past, the consumer would probably approach a transport company which would simply provide a lorry with some rough and tough looking workers. Today, the innovative house-moving company has discovered that by providing additional services (like packing and unpacking), materials (such as styrofoam, cardboards, cartons and papers) for wrapping breakable items, well-equipped container-trailer (to protect the items from the elements), and guarantee against breakages and damages during moving, it can easily raise the price of its services. More importantly, by providing these "augmented" services, it can also develop unique competitive advantages.

The creation of value-added activities really isn't a modern phenomenon of the distribution function. Middlemen like agents, wholesalers and retailers and salesmen have traditionally been important components of any distribution channel system. They have played various roles ranging from holding stock to bulk breaking, risk-taking, financing, extension of consumer credit, and even advertising. Indeed, their many different functions have helped to reduce the total marketing costs of bringing the product to the consumer. What is new is that distribution now encompasses a whole spectrum of activities and value-added services that it has become a viable and distinctive business on its own. Many conventional distribution companies like YCH and Freight Links now position themselves as **total logistics business**.

11.2.2 High Visibility of Some "Distribution" Companies

Distribution has been elevated to a higher status with the emergence of some high profile businesses which thrive on providing the core functions of delivery and transportation. Examples of such businesses include the airline and courier industries. In the case of the airline industry, it only grew rapidly after World War II. However, over the past fifty years, the growth in air transportation has been so phenomenal that many airlines now contribute significantly to their respective economies as well as to world trade and business.

Indeed, the airline business has extended beyond being an important means for the speedy movement of passengers across vast distances in a safe, reliable and comfortable manner. Over the years, the industry has moved beyond competing on the core service of providing air transport. Rather, many airlines now boast of their superb inflight service, flexible schedule, convenient and extensive flight connections, amongst others.

The high profile nature of the airline business has even prompted many countries to use their national airlines for strategic reasons, that is to retain control of the airlines and use them to advance the national interests. In fact, the success of an airline can even become a source of national pride in that it effectively can become a "flying ambassador" to project the kind of service that the country is capable of providing. Allow me to cite SIA again. SIA has not only brought much pride and visibility to Singapore, but the airline also contributes significantly to its gross national product and the businesses of other countries. In mid-November 1995, SIA announced a record US$12.7 billion deal for acquiring 77 Boeing 777 jets. The size of the order made world news and created much impact on the aviation world in that it even affected the relative market shares and fortunes of the two arch rivals in aircraft manufacturing — Boeing and Airbus. The order lifted the confidence of Boeing in that SIA is a major and leading international airline and its order helped to boost future sales of Boeing aircrafts to other airlines. On the other hand, Airbus suffered a severe setback as the loss could affect their bid for the businesses of other airlines.

On the cargo side, airlines have played significant roles in ensuring the safe and timely delivery of high ticket perishable items. For example, Sri Lankan crabs, Shanghai hairy crabs, New Zealand vegetables (like lettuces) and fruits (like kiwi and strawberries),

Australian beef, Norwegian salmon, and so on are airflown regularly into Singapore and other Asian cities.

The courier industry is another interesting business that only mushroomed over the last two decades. Its phenomenal growth has brought much attention to the role of distribution in the marketing process. Owing to the need for speed, convenience, reliablity, and personalized service, distribution now has its unique niche in the business world. Companies like Federal Express, DHL and UPS are now synonymous with quality service in the distribution of corporate and personal documents and parcels.

11.2.3 Emergence of Countertrade

Another interesting development that brings back the importance of the distribution function, and in particular, the role of the middleman, has to be the emergence of countertrade. Many countries in the developing world have resorted to countertrade as a way to arrest their trade disparity and to overcome shortages of hard currencies to pay for their imports. In such a trading arrangement, the seller is obligated to accept payment in the form of other products from the buying country that is equivalent to the value of the goods sold. However, the seller may not need the goods that have been exchanged nor have the expertise to dispose of the goods. As such, he has to rely on countertrade agencies who are actually sophisticated middlemen who specialize in bulk buying and selling of products at the international level.

Having acquired the goods, these countertrade agencies are then able to break up the bulk and then re-distribute the goods to their final destinations, earning a commission in the process. Here, it is important to point out that countertrade is a fast growing means of world trade among many countries today, especially between the developed and the less developed countries. Many countries in Asia are still developing and have to rely on the developed countries for machinery, production systems, and technology. Meanwhile, they simply do not have sufficient foreign exchange to pay for such capital goods. Countertrade provides a viable alternative for them to pay for the much needed capital goods to support their economic growth. Indeed, many government agencies in Asia like India, Indonesia, Vietnam, Myanmar, and so on rely on countertrade as a means of trading with the developed world.

11.2.4 New Shopping Preferences of Consumers

It is significant to note that in recent years, more and more companies are beginning to realize the importance of the distribution function even at the consumer's level. For example, retailing in many Asian cities has undergone drastic transformation. In almost every major city in Asia, whether it is Bangkok, Kuala Lumpur, Jakarta, Beijing, Shanghai, Seoul, Taipei, New Delhi, Hong Kong and Singapore, new and larger departmental stores are emerging rapidly. In particular, the big and established Japanese departmental chains like Takashimaya, Tokyu, and Seiyu have certainly made their entrances felt. Their arrivals signal the importance and confidence that these giant retail stores place on the future of the purchasing power of the Asian consumers.

Besides departmental stores, supermarkets and chain stores (including franchises) are also appearing very quickly all over Asia. They are replacing the old and mouldy corner shops. There are reasons for their success. For example, operators like NTUC FairPrice (a Singapore-based company) and 7-Eleven are able to enjoy economies of scale through large scale purchasing. As a result, they are able to pass on the savings to the consumers in the form of lower prices. At the same time, their greater financial strengths and stronger business contacts also allow them to constantly bring in new and better products, introduce improved services, and offer more efficient management (such as through computerized stock-taking and ordering, use of computerized accounting and financial systems, amongst others). Besides their speedier turnover of products within each store, they are also able to operate with fewer workers, resulting in lower operating costs. These supermarkets and chain stores also provide very modern, clean and pleasant shopping environment. They are all well-lit and air-conditioned, with well-planned layout that are all aimed at providing an enjoyable shopping experience. All these factors account for the higher customer traffic in the stores!

The winning edge of these large supermarkets and chain stores have not gone unnoticed by local businessmen and their governments. For example, in Singapore, Econ minimart have basically adopted and adapted the operating systems of these large chains. At the same time, the Singapore government is strongly promoting the establishment local chain stores through franchising as a means to counter competition from the retail giants from overseas, and to increase productivity through reduction of reliance on labour and increase in automation.

Besides Singapore, the local retail outlets in other Asian economies like Hong Kong, South Korea, Malaysia, and Taiwan are facing similar challenges from overseas competition. Even China, the last largest market for consumer products, encountered its own retail revolution with the arrival of the western fast food chains like McDonald's, Kentucky Fried Chicken and Pizza Hut. The Chinese authorities are now encouraging their own local businesses to set up chain stores to counter the foreign threats. The well-known operator of Peking-Duck heeded their advice and has since expanded its outlets.

With their physical increasing affluence, the Asian consumers are likely to exert greater demand on the aspects of shopping. In other words, they will want better shopping facilities and support services. This will put pressure on local businesses to upgrade their premises. At the same time, new and better shopping centres, locations and retail outlets will continue to appear in greater numbers especially in the larger Asian cities. I believe the retail revolution in Asia will continue for at least the next twenty years.

11.2.5 Advent of Technology

The impact of technology on the distribution function has been felt in many areas. To begin with, warehousing has benefitted tremendously through computerization and automation. Today, it is possible to stack and store goods literally from floor to ceiling with mininal clearance space between columns of goods. Yet, it is so easy to move them efficiently at the touch of a button. Indeed, with technology, automated warehouses can now optimize the use of space and labour and help manufacturers and marketeers move their goods efficiently. Even large retail giants like Proctor & Gamble has found that it is cheaper and more efficient to farm out its distribution function to professional warehouses.

At the retail level, an innovative distributor of liquified petroleum gas (LPG) in Singapore has integrated various communication media to provide an efficient delivery system to the consumers. The system works as follows. A consumer phones a retail outlet to place an order for a cylinder of LPG gas. The telephone message is automatically fed into a central computer which in turn transmits the order through a fax machine that is installed in a van or a truck that is on its delivery route. The driver who doubles up as a delivery man reads the transmitted faxed order and proceeds to fill that order. The result is higher productivity, more sales and greater profits!

Pizza operators like Pizza Hut use a similar approach. When a customer places an order through the telephone, Pizza Hut's computerized order system not only verifies the order, but is able to retrieve information on the client's previous purchases that depict his preferences! In addition, the system also estimates the delivery time needed for the pizza to arrive at the doorstep of the customer.

Perhaps the impact of technology on the distribution function has been the greatest in the logistics industry. Other than automated warehouses that use state-of-the-art robotics for packing, storage, and delivery of goods, the industry is now characterized by sophisticated application of information techology to manage the whole supply chain on a door-to-door basis. In addition, fully refrigerated containers are now available to ensure that even perishable products can arrive fresh for consumption.

So, what is becoming increasingly evident to many companies is that it is not just being able to manufacture a high quality product that's important. What is more important is that it must be able to bring these products to the customers, preferably right up to their doorsteps. At the same time, the products must arrive in the best condition, at the shortest time possible, and at the lowest cost possible. With technology, distribution is no longer confined to the physical movement of products, but to the management of the whole supply chain through the application of efficient information support systems.

11.3 Developing Effective Distribution Strategies

The secondary role that distribution was relegated to in the past has caused a lot of misunderstanding about its true function. This has hampered the development of effective distribution strategies. It is therefore necessary to address these false conceptions in order that the marketeer can have a different perspective about what distribution can achieve as part of the company's overall marketing strategy. Distribution truly has been the least exploited of the four Ps of marketing. Much can be gained by having a good understanding of what distribution can accomplish.

11.3.1 Product Characteristics and the Distribution Structure

It is commonly believed that if the product is small and cheap, then a long channel system should be used. By this, I mean the use of many channel members like agents, wholesalers, and retailers in a some hierarchical manner. In this system, the product therefore reaches the final consumer in an indirect and convoluted way. On the other hand, if the product is large, expensive and bulky, then a short channel system consisting of as few members as possible, is advocated. In this instance, it is assumed that it is better to reach the consumer in a direct and quick way.

What is important in distribution is to focus on the **consumer** in the design of the distribution system. This is because the consumer is dynamic or constantly changing, while the product tends to be relatively static and predictable. Let me illustrate with an example in the white bread business in Singapore. When Gardenia Bread first entered the Singapore market in the mid-1980s, it made a detailed study of the consumers before deciding how to distribute its bread to the consumers. It found, amongst other things, that the Singaporean consumers had arrived. Besides being willing to pay a premium for a high quality branded white bread, their purchasing behaviour were dictated by one key factor — convenience. As a result, Gardenia decided to penetrate the market through an extensive distribution system that covered every conceivable retail outlet, including those in the wet markets and the housing estates. This it did while charging a relatively higher price for its bread than the local bakery shops in the housing estates. The result was that it took the market by storm and within a few years, captured more than 50% of the white bread market in Singapore.

Interestingly, there was another brand of white bread, Sunshine, that was already in the market years before Gardenia. It had all the attributes of Gardenia: a good brand, prescribed due date to indicate freshness, information on the nutrients in the bread, so on. However, the problem with Sunshine was that its distributor focused on the product. It was then rather expensive and targetted largely at the expatriate community which enjoyed much higher incomes than the locals in the 1960s and 1970s. As a result, Sunshine was distributed exclusively through "upmarket" supermarkets like Cold Storage, FitzPatricks (now defunct), and Yaohan. Let's take a closer look at the approaches of the two bread companies and their respective rewards.

As Singapore consumers became more affluent in the 1980s, the previously expensive bread had become cheap to them. To them, paying a premium for good quality bread was no longer a problem.

Unfortunately, by designing its distribution around the product, the manufacturer of Sunshine bread failed to see the emerging opportunities that were appearing in the market. As mentioned earlier, the consumers were fast changing (dynamic), while the bread remained unchanged over the years (static)! The success of **Gardenia** in changing the distribution system by focusing on the changing consumer taught Sunshine a very useful and costly lesson. Today, wherever Gardenia bread is displayed, one can easily find Sunshine as well.

The lessons learned from the distribution of white bread should not be ignored by other distributors of products. What is important is to constantly review the demands of a changing market and its consumers. I believe that a revamp of the distribution methods of many products in Asia is long overdue. For example, paints are still being distributed through the corner hardware shops or paint shops which gives absolutely no advice on the use of the paints. Yet the new entrants into the home improvement and decoration market for products such as wall papers and venetian blinds have been able to reach out to their consumers through well-layout and appealing stores. Besides providing excellent displays of their products, they are able to advise and provide related services — aspects that are becoming increasingly important to the affluent Asian consumers. It is perhaps timely for distributors of paints to review their strategies before being threatened by their direct and indirect competitors.

11.3.2 Constraints of Physical Outlets

In the past, marketeers used to have the notion that distribution is constrained by the number of physical outlets. This belief was prevalent in the retailing and furniture businesses. A furniture retailer would therefore operate on the assumption that if he could not have more showrooms, he would not be able to sell more furniture. Car dealers operated on the same assumption that without showrooms, they could not sell cars. However, with innovative marketing approaches, this constraint no longer holds true. In Singapore and other larger cities in the Asia-Pacific region, exhibition organizers are now able to assemble numerous furniture dealers under one roof to display their great variety of products on a fairly regular basis. Often, the participating dealers even come from overseas.

The success of exhibitions in luring large crowds to the fairs are not confined to the furniture business. Today, exhibitions are used very effectively as marketing tools for consumer products such as hi-fi systems, electronic goods, books, computers, and household appliances; for luxury items like boats and aircrafts; for collectibles like antiques, watches, clocks, jewellery, and paintings; for specialized products like medical and military equipment; for industrial machineries; for home renovations, improvements, and garden equipments; for things relating to hobbies like ornamental fishes, flowers (orchids), stamps, coins and phone cards; for sale of overseas properties, golf clubs, and resorts; and even for services like education and travel services.

In sum, trade exhibitions have become new and effective distribution channels for reaching out to the Asian consumers. There are at least three reasons for their success. First, in gathering a large number of sellers from the same trade under one roof, the exhibition organizer is able to generate the "critical mass" effect — a powerful promotional pull factor in luring more potential customers. With so many exhibitors openly displaying their products under one roof, the potential buyer saves a lot of time in comparing products and prices. As such, he is likely to make a better and more satisfying decision in the process. Also, as the exhibition itself is very focused on the type of products or services on display, the crowd it draws are those who have an interest in the product. They are therefore potential customers. The marketing job is therefore made much easier; the marketeer needs only to focus on converting the prospect into a sale. Finally, with trade exhibitions, the market for the participating exhibitor is no longer confined to one location or the local market. His participation in various international exhibitions makes his market an international one.

In the area of services, the advent of the auto-teller machines (ATMs) has seriously challenged the need for physical branches in order to carry out basic banking services. Technology has also made home-banking a reality. Today, one can easily check the details of one's account by using the telephone. In some instances, bank loans can even be processed and approved through the telephone. Citibank has pioneered such a scheme in many Asian cities. Indeed, more and more banking transactions can now be done without the customer even having to step into a bank. In Singapore, ATMs are now used by customers to apply for shares in initial public offerings, to bid for certificates of entitlement (COEs) for purchase of cars and motorcycles, and even to purchase bank drafts. These are technological advances that transcend spatial and temporal constraints — you can now conduct selective banking services 24 hours a day, and even at faraway places!

Another development that has occurred in recent years that has eliminated the need to rely on physical outlets to increase distribution coverage is that of **direct marketing**. Today, direct marketing has made significant impact on the markets of Asia. By combining the strong promotional tools of television advertising and exploiting the increasingly efficient mail and courier systems, these innovative marketeers have extended their products beyond selling magazines, books and coins. They now cover a wide spectrum of household products, appliances, tools, and even clothing. Through attractively printed catalogues, and adopting a return policy with money-back guarantee, direct marketing has enabled some innovative marketeers from the United States and Europe to market their products to consumers in Asia. With technology ever advancing, direct marketing in the form of electronic shopping may soon become a reality in many cities of Asia as well.

11.3.3 Manufacturer's Influence on the Distribution Structure

A common misconception about distribution is that in most instances, the manufacturer has full control over the type of distribution structure he would like to use. Unfortunately, the fact is that the manufacturer may not be able to dictate how his product should be distributed. How the distribution system will be developed will depend on the channel member who has the most power. That member is commonly known as the channel captain.

Take the case of NTUC FairPrice supermarket in Singapore. Over the years, it has built up such a tremendous reputation in the grocery retail business that it has become a strong "captain" in the whole distribution system for groceries in Singapore. Moreover, owing to its great many widespread distribution outlets that are located all over Singapore, including in high density population areas, it has developed extensive market coverage as well as enormous economies of scale in its operations. In a nutshell, it has become a very effective and cost efficient channel system for any manufacturer or supplier. Thus, most manufacturers or suppliers of even branded products find themselves in weak bargaining positions as they need the NTUC FairPrice supermarket chain more than it needs them!

In so far as the manufacturer does not own the outlet, he loses much of the control. Often, it depends on the market structure. For example, in the less developed economies of Asia such as India, the

Philippines, Indonesia, Vietnam and Myanmar, cigarettes are still sold by the stick, and not by the pack. They have to be available at every convenient location — roadside stalls, coffee shops, hawkers' stalls, road junctions, and so on — thus requiring an extensive distribution network with multiple layers of channel members from agent right down to the final retailer.

In many Asian economies, it is not so easy for the manufacturer to dictate the distribution structure. Often, the distribution network will evolve in a "cobweb-like" manner with many tiers of dealers and retailers, many of whom may not have been authorized by the manufacturer. At other times, the distribution systems may be dictated by the respective national policies, social practices, and cultural peculiarities. For example, while retail pharmacies have emerged in some Asian cities, doctors are the key persons responsible for the prescription of drugs. In economies like Singapore and Malaysia, doctors also sell drugs directly to their patients. Thus, salesmen are still needed to market directly to the doctors as they are the ones to decide on what type of drugs their patients should take.

11.3.4 Conflicts Among Channel Members

Some marketeers are very concerned that there should not be any conflict among the channel members. Such a line of thought is fallacious; conflicts are often the reason for efficiency and competence. To begin with, anytime a company adopts a multiple channel system, that is, it has different types of channel members performing similar functions, with incentives based on quotas, conflicts are rather inevitable.

Conflicts are also inevitable when each channel member wants to maximize profits and maintain a high level of customer service. Afterall, these two objectives are conflicting, in that the attainment of one objective would compromise the achievement of the other. To maximize customer service, the marketeer has to carry a high level of inventory. This inevitably would push up costs, and hence reduce profits! Any shrewd retailer would conclude that it is not easy to achieve both objectives simultaneously unless he can push the inventory-carrying function to the wholesaler, and demand that the latter respond to his requests for stock instantaneously. On the part of the wholesaler, to maximize his profits, he should push inventory upwards to the manufacturer or downwards to the retailer! If pushing upwards to the manufacturer is not possible, conflicts between the wholesaler and retailer become unavoidable when both channel members strive to be efficient and profitable.

Of course, when it comes to the manufacturer, he has to push the inventory downwards to the wholesaler in order to maximize profits. There is no other way unless he is prepared to compromise his objective of profit maximization. In reality, conflicts among channel members are not necessarily a bad thing. Rather, conflicts show that there are vested interests by the parties concerned and reflect their quest for efficiency and effectiveness. In contrast, when there are no conflicts, the system may be inefficient, or worse still, dead! For example, the agents may have lost interest in the marketeer (manufacturer) and have decided not to distribute his products.

The idea of managing conflicts is not different from that of managing customers' complaints. When customers complain, the marketeer can be sure that there is something wrong with his product or marketing approach. However, when customers do not complain, it does not mean that the marketeer has done well. It could well be that the customers have given up hope on the marketeer, and have therefore boycotted the product!

11.3.5 Profitability and Efficiency

Using profitability as a yardstick to measure the efficiency of a distribution system is a tricky thing to do. Profits may be owing to market distortions or monopolistic situations created by the holding of patents or exclusive rights. At other times, the product may be enjoying temporary market advantage owing to its quality or other factors. Take for example, Honda, especially the Accord model, which was a car in strong demand in Singapore during the early 1980s. Its immense success allowed the distributor to enjoy good profits. However, many car buyers of Honda Accord would agree that the high demand for the car was caused more by the "push" factor created by a very good product than the "pull" effect created by the distributor. Some buyers would even argue that the services provided by the distributor at that time were far from satisfactory.

Similarly, Mercedes cars are selling very well in many Asian markets largely because of the strong brand name and high social prestige associated with the brand. While the local distributors may have put in some efforts, their contributions cannot be considered as significant. As it currently stands, the car sells itself in many Asian markets. It is a car that symbolizes social arrival and status. But, such a situation cannot be expected to last forever.

Besides profitability, what is more important is to focus on **channel productivity**. High productivity will always lead to efficiency, and ultimately to profits. With high productivity, profits become more sustainable. High profits, by themselves, do not necessarily mean that there is high efficiency or high productivity in the system.

Here, it is important to point out that many government organizations or government-linked companies in Asia are profitable but inefficient, largely due to their monopolistic positions. For them, the easiest way to make money is to adopt the "cost-plus" method in pricing. It is precisely to increase efficiency and productivity that many governments in Asia have decided to embark on massive privatization of their companies, including distribution services like airlines, shipping companies, telecommunications, electricity, and postal services.

11.3.6 Roles of Warehousing

I find it interesting that many managers tend to view the primary role of a warehouse as that of storage. I find this a backward way of thinking which is harmful to the overall productivity of the distribution system. I argue that the primary role of a warehouse should be to facilitate the movement or sale of products. And the ways in which warehousing roles are viewed determine how managers behave.

The reason for the existence of a warehouse is that the marketeer cannot find a buyer immediately. At the same time, it does not make good business sense to look for a buyer first, then source for the product — the opportunity cost would be very high. So, in order not to lose the sale, a warehouse is used to store the product so as to support the marketing of the product. However, if a manager views a warehouse only as a means for storage, he would feel less urgency when he cannot sell all his products because there is always a warehouse for him to store the goods. He might find ways to fill up a half-empty warehouse. And when he runs out of warehouse space, well, he would ask for more warehouse space — either by leasing or building! Worst of all, he may get worried when his warehouse is not full! This is because to him, the warehouse has to be full — the underlying fallacy of storage.

The irony is that storage is not free. Inventory costs money to buy and store, and they tie up much needed capital that could be gainfully used elsewhere to earn higher returns. In addition, some type of inventories depreciate over time, and can even be obsolete, like the case of fashion wear and high-technology products. Thus, there are risks associated with tying up unnecessary capital in inventories.

On the other hand, a manager who operates on the concept of facilitation is likely to be very delighted to note that his warehouse is half-empty. What's even better is that he would view himself as highly productive if he can operate with minimal reliance on his warehouse. To achieve this, he constantly has to be proactive, and look for customers to buy up all his stock. In this way, he will achieve higher inventory turnover and avoid tying up capital on unsold products. This is the approach underlying the "just-in-time" system that is so well practised by Japanese companies.

To Japanese companies, it is more important to manage the whole supply chain efficiently so as not to tie up inventory. Warehousing, afterall, is tantamount to a "just-in-case" system. The realization of not tying up capital in warehousing has prompted marketing companies like Proctor & Gamble to farm out its distribution function to professional logistics companies. This is because when one focuses on product movement instead of storage, other viable alternatives of facilitating movement may become evident. The approach of dispensing with warehouses taken by large marketing firms like Proctor & Gamble is likely to be followed by other companies, especially when logistics companies become more and more efficient in their management of the whole supply chain.

11.3.7 Buying from Selling to Versus Marketing Through

Traditionally, many distributors in Asia tend to operate on the concept of buying from any manufacturer that gives them the best deal and then selling to the retailer that gives them the best offer. This approach is not surprising considering the fact that many of these distributors operated historically as middlemen or brokers with the faintest idea of the need to add or create value to the distribution chain. This has resulted in very ill-focused businesses; many of them (especially the smaller distributors) would trade in all kinds of products. While this could be viewed as a very flexible way of doing business, it does little to build up loyalty among members of the channel system. In fact, buying from or selling to is a myopic view of doing business as it tends to view each transaction on an ad hoc basis.

In today's highly competitive environment, what is needed more is to learn to market through the channel members, including the ultimate consumers. To apply this "through" concept, the marketeer must make conscious efforts to cultivate strong relationships with both the consumers and the distributors. The objective is to cultivate loyalty among channel members and customers.

The importance of marketing through channel members is that they are the ones who can often determine whether to promote or not to promote the product to the consumers. The power of the sales-person at the point-of-sale cannot be ignored. For example, it is not uncommon for someone who walks into a retail shop wanting to buy one particular brand of product, to end up buying a different brand, because of the influence of the salesperson. The question is: why does that salesperson advocate or recommend a different brand to the consumer? Among other reasons, one strong motivation is cer-tain: the marketeer of that brand that the salesperson recommends must have done a better job of relationship building with the dealer.

The amazing fact about mastering the "through" concept is that the marketeer ends up using less effort and resources to distribute his products once he has established a strong relationship with his channel members. This is because the satisfied channel members and customers will be helping the marketeer to promote the prod-uct! Good sales pitches definitely can bring in more customers. In a way, by learning to "distribute through", the marketeer is leveraging on the resources, energies and expertise of the whole supply chain, right down to the final consumer. Tremendous synergy is generated in the process.

The need to build strong business partnership is made very evi-dent by well established companies like Hewlett Packard, IBM, American Express, NEC and Motorola. These companies organize regular activities for their dealers business partners, that include fully paid working vacations. In the case of Xian Janssen, one of the larg-est joint-venture companies in China, the management developed very creative and innovative ways to reinforce its relationships with various channel members in their supply chain. For example, it cre-ated incentive schemes to motivate dealers and distributors to meet and exceed their quotas. These schemes involve bringing them for very high quality training programmes overseas that include a vaca-tion component — all fully paid for! In addition, the company also sponsors influential decision-makers on training programmes as well. Their efforts in relationship building paid off handsomely.

As of 1994/95, Xian Janssen has become one of the most profitable joint-venture companies in China. In fact, it exceeded it sales forecast by over 50% in 1995!

11.3.8 Location in Relation to Competitors

One of the misguided approaches taken by some marketeers is to locate their distribution outlets away from their competitors. The reasons for doing so include avoiding price and product comparisons so that their products will command the undivided attention of the consumers. This seemingly logical strategy is, in fact, short-sighted. This is because when a firm is sited alone by itself, the marketeer must perform at least three functions. It has to attract potential customers, identify them (since not every one who passes by is a potential customer), and then convert the prospects into sales. The overall cost to perform these three functions is high. Many small and medium-sized companies will find it impossible to do all these three things effectively and efficiently.

For many consumer products, it is often better, if not necessary, for the distributor to locate his outlet near those of his competitors. There are good reasons for doing so. When a group of competitive firms are located together, it has that "critical mass" effect that provides consumers with a wide variety of choices. The net result is that not only are they attracted to the cluster of outlets, but those who show up are principally those customers who have a strong interest in buying the product. Thus, the marketeer's job is reduced to only that of sales conversion.

The critical mass effect is clearly acknowledged by the management of large shopping centres. Without doubt, these shopping centres strive not only to be bigger and with a greater variety of stores, but they would consciously seek out well-established departmental stores and supermarkets as anchor tenants. This is because these anchor tenants have huge advertising budgets, and are able to pull in large number of shoppers on their own. The smaller stores can piggyback on their power to pull in the crowds.

In Singapore, this critical mass effect is clearly demonstrated when competitive firms choose to locate in one shopping area. For example, Funan Centre is largely known for computer hardware and software; Sim Lim Towers is known for consumer electronics; and Leng Kee Road is known for cars and motor servicing. In Hong Kong, there are also centres that cluster boutiques, textile shops, and even food outlets. It even has streets that sell only snakes and birds! Such clustering of shops selling similar goods are also observed in other Asian cities like Jakarta, Kuala Lumpur, Bangkok, Beijing, Taipei, Kaoshiung, Seoul, Tokyo, Osaka, and so on.

11.4 Conclusion

A marketeer must develop a broader perspective of the distribution function. He should not be circumscribed by conventional practices. Afterall, in today's highly competitive and technological environment, nothing should be viewed as cast in stone and distribution systems are no exception.

The management of a company's channel system can no longer remain the sole responsibility of the distribution manager. Functional responsibility is no longer enough. It now requires more attention and involvement on the part of top management. In particular, with advances in the areas of information technology, the distribution function can become a more strategic planning variable among the marketing four P's. In addition, it has to be integrated more into the marketing planning process. What is needed, however, is the freeing of the mindsets of the marketing manager and his corporate top management — to accept that the distribution function can now be managed in an innovative and creative way to add value and generate competitive advantages for the company.

12

Advertising and Promotion: Developing the Right Combinations

12.1 Introduction

Among the four Ps of marketing, advertising and promotion have got to be the most exciting and glamorous activities. With the advent of cable television and satellite broadcasting, and the progress in computer technology (especially in the form of the Internet and World Wide Web), advertising and promotion is likely to enter into another challenging era. What's more, as Asia continues to flourish, media advertising will increase by leaps and bounds. As it is, China is experiencing an astronomical increase in television ownership. As of 1995, it has one television set per 48 people, and the ratio is increasing very quickly. Even at its current ratio of 1:48, it is already way above the world average of 1:66. But what's significant is that many Asian economies are already enjoying television ownership ratios that are comparable to the developed economies. For example, the United States has a television-to-people ratio of 1:1.2 while Japan has a ratio of 1:1.6. The Asian NIEs like Singapore (1:2.7), Hong Kong (1:3.9), and South Korea (1:4.9) enjoy comparable ratios.

Besides the increase in television ownership, the liberalization of their respective economies have also allowed the mushrooming of many other forms of media. In particular, new and foreign media-related agencies have made significant inroads into Asia over the last five years. Newspapers, magazines, radio stations are all growing at phenomenal rates. It is inevitable that media advertising in Asia will be in for the golden years for at least the next twenty years.

12.2 Which Media to Use

To begin with, there are many means of promotion that the marketeer can adopt. Some of these main forms would include advertising, direct sale, public relations, sales, and word-of-mouth publicity. Of these, it is important to point out that word-of mouth publicity cannot be bought directly, while public relations is more of an indirect way of promotion. The use of any one or a combination of these means would depend on several factors.

12.2.1 Characteristics of the Target Audience

No matter how good a product or service is, its sale isn't possible unless its benefits are conveyed to the consumers through some promotional media. However, to do this effectively, the marketeer must know the characteristics of the target audience. By this, I mean understanding the various attributes of the consumers such as demographic factors like income, education, and occupation; and psychographic and lifestyle factors like his activities, interests, and opinions. This is because different target audience characteristics will affect the kind of promotional tools the marketeer can use. For example, if consumers are lowly educated and poor, it may not be possible to use media like the newspapers and television. Instead, the radio may be a more effective medium for reaching out to the consumers.

In the case of many of Asia's newly-opened economies like India, Vietnam, Myanmar and Cambodia, the television set is still beyond the means of the average households, especially those residing in the rural areas. At the same time, their literacy levels are still so low that printed materials like the newspapers and magazines would have no impact on them. In contrast, the radio is readily within their reach, and is hence the best medium for advertising to households in the rural areas of Asia.

Many Asian cities on the other hand, are very advanced even by western standards. They have very good infrastructure, including communications systems. Many of them are also very cosmopolitan and the consumers are fairly well-educated. It is in these Asian urban cities that the conventional audio-visual and printed media are likely to have the most impact. Interestingly, these cities are also densely populated. The marketeer has immense opportunities to reach out to the masses.

12.2.2 Characteristics of the Product or Service

The characteristics of the product or service will determine how easy or difficult it will be to put a marketing message across to the consumers. Some products and services are more complex than others and, as such, are more difficult to understand and use. At times, they are also very costly. A good example is the encyclopaedia. Despite using newspapers and magazines as supporting promotional tools, the marketeer of encyclopaedias has found that it is still more effective for a salesman to personally explain the product to prospective customers to clinch sales.

Besides encyclopaedias, many office products like photocopiers, fax machines, computer hardware and software also require demonstration of use of the product in order to sell it. Such demonstrations are necessary to help overcome the fear of adopting a new and strange piece of equipment. Here is where the direct marketing approach comes in. As a matter of fact, many big ticket consumer items require the direct selling approach as well. For example, while a normal vacuum cleaner may be bought off the shelf, upmarket models like Electrolux, Hoover and Miele are sold directly to the consumers through house-calls.

So it is by knowing the characteristics of the product or service, that the marketeer can decide on its best promotional medium. The importance of this cannot be underestimated where Asian markets are concerned because of the great disparities in income, education, culture, social mobility and other demographic factors in these markets. These are the determining factors of the impact of an advertisement on consumers.

12.2.3 Stage of the Product Life Cycle

The stage at which a product is at in its life cycle also determines what kind of promotional methods are suitable. For example, at the introduction stage, there is a need to create awareness among consumers. For products or services at the introduction stage, it is not sufficient to use only one promotional medium to achieve awareness. Very often, it is necessary to use different forms of mass media such as newspapers, magazines, and television advertising in order to create the impact. Then, for some products that are more complex (for example, vacuum cleaners, air-conditioners, and hi-fi systems), it may even be necessary for the marketeer to participate in trade shows and exhibitions in order to provide exposure of the products as well as demonstrate their use.

However, at the maturity stage of a product, the marketeer may have to rely more on sales to promote the product. This is because at this stage, many consumers are already aware and familiar with the products. What is more pertinent is to maintain consumer loyalty among existing customers, and if possible, to "steal" market share from competitors. The toothpaste industry is a good example of a matured industry. Despite its many efforts to extend the life cycle of toothpaste through various product improvements like adding fluoride or calcium to it and, anti-tartar control and gum control compounds, and so on, the marketeer in this industry still has to rely heavily on sales promotion as a means to protect or gain market share. Advertising is only used when a company introduces a new product feature or announces a sales promotion.

12.2.4 Availability of Financial Resources

Certainly, the amount of resources available to the company will influence its promotional policies and objectives. For example, if the company is financially very strong, it can use a particular promotional medium more intensively, and use other forms of media as well. This is where small and medium-sized enterprises (SMEs) cannot compete with the big companies. As a result, these SMEs tend to get a free ride from the promotional campaigns of the larger ones. Observe that often when the anchor tenants (usually large departmental stores) of shopping centres decide to advertise their annual sales, the smaller tenants in these centres would follow suit with their own sales — without the need to advertise! What they basically would do is to use in-store advertising — that is, they simply put up prominent "sale" display signs to attract the consumers who are drawn into the shopping centres by the advertisements of the anchor tenants.

The power of the purse is something to be reckoned with. Besides the retail industry, many brands in the cosmetics and fashion industries are built up through sheer heavy investment in advertising, and often through the use of multiple promotional means. It is common knowledge that such industries invest as much as 20% of their sale revenue in advertising and sales promotion. In doing so, they literally "buy" into the business, and then they invest heavily to build up the brands over time. For such businesses, the smaller competitors who are not prepared to pump in more and more money to build up their brands and buy market share, are unlikely to be successful.

Here's where large foreign competitors with established brand names tend to have a decisive edge over many local manufacturers in Asia. For them, there are economies of scale to be reaped in advertising their brand names heavily in Asia as they are already well recognized worldwide. It therefore comes as no surprise to find that western designer brands of clothings and fashion wear, and even fast food chains like McDonald's and Pizza Hut are able to gain very rapid footholds and market shares in many Asian cities. In contrast, due to the lack of financial resources, and the relative ignorance of the importance of brand building, many Asian manufacturers are facing strong challenges ahead. They have to weather the aggressive onslaughts from these established foreign competitors.

12.2.5 Corporate Objectives

Next to financial resources, the corporate objectives of the company would also determine which media to use. For instance, how does the company view the importance of building up brand and corporate image? Specifically, how does it view the role of advertising and promotion in the building of its product's image? As mentioned earlier, advertising and promotion have been used extensively by the cosmetics and fashion industries for this purpose. However, image doesn't need to be built entirely through heavy investment in advertising and promotion. At other times, it can also be accomplished through the other three Ps of marketing such as by building a high quality product, setting high prices, and using exclusive distribution outlets. The point I want to make is that advertising and promotion aren't the only ways to build a company's reputation and that of its products. For example, in the industrial and commercial markets, suppliers often build their reputations based on high quality products, reliable delivery schedules, attractive financing terms, and efficient after-sale services.

Established American corporate giants like Motorola, IBM and Hewlett Packard are examples of companies who base their reputations on the excellence of their products and services. They have used this philosophy very well in the various Asian markets that they operate or invest in. Their strong presence, high visibility and image extend beyond relying on advertising alone. They adopt what I term a "total systems approach" to promote their corporate image in Asia.

215

12.2.6 **Availability of Media and their Characteristics**

Interestingly, the availability of media and their characteristics such as costs and effectiveness should also be considered. Not all media that are deemed effective in the West or the more advanced Asian economies like Japan, Hong Kong and Singapore may be suitable for other Asian economies like Indonesia, China, Myanmar and India. At times, it may be necessary to explore other more effective forms of media. For example, the conventional wisdom is that if a product is intended for the mass market, television and newspaper advertising would be desirable. However, they can be relatively expensive and companies may have tight promotional budgets.

The high costs of the mass media have deterred many Asian SMEs from developing systematic ways and well-thought out strategies to promote their products or services to their consumers. Often, they tend to rely on less effective, but affordable means to get their messages across to the consumers. But do not conclude that SMEs have no effective advertising media at their disposal. What is more important for the SMEs to do is to seek out the "right" media for their purposes. For example, many automotive suppliers, who are basically SMEs, have cleverly used specialized motor magazines to reach their target audience. Some SMEs cleverly use the fax machines to advertise their products or services to the consumers, thus making the latter bear part of the advertising costs! Others have also resorted to paging selected consumers, making their promotional pitches when the consumers call back.

In the case of Asia, radios, cinemas and billboards are widely available, and when properly exploited, can be very cost effective in reaching target audiences. In other situations, direct demonstrations of the products may be necessary. As such, direct selling through a well-trained salesforce (bearing in mind that labour costs is still very low in Asia) can also be explored. In fact, by using direct influence and leveraging on word-of-mouth communication, the impact can be very significant. This is because such a promotion technique allows the advertiser to tailor his or her sales pitch to the level of his or her consumer. At the same time, it allows for interaction with the prospective customer, giving ample opportunities to remove any doubts in the mind of the consumer.

12.2.7 Industrial and Competitive Practices

Industrial and competitive practices must be considered as well when a marketeer is deciding on his promotional strategy. While it is important to be creative and "different", it is also necessary to observe industrial norms and practices. For example, the fast food industry is characterized by heavy television advertising — it is the most effective medium in reaching out to the highest number of audience possible. Many of the major players in this industry use it effectively to enlarge their market share. So, any newcomer into this industry cannot afford to do without television advertising, expensive as it is.

There are good reasons to follow industrial and competitive practices. For one, they are likely to have evolved over a fairly long period of time, emerging as the most effective way of reaching out to the right people. For another, consumers would have developed certain search habits with regards to where the advertisements would be expected to appear. Hence, any departure from this industrial norm on the part of the marketeer would require the consumers to invest in new search efforts. Finally, there are a lot of experiences that can be learned and improved upon by studying the industrial and competitive practices. In other words, there is no need to re-invent the wheel; learn from what's been tried and proven, and then improve upon it.

12.2.8 Legal or Statutory Constraints

Finally, the legal or statutory constraints as well as professional ethics should also be considered in the choice of promotional media to use. For instance, the governments in some Asian countries like Singapore and Malaysia have tried to discourage cigarette consumption by implementing various anti-smoking measures. These measures have compelled many cigarette manufacturers to diversify into non-cigarette businesses like packaged tours, costume jewellery, designers' clothings, and so on. What is interesting to note is how some cigarette manufacturers try to circumvent regulatory restrictions. For example, mass media advertising of cigarettes through television is banned in Malaysia and Singapore. But don't be surprised if some particular scene or jingle of an advertisement of a vacation spot or holiday package brings back memories of a brand of cigarette!

Cigarettes aren't the only products subjected to regulation in advertising. In the more conservative Asian economies, especially those with strong Islamic cultures for instance, advertisements of feminine products like sanitary pads, brassieres, and panties are not allowed to be screened during prime time of television shows — a period when the viewership among children is highest. Advertisements for services like health care and legal counselling are also not permitted in many Asian countries. For such businesses, what consumers have to say about a product constitutes its advertisements. A positive impact comes only as a result of consumer satisfaction with the service provided. In the case of health care, some hospitals in Singapore have creatively exploited their public relations arm to generate publicity for their hospitals. For example, they would constantly develop newsworthy events for media coverage as well as make efforts to court media representatives.

Altogether then, a marketeer must not rely only on a single promotional method to market his product or service. Rather, he should carefully evaluate how each of the promotional media can best serve him, given the limited corporate resources. In the final analysis, he may have to use a mixture of various promotional methods in order to effectively convey the benefits of his product or service to his target audience.

12.3 Reach and Frequency

Among the various issues in advertising, the key issue has to be determining the amount that needs to be spent to gain maximum impact. This brings to mind two related aspects of advertising — reach and frequency. By "reach", I mean the extent of market coverage desired by the advertiser, while "frequency" refers to the level of intensity needed for any specific market that the advertisements are targetted at. Let me point out these two approaches are not mutually exclusive. More often than not, they are used hand-in-hand. However, there are situations in which their emphasis may differ.

12.3.1 When Reach is More Appropriate

There are three general situations in which the marketeer should focus more on "reach" rather than "frequency". These situations include when the target market cannot be defined clearly, when the product enjoys a strong brand franchise and when the purchase cycle is not very long.

Undefined Target Market

When the target market is not well defined, it becomes important to reach out to as many potential customers as possible. This can come about when the marketeer is not sure who exactly his potential customers are. A good example is the introduction of bottled mineral water and water filters to the Singapore market in the early 1980s. Unlike many other Asian economies, it is perfectly safe in Singapore to drink directly from the tap. But at the same time, Singaporeans were getting more and more affluent, and there could be possible demand for such products, despite their initial high prices. However, it was difficult to assess where the demand would come from. As a result, the marketeers of bottled mineral water and water filters chose the reach strategy in their promotional efforts. As it turned out, these products became very successful.

A reach strategy is also necessary when the market cannot be segmented at all, that is, the product is targetted at the mass market. Good examples include commodity-type products like gasoline, soft drinks, tissue and toilet papers, white bread, and rice. At other times, the product may be new, and the marketeer does not know exactly how his target audience looks like. In such situations, the marketeer has to try to reach as many of the potential customers as possible. Thus, mass media like the radio, television, newspapers, and magazines are used to supplement and comple–ment each other so as to generate maximum market coverage. While such a strategy may appear more like a "shotgun" approach, it none–theless will create greater awareness for the product, especially if it is new.

A good example of the use of a reach strategy is the 1993 floata–tion of Singapore Telecoms shares which was one of the largest public listing exercises ever undertaken in Singapore as well as in Asia. Extensive advertising media were used to reach out to al–most every adult Singaporean: full-page advertisements in all the local newspapers, television commercials, radio broadcasts, direct mail and public briefings. Besides exploiting every available ad–vertising medium, the publicity efforts were done in all the four official languages of Singapore — English, Chinese, Malay, and Tamil. It was a campaign that was highly successful: almost every adult Singaporean ended up holding some Telecoms shares. In addition, the strike price, as a result of excessive demand for the shares, was set at a relatively high level.

The use of mass media to reach out to a large sector of the population is not new to Singapore. Its government is known to use mass media frequently to convey important national policies and promote social campaigns. Some of these more notable campaigns include those that promote healthy lifestyles, courtesy, and increasing the family size. The successes of the Singapore government in using the mass media to reach out to its population for the purpose of educating and informing the public in order to fulfil social and economic objectives have prompted several other Asian economies to follow suit. Malaysia, Hong Kong and even China are adopting the Singapore's approach in their social campaigns as well.

Besides governments and their related agencies, the use of mass media by private sector businesses to reach out to new consumers are fast catching on in the newly emerging economies. In fact, this is the typical approach adopted by many marketeers in their advertising campaigns in China, Vietnam and India. In the case of China, the television is likely to emerge as an important medium for advertising. Within a short span of fifteen years, after opening up to the outside world, China now boasts of the ratio of one television set to forty-eight people as of 1995 and it's not stopping at this ratio either. By the year 2005, every one in twenty people is expected to own a television set. The growth of advertising in China can also be measured by the increasing number of advertising agencies. As of early 1994, there were thirty-one thousand advertising agencies in China. What is significant is that fifteen thousand agencies were set up in 1993 alone!

Strong Brand Franchise and Weak Competition

When a company has a strong brand name, it is possible to capitalize on its franchisees through a reach strategy. As such, the use of a greater number of advertising media to reach out to a wider consumer audience would be a logical approach to take so as to capture a larger market share. McDonald's, Burger King, and Pizza Hut commonly use the mass media for this purpose. These fast food chains have very strong brand names that allow them to take full advantage of reaching out to the mass market, more so when they are able to complement their marketing efforts through franchise outlets.

At times, a strong brand may also allow the marketeer to expand his range of products or even introduce another model. For example, the marketeer could capitalize on the strong brand image of the current product to reach out to other customers. The strong brand of Mercedes as a prestigious car has definitely helped it to successfully launched its smaller model 190E into the Asian market. Similarly, BMW used the strong image of its upper-end cars to propel the sales of its smaller 3-series models. Many Japanese manufacturers have also cleverly exploited their brand successes in consumer electronics to launch many other similar household products including appliances (for example, Sharp has used the same brand on products ranging from television to washing machines, refrigerators, telephones and even fax machines).

In the same way, the South Koreans have been able to introduce more products successfully in recent years as a result of their widely accepted brand names like Hyundai, Goldstar, Daewoo and Samsung. Like Japanese brands long ago, the Korean brands were initially not well known. However, by investing heavily in brand building and development over the years, these brands have built up strong franchises that are now easily recognizable. By labelling new but different products using these established brands, the South Korean manufacturers have been able to successfully reach out to more customers and markets. They use the reach strategy appropriately in promoting and advertising their products, something that they learned very well from the Japanese.

The use of a reach strategy in exploiting the power of a strong brand franchise to introduce other products can best be illustrated in the case of cigarette companies. When threatened with the prospect of being a declining industry (as a result of many anti-smoking campaigns, legislative restrictions, and health hazards caused by smoking), many cigarette companies like Dunhill, Camel and Marlboro have cleverly diversified into non-cigarette products. In the beginning, they focused on high-value added products that are small and personal so that the packaging can be made to look like the cigarette packs! This is to exploit brand association effects. Thus, companies like Dunhill started with ties, tie-pins, cuff-links, wallets and belts. Today, it markets a full array of personal products that includes shirts, men's colognes and fragrances, spectacle frames, and so on. In fact, they have become very prestigious brands that command high prices. These branded products could not have come at a more appropriate time for the various markets in Asia where established brands are in great demand.

Infrequent Purchase Cycle

A reach strategy may also be necessary in situations where the purchase cycle of a product is infrequent. This occurs in the case of high ticket products like cars, personal computers, television sets, hi-fi systems, and cameras, and for services like housing loans and packaged tours. The whole point for using a reach strategy for such products or services is to generate as much publicity about them as possible, and to widen the market coverage in order to reach more potential customers.

There is also another reason for the use of a reach strategy for infrequently purchased products or services. Owing to the long lapse of time between one purchase and another, the product or service may have undergone significant changes and there is a need to inform the consumers of the new features of the product. Good examples include cars and cameras. The number of new features that are added to a new model is normally very significant, and it is necessary to highlight these new features. In doing so, the marketeer may even convince some consumers to upgrade to the newer and better model.

12.3.2 When a Frequency Strategy is More Appropriate

The frequency of advertising has to do with the intensity of advertising and there are some rules of thumb in applying the frequency principle in advertising. To begin with, common sense dictates that one exposure, whether in print or by the audio-visual method, is definitely of little value: it may be missed or its message not fully understood the first time its audience hears it. The audience needs to be exposed to it a number of times. With increasing exposures, the impact on the target audience is likely to increase. However, this increasing return will only apply up to a certain level of exposures, beyond which diminishing returns will set in.

Complex Story

A frequency strategy is needed when the product is rather complex and where the advertising message is conveyed through a complex story. Under such a situation, in order for the target audience to grasp the message, many exposures are needed. This is true of products like cameras, cars, and other consumer electronics. For this reason, advertisers of sophisticated products tend to rely on the printed media such as magazines and newspapers to convey the complex story. This is because such print media allow the consumers sufficient time to comprehend and digest the message at their own pace, something that time-constrained media like the television and radio do not allow.

The greater reliance on the print media to convey complex product or service stories does not mean that there is no role for audio-visual media. More often than not, they can be used very effectively to complement the print media, especially in generating awareness and excitement about the product or service. Audio-visual media like the television can also be used effectively to project the image and prestige of the product or service. For example, the marketeers of luxury cars like the Mercedes, Lexus and BMW often use the television to introduce their new models.

Strong Competition

In general, when a product faces stiff competition, the marketeer may have to pay more attention to the frequency issue. This is because as the level of competitive "noises" increases, the marketeer's product faces the danger of being crowded or squeezed out if it does not increase its level of exposure of the product. In other words, the marketeer has to take into account the "attrition rate" that would occur in a highly competitive advertising environment.

Here, it is important to point out that the the crowding out effect may not come from direct competitors, but from indirect competitors as well. This is because many products and services offered today have substitutes, even if they appear dissimilar. For example, a consumer may substitute a vacation tour for a home entertainment system as both categories of purchases actually compete for the same pool of discretionary spending dollars of the consumer.

As Asia continues to enjoy healthy economic growth rates and affluence, marketeers will find more and more competitors going after the discretionary incomes of the Asian consumers. This is probably causing many marketeers to advertise very aggressively in many new cities of Asia, when it appears that many Asian consumers are not yet able to afford the products being advertised. This is done deliberately to win the minds of these potential consumers. It is actually done in anticipation of their acquisition of purchasing power to afford the products. Consumers having constantly been bombarded with advertising messages, advertisers believe, will be instilled with a desire for their product or products. So by the time they acquire the purchasing power, advertisers also believe their efforts will pay off in having created top-of-mind recall.

Frequently Purchased Product

When a product is frequently purchased, and where brand substitution is rampant, a marketeer needs to constantly remind the consumer of his brand of the product. Otherwise, the "out-of-sight, out-of-mind" syndrome may set in. Many household products like soap and detergent fall under this category. For such products, the consumer probably has a few acceptable brands in mind, but is not particularly loyal to any one of them. More often than not, he or she is prepared to substitute one brand for another, especially when there is no noticeable difference in quality. In such situations, the consumer tends to be influenced more by lower prices or sales promotion in their purchasing decision. So there is a need to constantly remind the consumer of the presence of the brand through heavy advertising. Besides, it would serve to create the impression that the product is in great demand!

Resistance to Brand

Intensive advertising is also needed when consumer resistance to the brand is high. Consider when Japanese products were first sold in Southeast Asia, they were resisted owing to their poor quality. The Japanese manufacturers not only improved on the quality of their product over time and provided adequate product warranties, they also invested heavily in advertising and promoting their brands. Today, many Japanese brands have become household names and are recognised for their high quality.

Observe that the South Koreans are using the same strategy as the Japanese. Besides improving their products and pricing competitively, South Korean manufacturers have begun to invest heavily in advertising: more and more of Daewoo, Samsung, Goldstar, and Hyundai advertisements are seen in the various media these days. Given the market penetration achieved by these South Korean brands, the strategy appears to work just as well for the South Koreans as it did for the Japanese.

The idea of a need to invest in brand building through aggressive advertising and promotion is something that not many Asian companies seem to subscribe to. Besides the Japanese, and possibly the South Korean companies, many Chinese, Taiwanese, Malaysian and Indonesian companies do not seem to be adopting this strategy as part of a long term development goal for their companies. It is, I believe, a challenge that they have to face before losing out to the foreign established brands in the battle for the share of an emerging and huge market.

Well-Defined Target Market

When a target market is well-defined, the use of a frequency strategy is very appropriate. When the marketeer knows precisely who his target audience is, he is then able to focus his resources to achieve the maximum impact. A well-defined target market also allows the marketeer to advertise frequently to build customer loyalty towards his product. For this purpose, marketeers of automative products would regularly advertise in motor magazines, while women magazines are constantly filled with advertisements on cosmetics, fashion wear, and jewellery.

12.4 Other Factors Affecting Advertising Effectiveness

Let me reiterate that the reach and frequency strategies should not be treated as mutually exclusive. They have been used very effectively together. In bank loans and packaged tours advertising, reach and frequency approaches have been used hand-in-hand successfully.

Generally, television and newspaper advertising are used to generate awareness and publicity, while direct mailing and brochures are used to target intensively at prospective customers. But to think that the impact of any advertising on the target audience relies only on the reach and frequency approaches alone would be wrong. There are other factors that the marketeer must consider.

12.4.1 Extent and Length of the Advertisement

Other things being equal, a short television commercial (say, a fifteen second one) is likely to create less impact than a longer commercial (say, a thirty second advertisement). The impact would be even lesser if the storyline is complex. This is because a short commercial is more likely to be missed, and it is harder to convey a complex message. In the same way, a smaller-size print advertisement (for example, quarter page) is likely to attract less attention than a larger size advertisement (for example, a full page). In fact, a very small size advertisement might even be missed by the reader. A smaller advertisement may compromise the credibility of the advertiser, and hence reduce its impact. The advertiser may also be perceived as a small outfit or as running a fly-by-night operation.

12.4.2 Timing of the Advertisement

Related to size and duration of an advertisement is timing. For example, the exposure obtained from a television commercial aired during prime time or a popular programme is definitely higher, although the costs would also be higher. For some products and services, their demands are seasonal. As such, it is important to time their advertisements accordingly. A good example is that of festive goods and packaged tours. In the case of Singapore, most families would take their annual vacations during June and/or December as they coincide with the school holidays of their children. Thus, the months before June and December are often flooded with advertisements on vacations.

In the same way, weekend newspapers tend to have a larger readership and longer shelf lives. In particular, some types of advertisements are more likely to be noticed on weekends than on weekdays, especially if the contents require the reader to devote more time to "digest" them, or when the purchase decision requires more time for consideration. Advertisements on resort condominiums, packaged tours, garage sales, and pets are examples.

Beginning from the early 1990s, there has been great interest in overseas property investments shown by many wealthy Asian consumers in Hong Kong, Japan, Taiwan, Singapore, Malaysia and Indonesia. This came about largely because of limited investment opportunities at home and the relatively cheaper properties in countries like Australia, New Zealand, and Canada. As a result, many weekend editions of Asian newspapers were filled with advertisements on overseas property sales and exhibitions. The popularity of these properties could not have come at a better time — the falling prices of properties in countries like Australia, New Zealand and Canada, and the increase in property prices in many

Asian cities. Thus, these overseas developers and agents were able to capitalize on the right timing to market their properties to the Asian market.

Timing also includes taking into account any major world events that may increase readership (for newspapers and magazines) and viewership (for television). For example, marketeers of sporting goods may want to intensify their advertising efforts during major sporting events like the Olympics, Asian Games or Sea Games. These are events that never fail to attract large captive audiences. It is thus not surprising to find that some major brands of products that have a wide consumer base, like Milo and Ovaltine, often associate themselves with mass sporting events, while others with defined and narrow target audience like Rolex, would position themselves with more exclusive sports like golf and tennis.

12.4.3 Effects of Overcrowding

Another factor to consider is the effects of "overcrowding". For instance, when a television programme is very popular, it is likely to attract a larger viewership, and hence presents a fertile opportunity for the marketeer to reach out to more potential customers. However, if many marketeers choose to place advertisements in the programme, overcrowding will occur. The result is that there is bound to be a lot of unnecessary "noise" and "wastage" that diminish the effectiveness of all the commercials. Further, when a string of commercials appear one after another, the viewer may be tempted to take a break, causing greater reduction in the effectiveness of the advertisements.

When many similar marketeers choose to place their advertisements on the same day in a newspaper, however, the effects may not necessarily be negative. No doubt, there is also overcrowding, but the addition of one more advertisement need not be at the expense of the others. This is because unlike television commercials which tend to occur sequentially and are relatively brief, print advertisements can appear side-by-side simultaneously and have longer shelf lives. In fact, a vast number of competitive print advertisements on similar products or services may even create a critical mass effect for the interested readers. For this reason, the classified advertisements section and the employment pages never fail to find receptive readers.

12.4.4 Location or Positioning of the Advertisement

How an advertisement should be placed or located should be considered. In the case of print advertising like newspapers and magazines, different pages command different levels of exposure. In the case of a daily newspaper, the main section definitely receives more attention than the supplementary section. At the same time, there are certain pages of the newpaper that are read more than other pages. As a result of this, the advertising rates for the pages that enjoy greater exposure, tend to be higher.

What is worth exploring is the exact location of an advertisement within a page itself. It is commonly believed that an advertisement placed on the righthand side of an odd number page or lefthand side of an even number page of a newspaper may attract more attention than the corresponding side. Similarly, given the large page size and layout of a typical newspaper, it is likely that the top half may catch more attention than the bottom half of any page. This is an area that is yet to be proven by research, but which intuitively makes sense for the pragmatic marketeer who wants maximum mileage out of his advertising dollar.

The position of a television commercial amongst a long string of commercials is also an issue of interest. Intuitively it would appear that if many television commercials are clustered together, those that are sandwiched in the middle are likely to receive the least attention, and be squeezed out by the viewer who may choose to take a break or switch to other channels. In contrast, the first commercial that appears immediately after a programme is likely to be watched as the viewer does not have sufficient time to leave his seat or make the switch. Similarly, the commercial that precedes the resumption of the program is also likely to be watched as the viewer would not want to miss any part of the show.

12.4.5 Life Span of the Advertisement

Certainly, some media allow a advertisement to have a longer life span than others. In this regard, radio and television are the least preferred from the perspective of durability of the advertisement. Once the advertisement is aired or broadcasted, it is gone, and cannot be stored or retained for future references by the consumer. With tape and video-recording capabilities, one can argue that the life span of radio and television commercials can be prolonged. But a viewer normally does the recording for purpose of viewing the programme, not the commercial. Thus, in the case of a television programme, it is not surprising to find that the viewer would skip all the commercials by using the "fast forward" feature.

On the other hand, print media like newspapers and magazines have much longer life spans. Advertisements in magazines, in particular, can enjoy very long shelf lives, especially if the magazines are of a specialized nature so that readers keep the magazines for future references. *Fortune, Business Week, Asia Week,* and *Asian Business* are examples of such magazines. The advertisements in these magazines are seen again and again. More importantly, these magazines are often widely circulated, thus reaching a very big audience. This is what the Faculty of Business Administration at the National University of Singapore discovered about its advertisements on executive development programmes. While newspapers were used regularly, they did not appear to reach out to the right target audience effectively. Subsequently, magazines such as the *Asia Week* became very useful for advertising its various training courses.

12.4.6 Creativity and Congruency

In advertising effectiveness, nothing beats creativity and congruency. Creativity will always catch the attention of the readers or viewers. And consumers like to talk about interesting advertisements and messages. Some years ago, BMW came out with a very snobbish but highly creative advertisement when it advertised its luxury cars with these lines:

> "Rumours had it that the new BMW is very expensive. Wrong, it is very, very expensive."
>
> "The new BMW is not for the rich. It is for the very, very rich."

In its newspaper advertisements, Chivas Regal had generously used empty large blank spaces. They stood out and drew the attention of readers. Some car dealers in Singapore had deliberately inverted their advertisements, while others like Borneo Motors ran a series of advertisements as a sequel to market the Lexus.

Equally important is the need to advertise in the "right" programmes. By this, I mean programmes that have a high congruency with the contents of the advertisement. A good example of this is that during the screening of a television sequel on "The Teochew Family" in Singapore, a major distributor cleverly advertised his brand of rice throughout the show. This is because "The Teochew Family" was about a successful rice merchant who migrated from China to Singapore. Similarly, during the screening of period costume dramas, some enterprising companies cleverly dressed their advertising models in similar ancient costume with fascinating historical themes to attract the attention of the viewers. By the same token, many health drinks and products are advertised during major sports events like the Asian Games and Olympics.

12.4.7 Deliver What You Promise

In advertising, it is very important to promise only what the marketeer can deliver. Unfortunately, many marketeers have the tendency to promise more than they deliver. This can generate adverse publicity, especially if they are highlighted in the media. Angry consumers may then boycott his goods or services, and sanctions by official bodies and regulators may also be in order. To ensure such ugly situations do not develop, the marketeer should carefully study what he can or cannot deliver to the consumers. So, if a pizza operator in his advertisement promises to serve the customer within ten minutes after the customer has placed his order, he must ensure that this is done, regardless of the customer traffic within his store. If he cannot do so within the specified time, he may seriously want to think of compensating the customer, like allowing him to have the pizza for free. This is precisely the practice adopted by many pizza operators in America.

The use of "deceptive" advertising is fast becoming an issue in many Asian economies. This is because unlike the west, advertising is relatively new in Asia, and there is generally a lack of controls and regulations that govern advertising. As a result, some unscrupulous marketeers have exploited naive and vulnerable consumers. Such unethical advertising practices cannot be condoned.

12.5 Conclusion

I wish the secret to great success in advertising can be summed up by some simple cardinal rules. Unfortunately, this is not the case. While issues like reach, frequency, timing, location and placement, size and duration are all important in designing an effective advertising strategy, mastery of them alone do not guarantee success. In the final analysis, for any advertisement to be effective, there is still a need for creativity and sound planning. A highly creative advertisement generates excitement and attention and creates further publicity because it will have people talking about it. For this reason, creative talents are highly prized in this industry. Unfortunately, they are rare. For the majority of marketeers, they still have to rely on a systematic way of planning and executing their advertisements.

13

Public Relations and *Guanxi*: Added Punch for More Effective Promotion

13.1 Introduction

Marketing results in terms of sales, market shares, and profits cannot be achieved entirely by direct advertising and promotion. At times, it is necessary to rely on other marketing means to bring about the results. This is where public relations (PR) and personal relations come in. They represent the less visible, but equally important arm of the promotion function. Indeed, careful management of public and personal relations (or *guanxi* as it is commonly known in the Chinese-speaking world) can generate a lot of goodwill for a company that can be translated into long term sales and profits. Let me illustrate with an example.

A large condominium developer in Malaysia recently organized a free one-day seminar for over five hundred of its previous buyers, potential customers and business associates, including its bankers, accountants, suppliers, contractors and lawyers. The event was conducted without any sales pitch for the company's properties that were going to be launched. However, as a result of this event, the company was able to project itself as a caring and socially responsible developer. The result: the company scored in a grand way for its public image; a lot of enquiries about its future properties were generated, so much so that its potential clientele list ran into the thousands! The executive chairman of the company also complemented the company's PR efforts with his strong personal networking skills. He was able to get prominent Malaysian ministers, including the prime minister, to grace the opening ceremonies of the company's various condominium projects. Such visible and tremendous publicity can never be achieved by the usual marketing or advertising methods. The company, Sunrise Berhad, is known to be able to sell most of its properties without even resorting to heavy advertising and promotion.

We will first look at the many dimensions of PR before moving on to highlight some aspects of personal relations or *guanxi*. This is an area of increasing importance in Asia. It is a key dimension in doing business with and in China and the other Chinese-speaking markets of Asia.

13.2 The Need to Pay Attention to Public Relations

13.2.1 Courting Consumers More Fervently

There are several reasons why companies are now paying more attention to PR. To begin with, an increasing number of Asian consumers, especially those from the more developed economies, are no longer passive players in the market. Rather, with better education, greater affluence and exposure to various world events, they have become more critical and demanding about companies and their products. For example, the younger and more affluent Asian consumers are no longer hesitant to reject defective products and lodge complaints about poor products and services. They are no longer prepared to suffer in silence or attribute their poor purchases to bad luck. Indeed, consumer associations and small claims tribunals are now becoming more common in Asian societies. It is likely that such institutions will become more established in the years ahead.

As a result of the green movement, many Asian consumers have also become more conscious of protecting the environment and nature. As such, they would refrain from buying or would boycott those products that are harmful to the environment. The community at large now expects companies to be more socially responsible in their behaviour. It is therefore not surprising to find that some of the MNCs operating in Asia are leading the way in showing that they do conduct their businesses in socially responsible ways. For instance, they have begun to use more re-cycled products and adopted many anti-pollution measures. The British-American Tobacco Company (BAT), one of the biggest manufacturers of cigarettes, has a very comprehensive forestation programme and is very active in supporting other social programmes and activities. All these PR activities are pursued to project a kinder and softer image of the company and ultimately to win the support of more consumers.

13.2.2 More Creative Approach to Generating Publicity

As competition becomes more intense, and as the usual advertising media get more congested resulting in crowding out effects, there is a need to seek out more creative and different ways to market the company. PR activities feature prominently in this search process. This is because companies are beginning to realize that the publicity that can be generated through a well-managed media event far exceeds that of paid advertisements. For example, a favourable news coverage in the local print or audio or visual media captures more attention and generates better response than a very direct advertisement.

For some organizations, paid advertisements as a means for marketing, are not even open to them. In Singapore, for instance, some professions like lawyers, doctors, and accountants are not allowed to advertise their services directly. Similarly, hospitals are not allowed to engage in direct advertising and promotion. Yet, it is interesting to note how some of the more enterprising hospitals like Mount Elizabeth have cleverly orchestrated events that generate media attention. The earnestness with which these hospitals pay attention to PR can be seen from the fact that they even have PR and marketing departments. Besides managing media events, these departments are also responsible for the printing of educational materials on health, conducting surveys and handling addressing complaints of customers, besides other related functions.

13.2.3 Effects on Multiple Publics

Business operations have become more complex in that they affect many parties. At the same time, the actions taken by these parties — whether customers, employees, the community at large, the media, stakeholders or the government — can affect the ways business firms operate. Thus, it is important that appropriate attention be paid to them. As the conventional marketing means can only be applied more directly to customers and consumers, other methods have to be sought to woo the the other parties. PR activities are viable and logical alternatives to conventional marketing. Take the example of Nick Neeson's case on the speculative trading of derivatives that caused the 1995 collapse of Barings, one of the oldest merchant banks in the United Kingdom. It is a case which shows how one man's actions caused such tremendous repercussions around the whole world to the extent that many policy-makers, top bankers, regulators, analysts, amongst others, had to do much PR activities, including defending the trading in derivatives. Indeed, the impact of the activities of financial institutions on the rest of the economy is probably one of the most significant. Little wonder that many banks place a lot of emphasis on PR activities.

13.2.4 Image Building Over Time

PR can also be used effectively to complement the marketing and advertising efforts of a company. When properly managed, it can be a softer and more indirect way of building the corporate image. Consider when Singapore started national service in the late 1960s. The public's perception of the armed forces was a very poor one. However, over the last twenty to thirty years, the Singapore Armed Forces (SAF) embarked on a systematic and concerted effort to upgrade its image. Besides advertising, it organized open houses, conducted public seminars, held exhibitions, gave talks to schools and other institutions, invited participation from employers, educated parents of national servicemen through various channels and even offerred lucrative and generous scholarships to the brightest students to pursue university education and a military career. The result: the SAF is today highly respected; it enjoys a favourable public image.

Consider too how the police force in Singapore used to be shunned and feared by members of the public in the 1960s and 1970s. It was difficult then to solicit public cooperation in the fight against crime. But with PR efforts over the last ten years, policemen are today viewed as "one of us" by the public. With Neighbourhood Police Posts (NPP) performing some non-traditional police functions (such as recording the change of addresses for residents) and co-producing television programmess such as "Crime Watch", the bond between the public and the police further strengthened. This NPP concept in Singapore was learned from the Japanese. In Japan, policemen are well respected and enjoy tremendous cooperation from the people.

Besides the SAF and the NPP, there are many other examples of companies that engage in image building through its various PR activities. The well-known watch company Rolex, has been known for sponsoring major golf tournaments around the world for many years. As golf is a very prestigious sports for the rich and famous in most Asian countries, Rolex Singapore Pte Ltd has succeeded in building up a very strong image in Asia, one that it is likely to keep for a long time.

13.3 Effective Public Relations

PR is not about getting free publicity or advertising. PR is part of the communication strategy of a company, and therefore should be managed systematically and professionally. The difference between PR and advertising is that the process and the techniques and methods are different. Otherwise, managing the PR function would be like managing the advertising and promotion function. But it is not. If anything, they should complement each other. There are several guidelines to developing an effective PR programme which I would like to highlight.

13.3.1 PR Function Should be Proactive

To begin with, every organization should have a department or someone tasked with handling the PR function. It should not be an activity that is forced upon the company. Instead, a company should constantly seek out opportunities to publicize itself and its products or services, highlight its sales goals, market share, competitive positioning, entrance into new markets, new ventures and so on.

Proactiveness in PR also implies that the company adopts an offensive rather than defensive posture; that it be opportunity-seeking rather than problem-solving. Thus, the PR department of any company should be proactive. In other words, it should decide what it wants to see publicized, rather than respond to events that have already occurred. Of course, I do not discount the possibility that at times PR is needed to contain and counteract the negative publicity generated by events outside its control (for example, an air crash, an oil leak, or a tanker's explosion). However, an organization that has a proactive PR department or function will find that it can respond to crises better and more effectively.

13.3.2 PR Activities Should be Planned, Coordinated, and Timed

When an organization adopts a proactive attitude in its PR, it means it will ensure that all its activities are well-planned, well coordinated and well timed. In other words, they are not conducted on an ad hoc basis. They form a part of the marketing function. There must be a PR strategy that links it with the other marketing activities and functions of the company. In this way, it would complement the advertising and promotion activities.

The importance of good timing, coordination and planning is imperative in handling crisis when clarity, accuracy and sincerity are critical. This is where the professional skills and expertise needed are very much different from those involved in advertising and promotion. In a crisis (for example, responding to media queries about a factory explosion, a tanker's collision that caused severe oil leakage, an air crash, a building collapse, a major fire in a shopping centre, a train accident, a major loan default and so on), there is no room for conflicting information. It takes a high level of dexterity to manage the tremendous pressure from very many interest groups, affected parties and the media who will be clamouring for information.

13.3.3 PR Activities are Targetted

All PR activities should be directed at specific audiences, whether they are internal or external. Let us look at some of the major target audiences that a typical organization has to deal with.

Customer Relations

Existing and potential customers probably form the largest target audience for a company's PR activities. There are many examples to demonstrate the extent to which an organization would go to woo its customers so as to generate favourable publicity. The Singapore Tourist Promotion Board (STPB), for example, flies in tourists (all expenses paid) who had been cheated by unscrupulous shopkeepers to testify in Singapore's courts of law. SIA not only takes customer complaints seriously, but even has a department that is tasked with constantly monitoring statistics of complaints. Furthermore, it regularly conducts surveys among its travellers to determine the level of consumer satisfaction. Other companies like the NTUC Co-operative Ltd, Tangs Departmental Store, American Express Bank Ltd, and Visa publish regular magazines that are distributed free to their selected customers.

PR exercises are carried out frequently by companies in Singapore. In its efforts to provide quality customer service, Giordano, a retail fashion chain, even employed student spies to check on their stores. The act received almost a quarter of a page coverage in the *Straits Times* on 18 December 1991. The publicity was definitely

significant for the company. In 1993, Giordano even polled its customers to decide on the price of its polo t-shirts. It was an event that
also generated significant local media coverage. To support the fine
arts, large companies like the Keppel Corporation Ltd, frequently
book full theatre or concert shows for clients. Similarly, Hour Glass
Ltd, one of the large watch retail chains, often organizes exhibitions
of exclusive jewellery watches and clocks.

Owing to the high prices of cars, the dealers in Singapore are
particularly active with their PR activities. Tan Chong & Sons Motor
Company (S) Pte Ltd took out a 16-page newspaper supplement in
both the *Sunday Times* and *Lianhe Zaobao* on 8 December 1991 to
announce its five new car models that had yet to arrive in Singapore.
It is not alone in doing this. Cycle & Carriage Ltd (agent for Mercedes
cars), Borneo Motors (S) Pte Ltd (agent for Lexus and Toyota), Performance Motors Ltd (the agent for BMW), Malayan Motors (the
agent for Jaguar), and many other dealers also frequently take up
large advertisement spaces and television time slots to announce their
new car models that will soon arrive. Some of these dealers such as
Singapore Motors (the dealer for Saab), even throw in cocktails
and elaborate receptions to entice their potential buyers and current car owners to view the new models.

Community Relations

The Coca-Cola company in Singapore budgeted S$200,000 to be given
away to Singapore athletes who won gold medals at the 1991 Manila
Southeast Asia Games. This amount was overtaken two years later by
Asia-Pacific Brewery which pledged S$500,000 for an Olympic gold
medal. While these amounts may appear high, they pale in comparison to those offered by other Asian countries. Malaysia and Indonesia, for example, are known to reward their badminton players very
handsomely with land, houses, and cars for winning major events like
the Thomas Cup and the World Cup. Many of their players became
overnight millionaires while the sponsoring companies were cheered
for their community spirit!

In an attempt to make sports a professional concern and make
them more attractive to spectators, many companies in Singapore
have begun to sponsor or adopt teams in games such as soccer, basketball and table-tennis. In Malaysia, Indonesia, Hong Kong, Thailand, Japan, South Korea, Taiwan and the Philippines, corporate
sponsorship of sports have an even earlier history. China has also

begun to actively reward her sportsmen and sportswomen over the past few years. An increasing numbers of major Chinese companies now regularly pledge high financial rewards for their athletes who win in major world events. Without doubt, companies have found that financial support for sporting events is a very powerful means to rally the local people and indirectly win recognition for the sponsors as well. What is more, as many Asian economies are becoming very interested in sports, sponsoring sporting events is definitely viewed as a strong community relations activity, as well as a means of winning political favours from the government.

Besides sporting events, there are other forms of community relations activities. The Hour Glass Ltd (Singapore) regularly sponsors the fine arts and other public events. Pico Art International contributed several millions dollars to the Economic Development Board (EDB) of Singapore for the development of creative talents in Singapore. The four big local banks in Singapore — Oversea-Chinese Banking Corporation Ltd (OCBC), Development Bank of Singapore (DBS), Overseas Union Bank Ltd (OUB), United Overseas Bank Ltd (UOB), — and other companies are very generous in giving scholarships to worthy persons or causes and making donations to charitable organizations. Other companies have adopted old folk homes, welfare homes and even animals in the zoo. Note too that MNCs operating in Asia are also very active in offering scholarships and other kinds of sponsorships. Some major MNC donors include Glaxo, Motorola, Hewlett Packard (HP), Singapore (Pte) Ltd, and many Japanese companies.

Of late, as a result of the green movement, many companies operating in Asia have begun to organize or participate in various campaigns that are aimed to protect the environment. In doing so, they hope to project themselves as responsible organizations that care for the future of the world. British Petroleum (BP) even changed its corporate colours to green, to reflect its support for a green environment. As mentioned earlier, British-American Tobacco Company (BAT), one of the largest producers of cigarettes, tries to counter and supplant its negative image of being a perpetrator of ill health by being very active with its forestry and forestation programmes. In fact, as of 1995, it has replanted more trees than any other company in the world. Meanwhile, an increasing number of companies (McDonald's is one of them) are looking at how to use more recycled materials for packaging and in other areas. To support the concerns for the environment, some companies have also attempted to develop products that are not harmful to the ozone layer of the earth. For example, all the major car manufacturers strive to produce cars that are more fuel efficient and less polluting while petroleum companies are developing and promoting the consumption of lead-free gasoline.

In sum, companies engage in community-related activities in order to project a softer and more caring image of themselves; to counter the general perception that business is a cold blooded and profit-driven concern. The need to engage in community relations takes on greater significance in Asian economies for various reasons. First, despite having to rely on foreign investors for economic prosperity, many Asian societies still harbour a feeling of being exploited by foreign "intruders". This is carried over from the past or from the experiences of colonial times. Second, businessmen generally do not enjoy high social status in many Asian societies. Historically they were despised and viewed very much as unscrupulous opportunists. Finally, from a cultural perspective, Asians generally hold the view that those who are more privileged and have benefited from society should repay by giving portions of their gains back to society. Thus, companies, especially those from overseas, should take heed and be more proactive in the sphere of community relations.

Media Relations

More and more Asian companies are now paying attention to cultivating relations with the media. Some have begun to host lunches for selected key media personnel. Others issue press releases and organize events that may generate media attention. Certainly, Asian companies are beginning to realize the importance of the media in influencing public opinion about them. In an effort to solicit favourable reports, some companies in Taiwan, China, and Hong Kong have resorted to giving "red packets" to journalists and television crew members for covering their events.

In the west, as a result of the degree of freedom enjoyed by the press and the lack of censorship against them over the years, the various media have become so powerful that even politicians have to court them fervently. This is because the western media can effectively destroy or build up a candidate as more and more voters rely on the television and newspapers to form their impressions. I am of the opinion that it is this unchecked power of the media that have caused some of them to become increasingly irresponsible. In their attempt to increase readership or viewership, sensationalizing and distorting issues are not beneath them.

While the power of the media in this part of the world may not be comparable to that of the West, it is nonetheless important to pay attention to them, especially when the number of media is small. Imagine, if there were only one press in a country, a company that incurs its displeasure may find the press suppressing or censoring any news or events favourable to the company but playing up news that are detrimental to the company.

Stakeholders Relations

Annual reports no longer merely comprise financial tables, figures, and generally cold statistics Instead, they are lavishly splashed with full-coloured pictures, graphics and other eye-catching features. This is because companies have come to realize that even annual reports can become important communication tools to relate to their shareholders, potential investors, bankers and even suppliers and customers.

It is no longer uncommon for companies to engage professionals to help them design and edit their annual reports. A handful of companies like Shell Singapore, the Straits Times, and the Telecommunication Authority of Singapore (TAS) even commission the production of souvenir corporate books to celebrate special events. As Asian companies continue to grow and prosper and as more of them get publicly listed on the stock exchanges, relations with investors, bankers and financial analysts will become increasingly important in the years ahead.

Government Relations

The role of the government in affecting business operations cannot be discounted in Asia. If anything, many Asian governments have strong influences on the business sector, and often participate actively in business as well. It is therefore not surprising to find that more and more chief executive officers (CEOs) and senior managers of companies are now sitting on various government committees and board of government institutions. These CEOs are there not only to contribute, but to network as well. In fact, statutory boards like the TAS, the STPB, the National Productivity and Quality Council (NPQC) and the EDB are well-staffed with private sector directors.

In the 1985 economic recession of Singapore, the number of public and private sector CEOs and senior managers represented on the various sub-committees and working groups of the Economic Committe ran into hundreds!

Government relations are very important in Asia. After all a lot of business transactions and deals in Asia have to do with the government or government-linked companies. In fact, in many Asian economies, the government and government-linked companies are major players in business. For this reason, Bill Gates and many other top corporate executives of MNCs are keen on meeting top Chinese officials such as President Jiang Zeming when they visit China, President Suharto when they visit Indonesia and Prime Minister Mahathir when they visit Malaysia.

Employee and Channel Members' Relations

Besides ensuring that its activities are targeted at specific audiences outside the company, a company or organization must also be concerned with its internal publics. Here, there are two very important publics that require attention: the employees of the organization and its channel members such as agents, distributors and dealers.

In the area of employee relations, Apollo Hotel Singapore, like many other companies in Singapore and the region, honours one employee a month through a "best employee scheme". Many companies today provide training programmes, publish in-house newsletters, conduct regular employer-employee discussions, host annual dinners and organize regular social and sporting activities for their employees. Some organizations even go to the extent of arranging "all expenses paid" annual vacations for their employees. These activities cost money, yet many companies would not hesitate in providing them as they see them as means to maintaining morale and increasing productivity.

Other companies like Drew and Napier (a large law firm in Singapore) are known to charter a whole airplane to take their employees to annual corporate retreats and holidays. Sunrise Berhad, Yeo Hiap Seng Ltd and NEC of Malaysia, on the other hand, would organize cruises and other types of group holidays for their employees, usually on an annual basis. Often, they would even allow the employees to bring along their family members so that the whole event can become their annual vacation as well. In doing so, these companies hope to secure their loyalty and boost their morale.

In the area of channel relations, Xian-Janssen, one of the largest and most profitable joint-venture companies in China, has a very creative way of recognizing the performances of its dealers. Instead of paying them directly (which might not be politically acceptable), Xian-Janssen credits the incentive payments into a training account which can be used to send the dealers for overseas training courses. This scheme, implemented since 1993, has received very favourable responses both from the Chinese government as well as the dealers themselves. It is indeed a very clever PR exercise.

On the other hand, large Japanese manufacturers are known to reward their high performing dealers with very generous perks that include free holidays, conventions and the likes. Of late, some American companies operating in Asia have begun to do likewise by hosting annual dealers' conventions that encompass both work and vacation. However, in contrast to the Japanese companies which tend to have high social and leisure content in their conventions, the American approach is still largely work-oriented. From a PR standpoint, the American companies may have some way to go in terms of bonding with their employees.

13.3.4 PR Activities Must be Objective-Driven

There should be a very well defined purpose in every PR activity. PR activities are not intended to be charitable acts by themselves. They are not free publicity given to the company, but rather are the results of well-planned and proactive actions on the part of the company. In other words, there must be a PR strategy that contributes to the overall strategic planning and management decision making of the company. The following are some of the possible PR objectives:

1. To nurture relationships with key publics.
2. To systematically inform the internal and external publics about interesting events of the company.
3. To contribute to the company's profits by minimizing the costs of resolving conflicts such as labour disputes, strikes, boycotts, law suits and so on.
4. To increase corporate profits by improving relations with customers, dealers, media, government officials, amongst others.

5. To project the company as a socially caring and responsible organization.
6. To improve the corporate image in the local community.
7. To project the company as the best place to work.
8. To improve the company's image in the eyes of the government.

In order to determine whether the objectives are accomplished, there is a need to assess the effectiveness of PR campaigns both in the short and long term. In other words, there must be control mechanisms, feedback procedures and evaluation processes to determine the success or failure of PR campaigns. Unfortunately, this is an area that is very difficult to measure. It is precisely for this reason that PR can end up getting the back-seat treatment. This is because unlike an advertising or promotional campaign where the impact can be measured in terms of increased sales, the contributions from PR tend to be more indirect and long term. Ironically, it is often relegated to the peripheral of the company's management, often called upon only to do "damage control" of crisis — a rather late course of action.

13.3.5 The PR Function Must be Top-Directed

In order for the PR function to gain its due respect and recognition, it must be directed from the top. I recall one PR manager of a large bank in Singapore once asking me the justification of the existence of his department. I candidly replied that it all depended on the magnanimity of his CEO. The support of top management is absolutely needed for the PR department or personnel to function effectively. I would even advocate that the PR function should be directly under the jurisdiction of the CEO.

The CEO is the best PR person for the company in that he would be in a position to network in important circles and promote the company in terms of providing newsworthy items and granting interviews. In addition, by playing the lead role, he can also project a stronger and better image for his company.

13.3.6 PR Activities Should be Multifaceted

Finally, the PR function cannot be easily defined and it cannot be confined to a specific area. Instead, it should cover a wide area of activities that include corporate communications, management issues, investor relations, lobbying, community affairs, public affairs, media relations, handling of interviews, government relations, product and service publicity, sponsorship of events, management of donations, hosting of site visits, reception and briefing of visitors and management of crisis.

In terms of the tools, methods and avenues available for the conduct of PR activities, they should also not be confined to the conventional means. This is where creativity and innovation are much needed so that novel ways can be found to generate publicity and attract media attention. For this reason, if there are insufficient skills and expertise available within a company, it must be bold enough to seek external PR consultants. However, the best advertising firm may not be the best company to do the PR job! This is because the skills and expertise needed for the conduct of public relations are very different from those of advertising and the target publics may also differ significantly. At times it may even be necessary to engage different external consultants for the various PR activities involved.

13.4 *Guanxi* and Personal Relations

Guanxi, translated roughly as "personal relationships" or "connections" or "personal networking" has become a new buzzword for doing business with and in China and with the Chinese businessmen in Asia. In reality, personal relations and networking are not unique to China and the Chinese entrepreneurs. It is the norm for doing business among small companies in many societies and cultures such as the Italian, the Jew, the Indian, the Arab and the Malay communities. However, to many Chinese, *guanxi* takes on greater significance in that it is tied to the Confucian ethos of family obligations and reciprocity. Furthermore, as Chinese family entrepreneurs have gotten a foothold in almost every Asian economy and the rest of the world, the networks created are something that cannot be easily ignored nor discounted. Given the rise of the Chinese economy, and the increasing trading and investment activities of overseas Chinese in Hong Kong, Taiwan, Singapore, Indonesia, Thailand, the Philippines and soon, Vietnam, *guanxi* has taken on greater significance.

But *guanxi* has also sparked much moral debate. This is because it is an informal alternative to the western legal framework, and has thus prompted critics to point out the potential dangers in its eroding the authority of the law. Critics have come to equate *guanxi* with bribes and corruption. However, this stems from a very narrow understanding of *guanxi*.

13.4.1 Understanding *Guanxi*

Guanxi is very much part and parcel of Chinese tradition and culture. Historically, the Chinese had very weak legal systems and framework. In terms of the social mindset of the Chinese, they tended to place emotions (*qing*) first. This is followed by logic or reason (*li*) while legality (*fa*) is ranked last. In other words, the traditional Chinese would only resort to legal resolution last. To take someone to court is to ignore emotions, and is tantamount to not "giving face" to the other party. It would be the end of any relationship. This hierarchy in the Chinese social mindset is in sharp contrast to that of a typical westerner where the reverse order would apply.

Qing or emotions are unfortunately, relations-based, and often on a very personal basis. Moreover, *qing* takes time to develop and is also linked to the Confucian ethos of reciprocity. It is therefore not surprising to find that the Chinese tend not to trust "outsiders" in the conduct of their businesses. They tend to rely heavily on immediate family members and relatives. They also tend to extend their friendship to those from the same clan or those who share the same ancestorship. For an outsider to earn the trust of a Chinese, he will have to break into this close network by investing time, money and effort to cultivate the social bond. Thus, giving presents is not only an act of showing respect, but also serves to build a relationships on a more personal basis. Given the strong Confucian ethos of reciprocity, it then becomes "natural" to have favours done in return.

Unfortunately, over the years, with the fast opening and growing market in China and elsewhere in the Chinese-speaking world, the building of *guanxi* becomes more of gift-for-favour exchange to the extent that it has become a euphemism for bribery. To put it more candidly, it has been abused and has a way in which payments are made to influential officials or contacts of a country's government in order to solicit business deals. Given the fact that the Chinese are not known to rely on written contracts (actually, they tend to negotiate beyond the written contract), trust and mutual obligations become the norm for doing business. Thus, this informal but personal relationship of *guanxi* has become a necessary evil, at least for the next ten to twenty years.

While *guanxi* is a term commonly known to the Chinese-speaking world, and in particular for doing business in China, personal relations and networking are very much the norm in doing business in many other parts of Asia. Personal relations and contacts are very much needed not only to secure big government contacts, but to solicit large private sector businesses deals as well. It is something that cannot be avoided if one wants to do business in Asia.

13.4.2 Learn to Manage, Not Avoid *Guanxi*

While *guanxi* and personal relations may be something very alien to those who know only the western way of conducting business, it is a phenomenon that has to be confronted and managed to one's advantage. There is no way to avoid it, unless one is prepared to forgo the Chinese market as well as the other markets of Asia. As it is, there are not many Asian societies are like Singapore and Hong Kong where the legal frameworks are more established and the laws are enforced. Thus, instead of rejecting and condemning such social practices, companies should show respect and patience so as to gain a deeper understanding of the underlying cultures and turn them into business opportunities.

To excel in marketing and doing business in Asia, a company has to learn the art of personal networking. This is where it must be prepared to dig in for the long run, and be prepared to invest in the long run. It must not begin by asking, "What's our bottomline or return on investment?" Instead, it must ask, "How much are we prepared to invest?" and be prepared to wait for the returns over a longer time horizon. It would even be better if some of these companies would adopt the Japanese, the Korean or the overseas Chinese approach of viewing their investments in China and other Asian markets by asking, "How much are we prepared to lose?" The three questions mentioned above obviously reflect completely different approaches to how the business would be conducted.

Interestingly, in the area of marketing, many renown western scholars like Philip Kotler and Jagdish Sheth have recently been advocating the concept of relationship marketing. Obviously, these marketing gurus have come to realize that there are limitations to the conventional approach of using only the 4Ps of marketing. Instead, there is a need to build relationships all round — with customers, suppliers, distributors, government officials, lobby groups and the general public — so as to create a more favourable image towards the company and its products or services. There is likely to be a gradual convergence of views with regard to the issue of personal networking and relations as an important component for doing business. What may differ is the approach used to build the networks.

13.4.3 Be Legal and Moral

While it is true that any company who wants to do business in Asia must learn to cultivate good *guanxi*, it must not do so at the expense of breaking the law or engage in unethical practices. Obviously, given the relatively undefined legal boundaries for doing business in Asia, the temptations are there for any company to engage in "below the board" methods and means in order to solicit business deals. It is such indirect encouragement by companies that actually compound the bribery and corruption problems that exist in some Asian economies.

To eradicate grey business practices, companies themselves must make conscious attempts not to succumb to demands for personal payments and bribes. Of course, it is very difficult to expect that the problem will disappear overnight. However, companies can learn to circumvent the corrupt practices over time if they learn to develop more creative ways of rewarding their local counterparts. For example, outright payments to personal bank accounts are both illegal and unethical. However, creating scholarships and training places is definitely legal and are very praiseworthy. Similarly, large personal gifts may be questionable, but leaving behind product samples may be acceptable.

At the end of the day, my advice would be that every company should strive to be both legal and moral in everything it does. I cannot stress enough of the need to ensure tht everything a company does is above the board. Unfortunately, unlike legal frameworks by which it is easier to establish clear boundaries, the issue of morality is more subjective so that it is difficult to agree on a definite code of conduct. Not only does the moral code of one culture or society differ significantly from another, even within the same culture and society, individuals can differ significantly in terms of their moral perception. Thus, it is essential for every company operating in Asia to establish its own code of ethics. Only then can the employees know how to go about conducting themselves in the course of business. This is particularly important for those involved in the marketing function as they are the front line staff of the company. They interact most with external parties and are therefore most vulnerable to getting entangled in questionable business practices.

13.5 Conclusion

In the past, many top executives had great difficulties in evaluating the returns on money spent on PR activities. The failure to develop clear criteria in deciding on the types of PR activities to be involved in also compounded the problem. The result was that more often than not, expenditure on PR activities tended to be frowned upon and viewed as something to be avoided. This lip-service treatment to PR activities was clearly evident in that in many instances, the department, if it existed at all, had to rely on the magnanimity of the CEO. In the event of a budgetary squeeze, it would probably be one of the first departments to be sacrificed.

Fortunately, the situation is now changing. Asian companies are beginning to realize that PR is not about getting free publicity. They now understand that PR can be a key component of the corporate communication strategy which in turn forms part of the overall corporate strategy. At the same time, it can be managed proactively like the advertising and promotion function. Approaches, techniques and methods used in PR may differ from those of advertising and marketing. Fortunately, there are now quite a number of firms offering PR services, including international companies such as Hill and Knowlton. Thus, the PR function need not be confined to ad hoc activities. There is now professional help to put together coherent and effective campaigns with well defined objectives and target audiences.

Many Asian companies have themselves begun to establish formal PR departments or have specific officers who are designated to handle PR. Thus, the PR function has probably become another important **P** to the existing 4Ps of marketing — **p**roduct, **p**ricing, **p**romotion, and **p**lacement (distribution). This fifth "**P**" of the marketing mix variables is something that cannot be ignored.

In Asia especially, personal relations and networking is an important dimension of doing business, especially in the realm of marketing. This is because culturally and socially, many Asian societies thrive on relationships and friendships and place more faith in the individuals than written contracts. There is therefore, a need to establish personal credibility and contacts in order to secure business deals and contracts. A high level of interpersonal skills, patience and understanding are needed in order to establish such personal relations. Such *guanxi* cannot be achieved overnight and companies must learn to adopt a longer term perspective. Ignoring aspect of *guanxi* of doing business in Asia would be tantamount to missing out on the immense opportunities in the growth in the region. Perhaps, in the case of doing business in Asia, it is timely that personal relations and networking be added as the sixth **"P"** to the list of marketing functions.

14

Marketing of Services: Helping Businesses to Prosper

14.1 Introduction

The tremendous economic growth of Asia leading to an ever increasing demand for consumer goods is also accompanied by the demand for services. In fact, the demand for services is a trend that is likely to continue because of increasing affluence, rising education, more leisure time, longer life expectancy and higher woman labour force participation rate. Each of these factors generates its own demand for services.

To begin with, higher incomes have generated demands for discretionary and luxury services. Golf and country clubs, squash and recreation clubs have mushroomed in countries like Malaysia, Singapore, Indonesia, Thailand, and Taiwan over the last few years. Upmarket hair saloons and barber shops, landscaping and garden maintenance services, and even banking, insurance and credit card services have experienced very significant growth. In particular, many big ticket items are now sold with a string of services attached. For example, luxury cars like Lexus, Cima, Jaguar, Rolls Royce, BMW and Mercedes (higher-end models) are now sold with free servicing and maintenance for up to three years. Some innovative agents even provide free pick-up and delivery services, including a replacement car during the period in which the owner's car is in the workshop. It is also not uncommon to find that an engineer has been specially assigned to oversee the maintenance of the car!

Education has been largely responsible for the demand for the fine arts, theatre plays and concerts. Education, together with increasing income, has created what is generally known as the "yuppy" lifestyle among the younger consumers aged between twenty-five and forty-five. This group of consumers spends a considerable amount of their time and money on services related to a modern trendy life-style. It is this group of young consumers who account for the increasing patronage of classical and popular concerts, theatres, plays and others. In the more affluent Asian cities like Tokyo, Hong Kong, Taipei, Seoul and Singapore the governments have been prompted to stage annual festivals of arts. National arts councils, arts centres, concert halls and museums — all designed to cater to the more aesthetic and gracious aspects of modern living of the 21st century – are now found in these countries.

With more leisure time, there is also a greater demand for travels and tours, cooking lessons, *Taichi* lessons and many other hobby-related services. Longer life expectancy, on the other hand, accounts for the greater demand for healthcare services. In recent years, many hospitals, specialists' clinics, gymnasiums and health clubs have emerged in many Asian cities. In particular, well-known private hospitals and health care centres like Mount Elizabeth and Gleneagles have begun operations in many major Asian cities.

The higher rate of participation of women in the labour force has also generated the demand for house-cleaning services, domestic maids and for nurseries and creches for toddlers. Economies like Malaysia, Singapore and Hong Kong have all experienced tremendous amounts of import of foreign maids in recent years. Also, with more married women working while at the same time having fewer children, many families are now spending large sums of money on their children in various types of services like home tuition; piano, guitar, organ and violin lessons; calligraphy and painting classes; ballet and dancing classes; grooming and enrichment courses; and so on. As a result of the new but strong support of many Asian consumers, the service industry has begun to emerge in a very significant way over the past ten years. Indeed, its importance is likely to increase dramatically over the next ten to twenty years. The strongest indicator has been the emerging market for the fine arts. Creative talents like artists, painters, calligraphers, sculptors, pianists, singers, actors and actresses, musicians, deejays and even comedians have found increasing demand and appreciation for their works among Asian consumers. They no longer need to venture to the West to earn a living.

14.2 Differences between Products and Services

As many countries in the Asia Pacific region will increase their demand for different kinds of services, there is a need for the marketeer to improve the marketing of services which is rather different from marketing products. Table 14.1 summarizes some of these fundamental differences. Based on the different characteristics of services, there are several important implications for the marketeer.

14.2.1 Giving a Service Physical Representation

As a service consists of a series of activities, and tends to be intangible and abstract, the marketeer will have to pay closer attention to

TABLE 14.1 Differences between Products and Services

Products	Services
1. A thing or physical object with tangible attributes	1. An activity or process with intangible attributes
2. Attributes or product features can be demonstrated objectively	2. Attributes or service features are often perceived subjectively
3. Homogeneous and can be standardized	3. Heterogeneous and are difficult to standardize
4. Production, distribution and consumption can occur as separate activities	4. Production, distribution and consumption often occur together as a series of related activities
5. Fewer points of contact between the service provider and the consumer	5. Many points of contact between the service provider and the consumer
6. Consumers are usually not involved in producing the product	6. Except for services performed on objects, consumers usually participate in the production process
7. Core benefits and quality of the product are determined during manufacturing	7. Core benefits and the overall service quality are determined when the consumer is being served
8. Can be stored with little loss of value	8. Cannot be stored and tend to be perishable over time
9. Ownership is transferred to the consumer when the sale is completed	9. Ownership usually remains with the supplier

making service understood by his consumers. Unlike a product which can become a marketing tool by itself, the marketeer of a service will have to seek ways and means to give a physical representation of his service in order to make. Such efforts to make his service "seen" and "felt" will also have to include how he wishes to depict his service offerings. For example, hotels, hospitals and restaurants make full use of their buildings, furniture and fixtures, interior decorations, lightings, other physical facilities and equipment as ways to reflect standards of their services.

One good example of how a service provider can make his service somewhat concrete is that of the executive education programmes conducted by the Faculty of Business Administration (FBA) at the National University of Singapore (NUS). Education is an abstract thing, and it is very difficult for participants to visualize the kind of training that they would be going through, say, over a two-week period. However, the need to convey to them that the experience will be worth their while is critical in view of the fact that the course fees are very high. They can be higher than the total tuition fee for a university degree!

The FBA of NUS adopts a total approach in making its executive programmes "felt" and "seen" by exploiting the range of service offerings from the core to the augmented levels. Among other things, it provides:

• Customized reading materials, folders and other stationery;
• Personalized name tags and labels;
• Group photographs and addresses of participants;
• Souvenir T-shirt, plaque and certificate;
• Access to university facilities during the programme period;
• Hotel-standard teas, lunches and selected dinners;
• Mid-programme "surprise" function;
• Affiliation to the alumni of the FBA;
• Free invitations to future executive seminars conducted by the FBA; and
• Others.

All these additional services and products are designed to enhance and facilitate the learning experience of the executives. While they help to make an executive's experience enjoyable and memorable, they also give him the opportunity to extend his business networks beyond the duration of the programme.

14.2.2 Focus on Service Personnel

In the case of a product, it is often easy to standardize its features through automation and technology. For instance, car manufacturing is today highly automated through the use of robotics. The result is that every car that comes out of the factory line is identical in quality and performance. As such, the consumer can have absolute confidence in picking his car, regardless of whether it is one that comes out first or last in the production process.

Automation is often not possible for many services, especially for those that rely on people to deliver them. For such "high contact" services, the service providers are often placed in close interaction with the consumers of the services. The result is that the interaction between two individuals – the provider and receiver of the service – is likely to produce non-identical results. This is because no two customers are alike. They differ in terms of personality, mood, attitude, behaviour and so on. Each of these factors would impact on the performance of the service provider who is equally affected by the same set of factors as well. In addition, the service provider's mood and behaviour may also change over the time of a day. The setting of the interaction between the service provider and his customer would also impact on the outcome of the quality of service provided. In sum, the chances for wide fluctuations of service standards are very likely if the "production process" is not properly managed.

It becomes very essential that service providers be well selected and trained in order to ensure that the quality of the service delivered is consistent and high. For this reason, SIA conducts training for all its employees throughout the year. It is very rigorous in the training of the cabin crew as they are the front-line personnel who have the greatest interface with the customers. It is no exaggeration to state that their performance would significantly affect the perception of the service offerings of the airline, and to some extent, its business and profitability.

That services are likely to be heterogeneous means that the marketeer has to pay closer attention to supervision and control of his employees' performances. In particular, performance standards have to be clearly spelt out. Some established service companies like banks, hotels and hospitals have developed operating procedures and systems so as to minimize variations in service standards. In addition, training and retraining are also frequently carried out, which are especially important when production, distribution and consumption occur as a series of related activities (as in the case of fast food). A weak product can rely on a strong agent to overcome its shortcomings by stepping up efforts in areas like pricing, promotion and distribution. But such options are typically not available to many services.

14.2.3 Managing Points of Contact

Unlike the sale of a product, a service transaction can consist of a stream of related and unrelated activities that can stretch over a fairly long period of time. Consider the marketing of a packaged tour. It does not end when the customer places his booking. It marks only the beginning of a relationship that may stretch from a few days to possibly a month. During this period, each of the activities will have to be managed carefully as there will be many **points of contact** between the service provider and the consumer. Hence, it is not only necessary for the marketeer to identify the various points of contacts, but to prioritize and rank them as well in order of importance.

Here, I must caution against just focusing on the front end of a service transaction. Rather, managing the **process** and the **tail end** are equally, if not more important, than the front end. This is because the front end is only concerned with getting the sale. However, how the process and the tail end are handled will determine whether there will be repeat and recommended sales — both very important for the future health of the company. In fact, if the service provider is able to capitalize on building up the social relationship with the customer through skilful handling of the various points of contacts over time, he may even help to build customer loyalty for his company. Moreover, favourable word-of-mouth communication is generated as well. This is particularly important in view that services depend a lot on recommendation, especially from those who have consumed the services before. For this reason, when outstanding service companies like SIA and McDonald's consistently receive accolades from their customers, these unsolicited testimonials act as very powerful tools in advertising and promoting their services.

The fact that production, distribution and consumption are often inseparable and are experienced simultaneously as the customer participates in the production process makes the marketing process of services unique. The performance of the service, in fact, has become highly visible. In other words, as the consumer is highly involved in the production process, he has every opportunity to scrutinize and evaluate every activity of the service to the smallest detail! This presents a tremendous challenge to any marketeer in that the standard of service would be determined there and then. For example, the marketeer would have to ensure that his service provider is well-trained and has the necessary professional skills to ensure a high level of service standard. At the same time, he must have the right attitude and behaviour in handling the customer. In particular, he must be equipped with skills in handling complaints and managing recovery in the event that something goes wrong in the execution of the service. So, in the case of a tourist guide, he must be trained to recover from an adverse situation like the cancellation of a major show or event as a result of delay in the journey, unavailability of tickets or other such circumstances.

14.2.4 Managing Opportunities and Time

In the case of a product, the core benefits are often determined during the manufacturing process at the factory. For a service, its value is often determined when the service is being performed on the customer or object. This can provide the creative and innovative marketeer the best opportunity to customize the service to the satisfaction of the consumer. Besides customization, a skilful service provider can even attempt to increase the total sales of the transaction by offering other related services to the customer. Take the case of selling life insurance. The smart salesperson does not aim at selling the basic coverage policy. Instead, he would try his best to motivate his client to increase the total amount covered as well as encourage him to take on additional coverages through various "riders". At times, he might even succeed in selling more than one insurance policy to his client. By managing the opportunities and time provided by his captive audience, he could even gather more information about the needs of the members of the customer's family, his friends and colleagues who are potential customers. Indeed, how the service provider manages such moments of truth will determine how much of repeated and recommended businesses he can generate for the company.

For many services, time is the constraining resource. Time cannot be stopped or stored. For example, in the case of a barber, hair stylist, lawyer or consultant, when no one steps into his store or office, sales for that time are, so to speak, lost instantaneously. On the other hand, if too many people show up at the same time, it is not possible to speed up the service substantially without affecting the service standard. To some extent, the marketeer can attempt to keep his customers by providing a conducive environment for them to wait, as in the case of a medical clinic. Still, for a sick patient, there is a limit to his patience!

With the provision of services, time has to be managed judiciously. Poor management of time can cost a company dearly. Service companies know this and they do pay a lot of attention to this aspect. In the case of fast food restaurants like McDonald's and Burger King, time utilization is carefully studied so as to get the maximum productivity out of every employee. For example, when there are slack periods, employees do not idle their time away. Instead, the crew members are scheduled to clean toilets, mop floors, polish windows, clear garbage and so on. In this way, these restaurants have been able to maintain a very high level of service quality.

Time management is not confined to the employees alone, but can be extended to the customers as well. Take the case of a well-known private hospital in Singapore. The top management studied in great detail how to occupy a hospitalized patient. It understands that a patient in a recovery ward can feel easily bored. He can also be very sensitive to the environment around him. As such, it would not be surprising if he begins to find fault with the things around him. Thus, it becomes crucial to fill the time of the patient before he gets impatient. His daily schedule is therefore carefully analysed. The result is a combination of various service offerings that include the provision of daily newspapers, meal menus, the careful and timely screening of in-house movies, the timing of visits and so on, to ensure that the patient is occupied. In this way, he is left with very little time to find fault with the hospital services!

Other innovative service operators like SIA have carefully planned their service schedule in such a way that air passengers will not feel that they have too much time on hand, nor feel cooped up in the aircraft. By filling the time effectively, the passengers will not feel bored, and at the same time, allows the airline to project a high level of quality service. In the same way, resorts like Haw Par Villa in Singapore and Tokyo Walt Disneyland employ crew members to conduct side-shows so as to minimize the frustrations of visitors who have to stand in long queues. Circus shows use clowns for the same reason — to kill time in between the change of programmes.

The fact that services cannot be inventorized makes the management of supply and demand an important concern of the marketeer since any unsold services are perishable and non-salvageable. In fact, for many services, it is not possible to stock up the supply. For example, any rooms that not occupied would affect the overall revenue of a hotel. The hotelier cannot hope to stock-up such unoccupied rooms in order to meet excess demand during another period. So, he has to learn to "synchronize" supply and demand in the management of the hotel. A hotelier would typically use a variety of strategies to improve the occupancy rate and total revenue of the hotel. These include the following:

- Using differentiated pricing to "smoothen" the supply and demand for rooms. This involves pricing room rates higher during peak periods so as to increase the yields and profits of the hotel, and lowering room rates during off-peak periods in order to stimulate demand.
- Targeting at local customers during the off-peak periods through attractive weekend packages.
- Targeting the food and beverage businesses more at the locals than the tourists, as this would ensure a higher year-round yield of revenue.
- Entering into long-term contracts with large clients and organizations. This includes providing rooms to packaged tour operators, airline crews, conventions and corporate meetings, often at greatly discounted rates.
- Charging higher room rates for walk-in customers and direct individual bookings.

The last strategy of charging higher room rates for walk-in customers and for direct bookings by individual clients may seem strange, as these are additional revenue above those made through group bookings. On closer scrutiny, it is a very sound policy. First, tour agencies, airline companies and large corporations provide the large volume of business that allows the hotel to enjoy the economies of scale in its operations quickly. Second, the revenue is very stable, with very little risk of clients not paying up. Third, these businesses, especially those from airlines and conventions, are normally of high profile, they provide good publicity and visibility for the hotel, boosting the hotel's image. Finally, convention attendees, corporate executives and airline crews are often not on tight budgets and are more prepared to use the other hotel services.

In contrast, there are higher risks associated with taking in individual hotel guests, whether they are walk-in customers or not. The problem of unpaid bills is often encountered with individual hotel guests and it is just too costly and difficult to sue an individual. Thus the strategy concerned is actually not a case of charging individual hotel guests higher rates, but giving more generous discounts to reputable groups and organizations.

The need to spread the occupancy rates over the year to avoid excess demand and excess supply situations in many service operations is very important. Like hotels, an airline cannot create extra seats and a hospital cannot stock up wards the same way that a retailer can stock up his goods to meet the strong demand during festive occasions like Christmas and New Year. On the other hand, an airplane seat not occupied and a bed without a patient means revenue foregone. Coping with varying demand in the face of supply constraint is indeed a challenging task. It requires the use of creative strategies to synchronize the demand with supply. As mentioned earlier, many hotels and vacation resorts have deliberately lowered prices during off-peak periods in order to attract bargain hunters, while deliberately raising prices during peak seasons in order to deter marginal customers. There is no reason why such time-differentiated pricing strategies cannot be applied to other services like haircuts, custom tailoring, bus and taxi rides and so on. Time-differentiated pricing as a means to smoothen the demand is certainly one area that needs to be further exploited by many Asian marketeers. But, there are some businesses such as medical, legal, accounting and consultancy services where it is relatively difficult to use time-differentiated pricing to synchronize supply and demand. Besides the difficulty of forecasting the demand, there are also ethical and professional issues to be considered.

14.2.5 Harnessing Proprietary Premiums

The fact that ownership remains with the supplier of the service means that the latter can have all the opportunities to improve his service standard without fear of losing proprietorship of the service. For sure, every other airline can copy the inflight service of SIA, but the myth behind the SIA girl can never be copied. As a result, SIA is able to enjoy healthy premiums on its tickets despite very stiff competition.

Similarly, the professional skills and expertise of an established lawyer, dentist, doctor, surgeon, accountant, consultant and trainer can never be robbed. Skilful management and marketing of such proprietary skills often translate into huge price premiums that can be unique only to that individual or service. For this reason, an increasing number of Asians are now pursuing careers in the fine and performing arts. This is because they have witnessed the handsome rewards enjoyed by successful musicians, singers, actors and actresses, painters, calligraphers and so on. Indeed, in the case of Asian movie stars, they are beginning to command hefty fees that are even higher than the salaries of top corporate executives. This is a trend similar to that of the West.

What is also fascinating about proprietary premiums enjoyed in the realm of services is that they can be extended into many areas. For example, many Asian movie stars now endorse products and appear regularly in all kinds of advertisement. In Asia, product endorsements and commercial appearances are no longer the domain of movie stars and singers. In recent years, sportsmen and sportswomen have also begun to realize that their skills and image can be harnessed in other areas as well. A good example is that of Fandi Ahmad, a well-known professional footballer in Singapore. His name and face can be found across a wide spectrum of products and services, including having his photograph appearing on transit cards that are used for subway travel.

Proprietary premiums are now enjoyed by educational institutions as well. Having recognized the importance of the paper chase in Asia, many British and Australian universities have begun to aggressively export their various degree programmes. Despite declining academic standards among some of these universities (some of them are not even tertiary insitutions of high academic standing), they have been able to attract many Asian students largely because of their reputation in the past. At the same time, there is a severe shortage of tertiary institutions in Asia. This shortage is aggravated by the increasing need for trained manpower as a result of the fast economic growth in this region.

14.3 Understanding and Managing Service Quality

One of the most difficult aspects of marketing a service has to do with maintaining its quality. This is because the service offering itself, as mentioned earlier, is abstract and intangible. On top of that, quality by itself is another abstract phenomenon that is very difficult to measure. Service quality is a challenging aspect that warrants greater attention.It is increasingly important for many Asian economies as they become more affluent. ISO 9000 is now pursued by service companies including construction companies, housing developers and even educational institutions. Even the civil service in Singapore has embarked on PS 21 (Public Service for the 21st century) to improve its service standards. At the same time, as more and more Asian government companies and agencies (for example, utility, public transport and telephone companies) are being corporatized or privatized, the quest for improvement of service quality is likely to increase.

Table 14.2 summarizes the major differences between product and service quality. In view of the different characteristics of services, how should one go about marketing and managing them? I would recommend the **STRIPE** approach — **S**election, **T**raining, **R**einforcement, **I**nforming, **P**lacement and **E**valuation. Let me eludicate these six principles.

14.3.1 Selection

Despite the advent of technology and automation, most services are still delivered by people. The high incidence of contacts between people in the service business would dictate that to achieve excellence in customer service, the process must begin with the **selection** of the right people for the job. This is because not everyone is disposed to serve others with the "slow to anger, but quick to please" attitude; nor does everyone smile naturally and readily and maintain a high level of enthusiasm. Someone once asked me, "Why is it that almost every air hostess of Singapore Airlines seems to smile so readily no matter how exhausted and stressed she is?" The answer, lies in the selection process.

Similarly, in the hotel industry, much attention must be paid to the selection of personnel, especially those who have to deal directly with the customers, such as reception staff and doormen. Indeed, careful selection of personnel for the service industry ensure that half the battle is won! Interestingly, selection of right personnel for the service industry should not be a major problem in Asia. Many Asian races (the Thais, Indonesian and Malays, amongst others) are known to have a very friendly and courteous nature.

TABLE 14.2 Differences between Product and Service Quality

Product Quality	Service Quality
1. Can be objectively measured and determined by the manufacturer	1. Is subjectively measured and often determined by the consumer
2. Criteria for measurement easier to establish and control	2. Criteria for measurement harder to establish and are often difficult to control
3. Quality standardization can be accomplished through investment in automation and technology	3. Quality harder to standardize and needs heavy investment in human resource training
4. Easier to communicate quality	4. Harder to communicate quality
5. Recovery on faulty products possible to ensure quality	5. Recovery on poor service difficult as cannot replace "faulty services"
6. Product itself projects the quality	6. Relies on the peripherals to make tangible the quality
7. Quality is enjoyed	7. Quality is experienced
8. Risks are often contained	8. Risks are often projected onto the customers (for example, in the case of a haircut or surgery)

Selection should not be confined to employees alone. Take the case of a packaged tour operator. The selection includes not only picking the right employees for the different job functions, but it includes selecting the right hotels, restaurants, travel routes, ticketing agencies, airlines, sites for visits and so on. In fact, the whole range of activities and events that affects the holiday maker has to be carefully selected so that he can have an enjoyable experience. In other words, selecting the right point of contact would ensure that the outcome of the service would be more favourable. There will also be less worry about any foul-ups.

14.3.2 Training

A good and thorough selection procedure marks the beginning of the winning formula in excellence in service offering. Equally important is to match it with well-planned and rigorous **training.** For example, SIA complements its stringent selection of friendly and courteous cabin crew with very rigorous training. They are taught to smile naturally, to have eye contact with customers and other social graces. They are also taught correct pronunciation of different languages. All these are undertaken to ensure that service is tip-top. Let me again point out that a consumer of services normally participates in the production process. This inevitably means that the production, distribution and consumption of a service occur almost simultaneously, and the core values and benefits of the service are determined while the customer is being served. The quality of the service is therefore dependent on the interaction between the service provider and his client, of which the latter can have a significant impact on the outcome of the quality itself. It is therefore important to solicit the cooperation of the client. SIA fully understands this, and thoroughly exploits the strengths of its superbly selected and well-trained cabin crew.

What futher complicates the overall quality of a service is that the execution of the service itself is often made up of a series of activities with many points of contacts between the buyer and seller of the service. The quality can therefore be affected at different points as well. To perform a service well, it is necessary to take an integrated approach, not a piecemeal one. Take again the case of a packaged tour operator, it is not sufficient to provide superb service when a customer comes into the sales office to book a tour. The same level of high quality service must be provided by the tour guide, the driver, the other local agents and so on. In other words, the focus is on the entire process from the beginning to the end. This, in essence, is how top-notch Asian hotels like the Oriental, Shangri-La, and Mandarin are run.

Although service quality may be very abstract and difficult to visualize, it can still be built up through systematic and comprehensive training. As the service quality is very much dependent on how it is delivered by the provider, the attitude and behaviour of the provider is critical. In the case of goods, the quality is determined by the product itself. Thus, at times, even the seller can get away with poor or no service. However, in the case of a service, the quality is in the act of the service itself. As such, the training must focus heavily on work ethics and behaviour so as to develop professionalism and skills in servicing the customer. More than anything else, reliability and trustworthiness, professional reputation and credibility are very important attributes of the service business. Such attributes can only be built up over time and with investment in training.

Interestingly, although many Asian economies are known for their good services, they (Japan is probably an exception) have not spend enough on both formal education and training as well as on-the-job training. There is actually a general lack of sustained training by companies to upgrade the skills of their employees. As of 1996, the amount of expenditure on manpower training spent by companies in Asia, except Japan, is less than half of those in developed countries. Concerned about the gravity of such a situation the government of Singapore legislated compulsory contributions by companies to the Skills Development Fund (SDF) for the training of lower-skilled workers. At the same time, it greatly encourages companies to spend more on training and manpower development. Singapore's national approach towards training is now followed by the Malaysian government and is likely to attract other Asian governments to do likewise in due course.

14.3.3 Reinforcement

The third STRIPE principle is that of **reinforcement.** Selection and training alone are not sufficient. As services are mainly provided by people who, by their nature, are subjected to changes in moods which inevitably affect the quality of service, the customer and server interaction can also affect the outcome of the quality of service. It is imperative that reinforcement is frequent. By reinforcement, I mean the need to constantly remind the employees of the importance of service, of what is expected of them in providing the service to the customers and in general, to remind them of the overall service mission of the company.

There are many ways to carry out reinforcement. These include selecting the best employee of the month, printing of a corporate newsletter to disseminate the importance of service, rewarding outstanding employees, forming work improvement teams to generate new service ideas and processes, amongst others. I would also include re-training and refresher courses as part of the reinforcement effort. In addition, positive behaviour should be publicly encouraged and rewarded, while negative behaviour should be corrected as soon as possible.

It does take time and effort to build up service quality, and even greater effort to maintain it. In the case of a product, a company can dramatically improve its quality standard through importation of the latest technology and automation, and establishment of very rigorous control systems to maintain the quality, but such means are not possible in the service industry. More often than not, it requires constant checks and auditing before errors can be detected. In the hotel business, for example, the amount of services provided at any one point in time is so great and varied that setting up any quality management and control system may be quite a nightmarish exercise. Yet such a system is indispensable, especially if the hotel concerned is a five-star hotel.

14.3.4 Informing

While reinforcement is concerned with the handling of the internal aspects of the organization, **informing** has to do with the handling of customers. As service offerings are intangible and abstract, it is important to give customers an idea of what to expect. A very good example is a recent case in Singapore which received considerable public and media attention. A clerk was charged over S$270 for a hairdo when she had expected to pay no more than S$70! It was the poor **information dissemination** efforts of the company that had produced rise to the wrong expectation.

The abstract and intangible nature of services has posed challenges to many marketeers in projecting the quality of their services to the consumers. In the case of bank, the building, decorations, furnishings, fixtures, and equipment are all used to somehow project a feel of the services provided and at the same time, a high quality, sophisticated and secure image. Similarly, hospitals have substantially upgraded their medical and non-medical facilities, spruced up their wards and beautified their environment to project the image of high quality medical treatment.

Despite its abstraction, service quality can indeed be communicated. However, to do it well, the marketeer must first have a clear and thorough understanding of the service itself and what it can or cannot do for the customer. This is because many services, unlike products, cannot be sampled. More often than not, a service has to be consumed in total. Moreover, unlike products which can be replaced in total or in part in the event of a breakdown without causing much damage and embarassment to the consumer, a poor service performed can bring about very serious and undesirable consequences. As such, the marketeer must ensure that he delivers what he promises. At the same time, as the opinion with regard to service quality is more subjective than that with regard to products, the service provider should not avoid making embarrassing claims like, "satisfaction guaranteed or money back". There is nothing to stop any customer from claiming dissatisfaction for the service performed!

14.3.5 Placement

The fourth STRIPE principle for ensuring high service quality is that of **placement**. By this, I mean putting the right person on the right job. Placement complements selection and training because having trained the right candidate, it is necessary to place him on the right job.

Nothing can be more ironical than assigning a well-trained employee to the wrong job. The first exposure of any employee to any service function is critical because it can build up his level of confidence or destroy lower it. An important thing to remember is that not all service jobs require face-to-face interactions with the customers. The key is to match the attributes of the employee to the requirements of job.

It is as important to remember that a person's interest in a job can change over time. Owing to, for instance, changes in his needs or his family's. The manager should not overlook the possibility that an employee (who does not seem to be performing) might have been "misplaced" in the first place. A case in point is that of SIA. In the past, its corporate policy allowed an air stewardess to get married. However, as soon as she started a family, she would be grounded. The problem with this policy was that, over the years, there were a severe shortages of experienced air stewardesses. SIA changed this policy in 1995 to allow married stewardesses with children to fly again. The revised policy helped SIA to solve its cabin crew shortage problem as well as provide additional manpower to help its expanding operations.

14.3.6 Evaluation

The final principle to ensure high service quality is that of **evaluation**. It is a principle that cannot be ignored if the service is one where there is a high incidence of interaction between the service provider and the client. The very fact that people are used to provide the service would demand that there should be constant monitoring in order to ensure a consistent and high service standard. Moreover, over time, the service offerings themselves may have to change owing to changing consumer tastes and preferences. Competition, new technology, changes in the economic, social or cultural environment, require that the service provider to constantly evaluate his service offerings. The truth is that, unlike products, service standards are very difficult to control and measure. The quality of a service is decided only at the point of its execution. Product quality and rejection rates can be pre-determined, including rejection rates. Service standards, unfortunately, are often not known until they are provided, often in full and by which time, is too late to redress the outcomes.

In the final analysis, service quality cannot be compromised. This is because unlike products, it is harder to engage in recovery work in the case of services. A faulty product and its component parts can be replaced and warranties are often possible without severe consequences. In other words, it is possible to make up for poor quality in products. For services, it is very difficult to do so. Often the damage is already done to the customer before recovery effort can begin. Think of the embarrassment caused by the spilled soup on the dress of the client; the trauma resulting from a poorly organized tour; the pain and agony as a result of a wrong medical diagnosis and surgery; the waste of time and money as a result of attending training courses that promise more than they deliver and so on. Poor services can be very costly physically, socially, economically and psychologically to the customer.

On the other hand, the payoff of quality service can be incredible, especially if the provider is able to maintain a high level of integrity, image and professionalism. That is why the established lawyer, doctor, consultant, entertainer, artist or musician can command a price that seems ridiculously higher than his average peer.

For institutional service providers, constant feedback surveys of their services are important. SIA, for example, conducts surveys amongst its customers regularly. I want to emphasize that it is not sufficient to rely on complaints by customers as a feedback mechanism. This is because when a customer complains, it is already a manifestation of great dissatisfaction because most dissatisfied customers do not complain! Instead, they may choose to boycott the service or speak negatively about the service provider. The point is, when a customer complains, the service provider knows that he must have done a terrible job. However, when the customer does not complain, it does not mean that the service provider has done a good job. He could have done the worst job of his life! Thus, it is better to take a more proactive approach – like conducting regular surveys – to find out more about how the company's services have been performed thus far.

14.4 Conclusion

Effective marketing of services is more an art than a science. The unique characteristics of services present interesting challenges to the manager. As many Asian economies continue to grow, the demand for services, and in time, high quality services, is likely to increase significantly. Marketeers should therefore take advantage of this situation. Without doubt, there is a multitude of niches to be discovered in this area. One startling example is that of the services provided for pets (such as grooming, training and so on) in cities like Beijing and Shanghai. One would expect that given the generally low per capita income of China, there would be no market for such services. Yet, amidst the masses, there is enough of the very rich to form a sizeable market for any creative and innovative marketeer. Similarly, hair-styling and personal grooming for the yuppies and nouveau-riche are mushrooming in many other Asian cities. If anything, the demand for services in Asia is likely to soar in the foreseeable future.

15

Going Overseas: Building the External Wing

15.1 Introduction

In recent years, as a result of the immense economic development in Asia, more and more MNCs have begun to actively invest in this part of the world. More interestingly, many large companies in Asia have also begun to invest in each other's economy. This trend is likely to grow stronger in the years ahead. Indeed, from the corporate perspective, the issue of going overseas would surface at some point of the company's development. There are many ways in which a company can choose to enter a foreign market. These entry strategies include exporting, licensing, franchising, joint venture and direct investment. Whichever entry strategy is used, it is important for a company to understand why a company chooses to go overseas in the first place.

15.2 Motivations to Go Overseas

There are many things that motivate a company to go abroad. These include necessity, the encouragement of the local government, as part of the strategic planning of the company, enticement of the host country and so on. In general, a company would venture abroad based on a combination of factors, although one or two of them may dominate.

15.2.1 Encouragement from the Government

Let us take the case of Singapore. Since the 1960s, the economic growth of Singapore has been propelled by investments from foreign MNCs. These MNCs not only brought with them their technology and capital, but they also helped to create abundant jobs for

Singaporean workers. More importantly, as these MNCs are operating in the global arena, they also launched Singapore-made products in the world market. Over the years, they have also helped to upgrade the level of skills of our local workers and management. This strategy of relying on MNCs served Singapore very well right up till 1980. Prior to this period, many of its ASEAN and Asian neighbours were more concerned with nationalism and political ideology than economic development. However, as its neighbouring countries began to embark on economic development and to open their doors to foreign investments from the late 1970s onwards, Singapore began to face very stiff competition. It has had to attract investments in more advanced technology in order to stay ahead. At the same time, it has had to continue to improve its business environment for businesses to find it conducive to operate in Singapore. However, in the longer term, new solutions have to be found if Singapore is to maintain its economic growth.

Beginning with the late 1980s, the Singapore government began to actively encourage Singapore companies to expand abroad. They began to offer a wide range of incentives to companies that wanted to venture abroad. Regularly, its minister would also lead delegations to explore business opportunities in the region. This **directive approach** is beginning to pay off in the 1990s. Today, many Singapore companies have become important business players in the region. Some of them, including City Development Limited (CDL), have even become world class players. Indeed, CDL took the London stock market by storm when it floated its Millenium & Copthorne (M & C) Hotels in late April of 1996. The listing attracted S$2.6 billion, was oversubscribed by almost seven times and opened with a 16% price premium on the first day of trading!

The directive approach taken by the Singapore government to encourage its companies to invest abroad is shared by many other Asian economies. The Japanese government has for many years been known to dictate when and where its large conglomerates (called *zaibatsu*) should invest. Through the Japanese Ministry of International Trade and Industry (MITI), it is even known to have coordinated the expansion strategies of these large Japanese conglomerates so as to prevent their competing directly against each other in the early stages of market entry. To some extent, the Korean government also adopts some of the Japanese strategies by directing where its *chaebols* (the Korean version of conglomerates) should invest abroad.

15.2.2 Push Factors Created by Limited Opportunities at Home

A company can also be compelled to go overseas. In other words, it invests overseas largely out of **necessity.** First, there may be limited market opportunities at home. This may be caused by strong domestic competition resulting in erosion of profits and market shares. Thus, to survive, it must look for overseas markets. Second, the company may be facing high costs of factors of production at home. This also reduces its profit. Investment abroad becomes a viable way to reduce costs. In fact, this was exactly what happened when China opened up its economy in the 1980s. Within a few years, many Hong Kong manufacturers of textiles, toys, shoes and other labour-intensive products moved their plants to Guangzhou and Shenzhen for reason of lower costs of production. Interestingly, despite their political differences, many Taiwanese businesses are doing likewise: they are moving their production plants to Fujian.

The third reason that a company may be forced to go abroad is the **shortage** of factors of production at home. While higher costs of production can be overcome by automation and increased productivity, the shortage of factors of production cannot always be overcome by paying more. For example, there is a limit to the supply of industrial and commercial land in a land-scarce economy like Singapore. For companies that need large factory spaces for production, they would have no choice but to seek alternative sites outside of Singapore.

Finally, a company may have excess capacity that is created by over investment or by a shrinkage in domestic demand. To exploit the excess capacity, it would be forced to seek export markets in order to take up the excess capacity and to enjoy economies of scale in its production. The Malaysian manufacturer of Proton Saga and Wira faces exactly this situation. It had to look for international markets for its cars from day one as the automobile industry is one in which economies of scale is very important. It is not economical to have small production plants for cars.

15.2.3 Enticement by Host Countries

A company may also be attracted to invest in another country because of the attractive incentives offered by that country. The use of incentives to attract foreign investment is a very common strategy adopted by many governments of the newly opened economies in Asia. The range of incentives are very widespread, ranging from tax exemption, accelerated differentiation, provision of land at generous rates and leases, liberalization of employment of expatriates, relaxation of foreign exchange controls, remission of earnings and so on. Incentive packages can be very attractive, especially when the company may be facing increasing costs of production and limited expansion opportunities in its home country. In fact, many companies investing abroad for the first time have been so overwhelmed by such incentives that they forget to investigate carefully the business environment which they are getting into.

Vietnam is a good example of a country offering attractive incentives. It has been very active in wooing foreign investments in the country over the past few years. Besides giving attractive incentives, it has even set aside its central planning in favour of the market mechanism for its economy. However, Vietnam's attraction begins to wane upon closer scrutiny. The country is still burdened by high inflation rates, huge government deficits, widespread corruption problems, unrealistic wage demands that do not correlate with productivity an irrational tax regime and a bureaucracy that hampers private sector operations. All these, in total, offset whatever incentives that are offered to the foreign investors.

To quite the same extent, India in its effort to woo foreign investment is also hampered by its internal problems which include a complicated political system that is beholden to sectoral interests and demands and a daunting bureaucracy. As a result, many foreign investors have been discouraged from doing business in India. A good case in point is that of SIA. Despite teaming up with the Tata Group, one of the largest and most respected Indian conglomerates and after countless rounds of negotiations for more than two years, it has yet to secure the rights to operate a domestic airline in India. Interestingly, SIA was invited to participate in the joint venture in the first place.

To be fair, however, it must be pointed out that many Asian economies face similar problems when they first opened themselves to the outside world. China encountered similar problems like those of Vietnam in the earlier years. Some of these problems such as corruption, low productivity, and poor management (especially among its state-owned enterprises) still persist today. Interestingly, China, owing to its size, presents a different challenge to the foreign investor today. Typically, it takes a very long time to obtain approval for projects in China. However, once approval is given, little controls are in place to check any abuses. At the same time, the farther away the project site is from Beijing, the more difficult it is to enforce control measures!

15.2.4 Strategic Plan of Company

A company may invest in overseas markets in a very **proactive** manner as part of its overall corporate strategy. In other words, it is a calculated approach and such an approach requires few incentives from the governments of both the home and host countries to encourage and entice the company to go abroad. The company would venture abroad on its own initiative and it is driven largely by its own assessment of market opportunities. Ideally, this is the way to enter any overseas market, especially if the company has the time and resources to conduct proper market research and feasibility studies.

Many Japanese companies exemplify this proactiveness of approach. After the Second World War, Japanese companies manufactured and catered mainly to its large domestic market. Having established their production skills and having attaining certain standards in quality, the Japanese companies began to export their products overseas. In the initial period, these products were exported under the brand names of other European and American companies. As they gained market knowledge however, the Japanese began to build up their own brand names. Even so, in the 1960s and 1970s, many Japanese companies concentrated on manufacturing products that did not compete head-on with the western giants. This can be observed in many product categories like cars, refrigerators, television sets, hi-fi equipment, amongst others. At the same time, the Japanese also chose markets ignored by the western competitors, such as the markets in Southeast Asia.

However, over the years, as the labour costs of the Japanese workers and other factors of production began to increase tremendously, the Japanese companies started to move their production plants overseas. This move towards overseas production was accelerated in the 1980s owing to the increasing value of the Japanese yen. Today, many brands of Japanese refrigerators, air conditioners, television sets and hi-fi systems are made in countries like Thailand, Malaysia and Singapore. Even with cameras, some brands in the lower price range, like Canon, are now made in Taiwan and other countries.

The Japanese experience is one of planned efforts. Note that its companies did not start off by going overseas. Instead, they planned their penetration of the world markets in a gradual and systematic way. They did not rush to enter the overseas market. Interestingly, the Japanese model has been copied very successfully by the Koreans. After establishing a very strong presence in its domestic market, several well known Korean *chaebols* like Hyundai, Samsung, Goldstar, Syangyang, and Daewoo have begun to invest more and more overseas by building their production plants and facilities overseas. Without doubt, more Asian economies will follow the lead of the Japanese and the Koreans.

15.3 Approaches to Entering Overseas Markets

There are many approaches to entering overseas markets. Every company may claim its own secret market entry strategy. I will highlight six approaches that are commonly undertaken by companies.

15.3.1 We Only Do It This Way

This is an arrogant way of entering overseas markets and many American and European companies are guilty of this practice. Owing to their financial strength and size, they tend to adopt the intimidating tactic of "only my way or nothing". This approach is also driven by the need to have control over the running of the business. Some western fast food chains for instance, still insist on pure franchises (whereby their fees are based on a fixed percentage of sales) when they enter the Asian markets.

I think this approach is all right so long as the company has very strong bargaining power and the host country needs its investment badly. Its position will be boosted if it has a monopolistic controls over technology or other exclusive rights. However, few companies in the world today can afford to take such a hardline approach. Moreover, this approach ignores market heterogeneity and the fact that market entry conditions differ from country to country. For example, the joint venture mode is preferred by the Chinese government. Direct foreign investment with 100% control is unlikely to be approved. Thus, to brush aside the joint venture mode, and insist on having 100% ownership would be tantamount to giving up investing in the largest market of the world today.

With increasing competition among companies wanting to invest overseas, the "we only do it this way" approach becomes rather immature and myopic. The business environment is very dynamic and fast changing. Hence, flexibility and adaptability are keys to business operations, especially when competing outside one's domestic market. In fact, owing to the immense market opportunities in Asia, some Asian governments like China, Malaysia and Indonesia have even learned to play one competitor against another to extract the best deal.

15.3.2 The Trial and Error Way

This approach is undertaken by companies which do not have the experience in operating overseas. Often, they would adopt one approach, only to discover later that it is the wrong approach to take. They would then try a new approach and could possibly fumble again. In fact, many small and medium-sized companies take to this approach largely because they do not have the time and resources to engage in proper market research and feasibility studies. However, there is no doubt that these companies are very earnest about operating overseas. What they need most is proper guidance. This is where the host country government can play an important role in helping such companies to become successful.

There are many examples of such companies which have failed in investing in China and elsewhere largely because of adopting the trial and error approach. Often, they are blinded by the seemingly attractive and immense opportunities and they fail to probe deeper into the businesses that they are getting into. By the time they discover the problems, it is often too late. The trial and error method is without doubt an expensive way to learn. The business world is filled with minefields. On the surface, things may look very good. However, there are many hidden dangers. This is where having a local partner helps to reduce the possibility of failure. However, it is important to choose the right partner, especially when operating in countries like China where business is based largely on personal connections (*guanxi*).

15.3.3 The Herd Mentality Way

This is one of the most fallible ways of going overseas. Like consumers, companies can be driven by the herd mentality too. It is especially true of investments and doing business with China. For example, many companies simply jumped onto the bandwagon when China opened its door to the outside world. These companies were tempted by the immense market opportunities in China. Few did much homework. They merely followed blindly. The property market in China provides the classic illustration of how many small investors were hurt in the process. Some developers from Hong Kong, Taiwan and even Singapore did not even know much about the background of their local partners when they went into joint ventures with them. A number of these overseas investors are still licking their wounds today because their local partners have either absconded with their money, or failed to live up to their promises and expectations.

Interestingly, it is acceptable to adopt the herd mentality so long as one follows the right leader. Unfortunately, the right leader is often hard to find! Moreover, even if one manages to follow the right leader, timing is a very crucial factor. Often, a company that follows ends up a late entrant with many missed opportunities. The property market in China again provides a good example. The early entrants have already made their money and recovered their investments. Those who entered later (after 1992) into the property development market have had to pay much higher prices for less attractive land sites and face increasing building and labour costs. The result is a big squeeze on profits.

15.3.4 The Jump-the-Queue Way

Another interesting approach to doing business overseas is by jumping the queue. This is done in several ways. First, physical proximity to the market confers distinctive advantages to the innovative company. For example, when China liberalized its economy, the earliest beneficiaries were companies from Japan, Hong Kong and even Taiwan. These companies (especially those from Hong Kong) were able to move way ahead of the traditional world players from the Western world in investing in China because of their proximity to the Chinese market. Today, Hong Kong tops the list of foreign investments in China — when it is not known to be a major player of foreign investments in any other part of the world.

Second, the cultural and social similarities of the investing economy to those of the overseas market also gives companies of the investing country, advantage to over those of other countries.

Most of the investments in the Guangzhou and Shenzhen areas are dominated by Hong Kong businessmen who speak the dialect as that used in Guangzhuo, namely Cantonese. Similarly, many Taiwanese investments in China are found in Fujian which has the same dialect (Hokkien) as Taiwan. Note also that a lot of overseas Chinese investment in China are made on the basis of dialect and on clan relations. *Guanxi* grants unique accessibility to the Chinese market, and allows the overseas Chinese investors from Hong Kong, Taiwan, Indonesia, Thailand and Singapore to literally jump queue over other investors from the western world. Even the Japanese *zaibatsus* and the Korean *chaebols* have found that they do not enjoy distinctive advantages over their smaller rivals from Taiwan, Hong Kong and Indonesia.

15.3.5 The Lowest Risk Way

This is a pragmatic way. However, a company taking such an approach may miss a lot of opportunities to make significant impact in overseas markets. For example, the most passive and lowest risk way of going overseas is through exporting. This can be done through using overseas agents or even using one's distribution systems. However, direct exporting is not enough for one major reason. It is based on the assumption that the home country has all the competitive advantages, such as lower labour costs, cheaper supplies and so on. It does not allow the company to exploit the advantages available in other countries. Thus, unless the company can either produce the cheapest or the highest quality products or both, it will become vulnerable to international competitors who may be able to produce the same products cheaper. Hence, with the opening of China, Hong Kong has lost almost all its competitive advantages in products like shoes, textiles, clothings, toys and other light industries. This is despite the fact that Hong Kong is one of the most competitive societies that has an abundant supply of high quality workforce.

In an era of a growing number of trading blocs, protective national policies among nations, and generally greater global competition, there is also a need to shift production to countries where the company can enjoy the most favoured nation (MFN) treatment. If the company does not seek out overseas markets, its international competitors will. Thus, going abroad is no longer a case of choice alone but one of necessity.

15.3.6 The Systematic Way

This is the strategic and analytic approach of entering overseas markets. On the surface, it would seem that much time and effort would be spent on trying to find out more about the overseas market that a company may be interested in. However, nothing can match meticulous planning that is based on market intelligence. In the long run, the systematic approach minimizes risks to the company.

As mentioned earlier, the Japanese experience in penetrating overseas markets has been one of a planned effort. In the initial years, the Japanese they focused on areas (which could be markets, products, services, designs, features, amongst others) where there were no competitors or where the competition was weak. The Japanese were opportunistic and visionary in their approach to the market and they were prepared to invest in the long term, which inevitably required a different perspective of risk-taking and risk-sharing.

It was when they had acquired the production and marketing skills and their products had attained world class quality that the Japanese companies began to take on their western competitors. For those products where they still had not reached the standards of the western competitors, the Japanese companies continued to avoid direct competition with their western counterparts. Clearly, theirs is a case of a planned and systematic approach to gaining footholds in international markets.

15.4 Core Capabilities and Resources

15.4.1 Natural Advantages

Before venturing abroad, it is important to know one's competitive advantages and core strengths. For example, comparative advantages may be those **endowed by nature,** such as the abundant availability of natural resources such as tin, coal, gold and so on. In the case of Malaysia, the abundance of tin allows it not only to export it in large quantities, but to develop its pewter industry as well. Today, Royal Selangor Pewter has become a world class producer of many souvenirs and other related items.

Similarly, Thailand has capitalized on its abundant supply of primary forest. It is particularly well-known for its teak furniture and related products. Burma, richly endowed with jade and rubies has however, yet to develop its cut jewellery trade. It has nonetheless been able to export much of its gem stones abroad. Amongst the Asian economies, China is probably responsible for the supplies of various gems and minerals like jade, amethyst, garnet, variscite, azurite, malachite and others. Many of these precious stones have traditionally been carved into decorative ornamental pieces that are displayed in palaces and in the homes of the rich and famous. With the opening of China, many of these pieces have become collectors' items. At the same time, China has also actively encouraged the growth of its various industries that use its rich natural resources. For example, the famous tea pots, ink blocks, porcelain and stone seals produced by China are today very much sought after by many enthusiastic collectors from Asia and the rest of the world.

15.4.2 Physical Advantages

Competitive advantages can be **developed** by capitalizing on physical factors like strategic location and deep seas. Singapore, for instance, has cleverly exploited its strategic location and deep seas to create strong industries in shipping and shipbuilding, logistics management and warehousing, entrepot trade, air services and so on. Unfortunately, unlike manufactured products, the services of such industries do not lend themselves to export. Only the knowledge and skills behind the creation of these facilities and their management can be exported.

15.4.3 Acquired Competitive Advantages

It is important to note that competitive advanages can also be created even if one does not have any natural or physical advantages. To do so would require the company or country to determine and discover its core competence. For example, Japan is not endowed with abundant natural resources. It also does not have a strategic location like Singapore. The current strengths of Japanese companies in various world markets for products and services have been the result of planned efforts. They were acquired strengths.

The same can be said about the diamond-cutting industry in Israel. Israel does not produce any raw diamonds. They are all imported from South Africa. Yet over the years, they have developed their skills to such a high standard that Israeli cut diamonds are deemed to be of the best quality in the world. Several Asian countries have begun to learn from the Israeli experience of developing their precious stones industry. India and Thailand are good examples. As a country, India produces very little precious stones such as emeralds, rubies and diamonds. India imports all of its uncut and unpolished emeralds from South America. Yet today, India has become a world centre for cut emeralds of the highest quality. At the same time, it has also developed a strong niche for lower-end cut diamonds and rubies. Similarly, Thailand is fast becoming the world centre for faceted and polished rubies and sapphires. It imports its uncut precious stones from Burma and other places around the world.

15.4.4 Establishing Proprietary Claims

In establishing their presence in various countries Japanese companies have cleverly developed strong brands over the years. Brand development should not be ignored especially when exporting or investing overseas. Today, the Japanese manufacturers are able to move their production plants abroad successfully because their brands have become familiar names among households and corporate boardrooms. Similarly, the Koreans have been able to make their presence felt in the world market as a result of the strong brand names developed by their *chaebols.* In contrast, the Taiwanese are facing some difficulties today. Many of their companies have been manufacturing other companies' products and as costs escalate, the foreign partners began to shift their operations to lower cost countries. The Taiwanese manufacturers are fast discovering that that their competitive advantages can gradually be eroded if they are handicapped by the lack of proprietary brand names. Today, the Taiwanese manufacturers, like their Singapore counterparts, are investing heavily in brand development.

It is interesting to note that the effects of franchising brands are not confined to manufactured products. Even services can be franchised when brands become well established. Well-known names abound in services like auditing and accounting (Coopers and Lybrand, Price Waterhouse, Ernst and Young are some of them), consulting (Arthur D. Little), advertising (Bateys), public relations (Hill and Knowlton), market research (Survey Research International) and so on. As in manufacturing, these firms thrive on building a strong corporate image and, at the same time, developing them. They develop systems that can be standardized and exported. The services offered by them are provided by the locals of the countries in which they operate. But what they bring to their business is their world class name and international business networks.

While all the top hotels in the world are located mainly in Asia (the Oriental in Bangkok, the Shangri-La in Singapore and the Mandarin in Hong Kong), the best hotel chains are still managed by western companies, especially those from the United States. The Sheraton and Holiday Inn are example of some of these. It is a recognized fact that American hotel chains are well-known for their management systems and expertise. Thus, when they combine these strengths with the naturally courteous and quick-to-please disposition of the Asians, the result is not at all surprising — world class hotels. But hotels are not the exception when it comes to top-notch operations in Asia. The best fast food restaurants, in terms of service standards and sales turnover, are all found in Asia!

But there is no reason why Asian service companies cannot develop strong brand franchises like their western counterparts. For example, there are many established law firms in Singapore such as Drew & Napier, Lee & Lee, Shook Lin & Bok, amongst others. These conpanies can easily organize themselves for expansion into the region. After all, as a result of its economic success, Singapore enjoys a tremendous reputation in many Asian economies such as China, India, Indonesia and Vietnam. These economies are trying to model themselves after Singapore and to learn the "secrets" behind her success story. As such, ample opportunities exist for many Singapore companies to expand their services to these economies.

Besides the legal service, other services where Singapore can enjoy competitive advantages when compared to Western companies include accounting and auditing, advertising and promotion, market research and feasibility studies, management training and education, urban planning, facilities and infrastructural management, banking and financial services and consulting. As it is, one of the more prominent architectural firms, RSP, and several local banks have begun to expand their services and operations into China.

15.4.5 Size is no Constraint

Interestingly, the small size of a domestic market is not necessary a hindrance to the development of local MNCs. It is really a double-edged sword. On the one hand, a small domestic market, like that of Singapore, does not allow for the development of some industries where economies of scale are important. For example, the automobile industry never took off in Singapore which continue its assembly operations in the 1960s and into the 1970s. In contrast, with a population base of twenty million, the Malaysian government was able to build up its automobile industry.

On the positive side, a small domestic market can, in fact, compel a company to look to the region or the world for business. SIA is a classic example. Its success today is attributed to a large extent to the fact that it had to compete in the world market from day one of its operations. It did not start off as a world class airline, neither was it a large company. It succeeded because it managed to find a niche in the world aviation industry by emphasizing on its inflight service. Its strategy then was well-planned, and its current world class standing is the result of great efforts.

Creative Technology, the well-known world class producer of the sound blaster, was similarly forced to operate outside of Singapore from day one of its operations. There was no domestic market to absorb its large volume production. As a result, Creative Technology focused on its operations in the United States, and today, it has become the pride of Singapore, especially because of its public listing on the United States Stock Exchange. Similarly, to be the world class player that it is today in hotel operations, the Hong Leong Group had to acquire hotels outside of Singapore. Today, with its CDL International and a listing on the London Stock Exchange, it has become a major player in the global hotel industry.

15.5 Some Things Don't Change

There are some fundamental factors that do not change even if a company decides to venture abroad. These include a good understanding of the market, the corporate objectives and resources and the competitive environment in which it would be operating.

15.5.1 Knowledge of the Market

The knowledge of the market is critical to the success of going overseas. By this, I mean a good understanding of the macro factors that determine the nature of business competition, including the economic, social, political, cultural and even physical factors. Let me explain with the case of Singapore. When the Singapore government advocated that Singapore companies should explore going international in the early 1980s, many companies took "international" to mean America and Europe. There is nothing wrong with going to America and Europe so long as Singapore firms know these markets well. Unfortunately, this was not the case.

Many Singapore firms were not familiar with the American and European markets. Culturally and socially, they were and still are very different from Singapore. More importantly, these are very advanced economies and the business players are all in the world class league. In other words, to compete for market share in similar products and services, the Singapore companies must be able to provide them at comparable quality and standards as those of their competitors. This is because Singapore is no longer a low cost economy that can supply labour intensive items like clothings, textiles and shoes. Consequently, the Singapore firms faced tough competition at the high end of the market from competitors from the United States, Europe and Japan, and also very tough competition at the low end of the market from low cost competitors like Hong Kong, Malaysia, Thailand and China. It was therefore not surprising that a number of them fared very badly.

As a result of these early failures, the Singapore government had to swiftly change its "battle cry" from **internationalization** to **regionalization** with the focus on the rest of Asia. There are several advantages in doing so. Firstly, many of the Asian markets are in the same time zone as Singapore and are very near to Singapore. Hence, control in the running of the business is easier. Secondly, many Asian economies like China, Indonesia, Vietnam and even India, have begun to open up very quickly to the rest of the world. At the same time, theirs have been high economic growth rates like many other Asian economies. Hence, it is more logical to focus on these growing markets than to direct long-distance efforts on the matured markets of Europe and America (many of these economies were stagnating in the 1980s; their growth rates in the 1990s have also been lower than those of most Asian economies).

Thirdly, from the social and cultural perspectives, the Asian markets are more familiar to Singapore companies as Singapore has the major Asian ethnic races among its population. Finally and most significantly, as Singapore is more advanced than many other Asian economies, there are many export and business opportunities for its companies. In particular, Singapore's economic success has become a model that many of these Asian economies aspire to emulate. In fact, Singapore enjoys a strong "brand image" in the eyes of many newly developing Asian economies. Thus, many Singapore companies are able to find relative superiority in what they offer, whether in products or services.

In sum, knowledge of the market involves answering six fundamental questions similar to that of conducting an indepth consumer analysis in domestic marketing:

1. Who are the consumers?

   This is basically a **targeting and positioning** issue. Whether it is marketing to overseas customers or local clients, a company must clearly identify the consumers that it is marketing its products or services to. This can be done through a detailed market analysis and segmentation. At the same time, it must learn to position its products or services as different from those offered by its competitors.

2. What do they look for in the product or service?

   This is essentially a **benefits offering decision.** Remember what has been repeatedly highlighted throughout this book. A consumer does not buy the product or service for itself. He buys the benefits that come with the product.

3. Why do they buy the product or service?

   This involves understanding the **motivation** behind the purchase. For example, is the product or service bought because it is cheap or for some other reasons. Understanding the reasons behind the purchase will help the marketeer to decide on the pricing and on what product or service features to emphasize.

4. When do they buy the product or service?

   This is an issue pertaining to **timing**. By knowing any specific period when the consumers choose to purchase the product or service will assist in production planning and inventory control. In addition, it will help the company to decide whether there is a need to use a differentiated pricing strategy as a means to spread out the demand over a period.

5. Where do they buy the product or service?

The answer to this question helps the marketeer to decide on what **distribution system and outlets** to use. For example, do they prefer to shop for the product at a departmental store, a specialized outlet or a neighbourhood store? Obviously, what works at home may not work equally well in another market.

6. How do they decide to buy the product or service?

This is a **decision processing** matter which is very important for deciding on the best advertising and promotion methods. Is the purchase decision made independently (for example, by the husband or wife) or jointly? In the case of families, do the children exert strong influences on the purchase decisions?

15.5.2 Corporate Objectives and Resources

The corporate objectives for going abroad are very important. Let me illustrate how important. There are many Western companies that are very active players in the Asian market. All of them want a big piece of the action in Asia. But there are distinctive differences in the way they approach the challenge. For example, McDonald's clearly knew what they should do when they entered the various Asian markets. Having observed that Western fast food is more a lifestyle phenomenon in Asia, McDonald's cleverly oriented all its advertisements and promotioned efforts in the angle of lifestyle. It deliberately played down the food aspects as its burgers were unlikely to be of greater value-for-money and neither were they likely to be tastier than the wide variety of Asian food. Furthermore, McDonald's also takes great pains to produce advertisements of Asian context, so that Asian consumers can relate to them. In order to get greater involvement from its local partners, McDonald's was also prepared to depart from its usual franchise mode of doing business. It was and is known to enter into even joint-venture operations. Undoubtedly, McDonald's is one company that has a **global orientation.**

In contrast, Burger King failed to recognize the lifestyle aspect in relation to its products when it first entered the Asian market. Instead, it took the easy way out by using many of its promotion materials and television commercials that were produced in the United States. Unfortunately, most of these advertisements were focused on the food aspect and failed to play on the lifestyle aspect. It took Burger

King several years to realize what it was missing. Efforts are now made to make its advertisements in Asian contexts and with more emphasis on the lifestyle aspect. Still, Burger King has always insisted on its pure franchise mode when it operates overseas. This has made it less flexible in responding to the different business operating modes in Asia. Furthermore, unlike McDonald's, Burger King has pork (or bacon) on its menu. This completely rules out its operating in the Islamic countries of Asia, such as Indonesia and Malaysia which have very large population bases. No attempt so far has been made to tailor its menu to suit the consumption habits of markets like Indonesia and Malaysia. Thus, while Burger King, with its operations in many countries, is definitely an international company, it lacks global orientation.

Besides western fast food chains, many other American companies also differ in their approach to the Asian market. The more enlightened companies have learned to re-direct and re-focus their strategies in Asia by shifting their regional headquarters and other important operations to this part of the world. They have also begun to actively seek out able Asian managers and manageress and train them to run their companies in Asia. Good examples include Motorola, Hewlett Packard and Allied Signals. On the other hand, there are many other companies which still try to direct their Asian operations from their home countries. In doing so, they are hoping to have more control over their overseas operations. Unfortunately, this may mean many missed opportunities. This is because many economies in Asia are growing very fast. As such, while opportunities come by quickly, they also disappear fast! To exploit such opportunities, there is a need to be close to where the action is.

In terms of resources, the company must ensure that it is capable of managing its overseas operations efficiently. Not only must it have adequate professional managers who are willing to work abroad, it must have well-planned human resource development policies that reward executives with overseas experience. If the necessary expertise is lacking, the company must be prepared to head-hunt and hire from elsewhere, and invest in the training of local personnel. Otherwise, its overseas operations may not be sustainable. This is one of the biggest challenges facing Singapore companies today. Many Singaporeans have become so accustomed to the good life at home that few are prepared to venture abroad, especially to other Asian economies where the living conditions are of a much lower standard than those at home.

Another important thing to keep in mind is that investments in many Asian economies do not yield returns very quickly. Hence, not only must the company be prepared to undertake higher risks, it must be willing to take a long term view of its investments. This inevitably means that it must have enough resources to see it through the difficult "hatching" period. Ironically, while many publicly listed companies do have adequate financial resources to venture abroad, the need to be accountable to shareholders in terms of showing strong performances and high return on investment (ROI) has constrained them from taking a long term perspective of investment. Not surprisingly, then, many Western companies find themselves somewhat handicapped when operating in Asian economies like China and Vietnam. In contrast, many privately-owned and family businesses from other Asian economies like Hong Kong, Thailand, Taiwan and Indonesia have found strong investment niches in China and Vietnam.

15.5.3 Nature of Competition

Competition abroad, if anything, is likely to be more intense with more players. On top of this, the uncertainty factor is even greater. Thus, it is important that the company does its sums correctly. For example, while a company may be a force to be reckoned with in its industry at home, it may find itself a small fish in a big pond in the international arena. Here is where it has to be very clear about its strengths or advantages. If the company's strengths are in owning and managing hotels, it may not be necessary for it to build hotels. This is because at any one point in time, there are always many hotels that are in the market for sale, while it takes many years to build just one hotel. The moment an operating hotel is bought, the cash register will start to ring. On the other hand, the moment a site is chosen to build a hotel, there will be several years of cash outflow before the first customer steps into the hotel. This is where many Asian companies should learn from the Western companies. Take the Holiday Inn, ITT Sheraton and Fairmont which are all well-known hotel operators. They do not build hotels and would even opt not to own the property if possible.

An alternative to focusing on one's distinctive strengths or advantages is to counter competitive threats by choosing areas (which could be markets, product ranges or product features) **ignored** by the competitors. To do so, the company must be very aggressive in seeking out markets, products or services in which there are hardly any competitors or where the competition is very weak. As I have mentioned time and again, the Japanese have exemplified this.

DHL International provides an interesting example of how an American company chose to focus on an Asian market that has been ignored long before its other competitors moved in. DHL is a very small and relatively unknown courier company in the United States compared to giants like Federal Express and UPS. However, while these larger courier companies were happily concentrating their businesses in the United States in the 1960s to 1980s, and ignored the rest of the world, DHL International found a vacuum to fill. Today, DHL International has built up an impressive track record in the Asian region, commanding over 40% of the market share. Its rival, UPS, has less than half of its share.

The world is a very big place. There is no need to rush into the same market like everybody else. In fact, the herd mentality may turn out to be very detrimental to a company. One must learn to study the competition carefully and choose markets, businesses and products which one can excel in. CDL (part of the Hong Leong Group of companies in Singapore) demonstrated this principle very well. Instead of jumping on the bandwagon of moving into China like many other Singapore companies, it chose a different strategy. Having noticed that many hotels in the western countries were facing severe difficulties and were on sale at rock bottom prices, CDL bought up many hotels in Europe and America in a quick succession. Among its prized catches are the newly listed North American and European company, the Millenium & Copthorne Hotels and the glamorous Plaza Hotel in New York (co-owned with Saudi Prince Al Waleed). Within just a few years, CDL has become a major player in the world hotel industry. It succeeds because it chooses to enter an area ignored by its other global competitors.

15.6 Conclusion

There is no secret formula for success in overseas markets. Even if there is one, it would be adopted by others soon enough. In a world where competition is ever increasing, there is a need to be more systematic and proactive in deciding on entering overseas markets. Asia is a very huge market. There are plenty of opportunities for the innovative company to exploit but there is a need to check that compulsion to give in to the herd mentality.

Index